The WRECK *of the* WILLIAM BROWN

The WRECK *of the* WILLIAM BROWN

A True Tale of Overcrowded Lifeboats and Murder at Sea

TOM KOCH

International Marine/McGraw-Hill
Camden, Maine • New York • Chicago • San Francisco • Lisbon • London
Madrid • Mexico City • Milan • New Delhi • San Juan • Seoul
Singapore • Sydney • Toronto

The **McGraw-Hill** Companies

1 2 3 4 5 6 7 8 9 10 DOC DOC 0 9 8 7 6 5 4

Library of Congress Cataloging-in-Publication Data
Koch, Tom, 1949–
    The Wreck of the William Brown : a true tale of over-
crowded lifeboats and murder at sea / Tom Koch.
        p.   cm.
    Originally published: Vancouver, BC : Douglas & McIntyre,
2003.
    Includes bibliographical references (p.   ).
    ISBN 0-07-143468-2
    1. William Brown (Sailing ship) 2. Shipwrecks—North
Atlantic Ocean. I. Title.
    G530.W65K625 2004
    910'.9163'4—dc22   2003065501

Questions regarding the content of this book should be addressed to
International Marine
P.O. Box 220
Camden, ME 04843
www.internationalmarine.com

Questions regarding the ordering of this book should be addressed to
The McGraw-Hill Companies
Customer Service Department
P.O. Box 547
Blacklick, OH 43304
Retail customers: 1-800-262-4729
Bookstores: 1-800-722-4726

Dedication

For the members of my watch:

John L. Daly
Warren Gill
Kenneth Denike
Walter Wright
Bill McArthur
Denis Wood
Jenny Young

Thank you

CONTENTS

LIST OF ILLUSTRATIONS

LIST OF PEOPLE ON THE *WILLIAM BROWN*

The records are inexact and varied. Some sailors are named in the depositions but are not on any official list. Some passengers may be listed twice under slightly different names, or incorrectly, or not at all. See the note in the introduction on the spelling of names.

Ship's Officers and Crew
George Harris, captain
Francis Rhodes, first mate+
Walter Parker, second mate
Isaac Freeman, sailor+
Alexander William Holmes, sailor+
Joseph Marshall, steward+
John "Jack" Messer, sailor+
William Miller, sailor+
Henry Murray, cook+
James Norton, sailor+
Charles Smith, sailor+
Joseph "Jack" Stetson, sailor+
1 unnamed sailor+
5 to 7 unnamed sailors

+ = in longboat
all others in jolly boat

Passengers Drowned with the *William Brown*
Mrs. Anderson & 3 children
Jane Anderson
Mary Bradley
Nicholas Carr, wife & 5 children
William Luden, wife & 10 children
Martin Morris, wife & child
John Davelin
Mary Connelly
Mary Jane Weil

Jolly Boat Passenger Saved
Eliza Lafferty

Longboat Passengers Saved
James and Ellen Black
Ann Bradley
Owen Carr
Sarah Corr
Mary Corr
Isabella Edgar
Jane Johnston Edgar
Jean Edgar
Margaret Edgar
Mrs. Margaret Edgar
Sarah Edgar
Susannah Edgar
Julie McCadden
Bridget McGee
Bridget "Biddy" Nugent
James and Matilda Patrick and child

Longboat Passengers Drowned
Ellen Aokin
Francis "Frank" Askin
Mary Askin
Charles Conlin
George Duffy
James Goeld
Robert Hunter
Hugh Keigham
James MacAvoy
Martin MacAvoy
George Nugent
John Nugent
Owen Riley
James Smith
James Todd
John Welsh
John Wilson

INTRODUCTION

IN 1841 A SHIP SAILED at maximum speed into waters where danger of icebergs was known to exist. It did this because speed meant profit and profit was the goal of the maritime trade, even when it endangered lives. As a result of its course and its speed, the ship struck an iceberg and sank. Because the ship, the *William Brown*, did not carry sufficient auxiliary craft, half of its passengers went down with the ship. At least fourteen, some say sixteen, persons saved to the ship's longboat were thrown overboard twenty-four hours later by sailors acting upon their superior's orders. One of those seamen was convicted a year later. The irony is that the man convicted, Alexander William Holmes, was the one hero of the whole sorry affair, the only crewman or passenger to risk his life in a selfless attempt to save another's.

That is what we know. The why and how and what might have been is the story this book tells. Its importance extends beyond the tale of nineteenth-century legal chicanery or the rehabilitation of the reputation of a long-dead sailor. The story of the *William Brown* is the story of how people get caught up in and destroyed by social systems that are supposed to protect them. It is also about how we construct ideals like "justice" and then accept constructions like "scarcity" that pervert those ideals in a way that is—or should be—indefensible. Finally, it is another example, if one is needed, of how complex events are reduced to simplistic tales, and how those tales are turned into clever but misleading metaphors. The result is that the lessons of history are turned into popular myths that are very different from the facts of the events themselves.

The story of the *William Brown* is important because what occurred in April 1841 was not an isolated event. It had happened before and it would happen again and again, the tragedy of one century presaging those of the next. It happens still today.

Seventy-one years after the *William Brown's* demise, the luxury ship *Titanic* sank in the same waters in a similar fashion. Both ships went down in April after striking at maximum speed an iceberg on the edge of the Gulf Stream. The captains of both vessels were experienced; they knew the waters they sailed and the potential dangers those waters held. Both vessels carried emigrants seeking a better life in North America. Neither carried sufficient auxiliary craft to permit the salvation of more than half the passengers on board. As a direct result, at least half the passengers—mostly poor emigrants—drowned.

In the nineteenth century, the very idea of scarcity's choice that today we know as "lifeboat ethics"—what to do and who to choose when critical resources are insufficient for all—was shocking, almost blasphemous. But by the first decades of the twentieth century, the fact of scarcity was so accepted that "rearranging deck chairs on the *Titanic*" became an almost instant synonym for futility in the face of limited resources. In both cases, early public reaction ranged from outrage to fatalism, the former mostly from working people and the latter typically from more moneyed folk, those who were the most likely to be saved when there was not enough for all.

From the *William Brown* to the *Titanic* and into our own time, the questions have been the same: who dies and who survives at what cost? When hard choices must be made, would we, could we do the same? Would we be so callous? Would we be so bold?

That ships sank with passengers aboard was a fact of nineteenth-century life, an accepted risk of the North Atlantic crossing. Nobody asked if these deaths were avoidable. Nobody questioned the myriad decisions by ship masters and owners that directly contributed to these disasters.

But to be saved from a sinking ship only to be killed by its crewmen was . . . exceptional. In the end, only one sailor, Alexander Holmes, was charged with one count of manslaughter on the high seas. Known to historians as *United States v. Holmes*, the story of his trial is a minor if recurrent footnote in the annals of law and moral philosophy, the first case to argue the "defence of necessity" and to examine the means by which people choose among themselves when scarcity reigns in their midst.

At one level, the story of the *William Brown*—of its survivors and its dead—is a simple narrative of shipwreck and eventual rescue that became a legal case with continuing resonance. At another, the saga is an overture to our times replete with the odour of politics and political cover-up. A nineteenth-century international *cause célèbre*, it was perhaps the first case in which political officials openly manipulated both journalists and legalists to assure that justice would seem to be done and yet in actuality would not *be* done. From the start, Alexander Holmes's conviction for "manslaughter on the high seas" was a foregone conclusion, a necessity of politics and commerce but not of justice before the law.

From this perspective, Alexander William Holmes was less a culprit or a tragic figure than a scapegoat whose conviction was required if the profitable nineteenth-century trade in goods and emigrants was to continue unhindered. His trial was not just an act of conscious justice or pioneering law but a carefully constructed morality play staged to reassure the thousands of emigrants then streaming from Europe to the Americas.

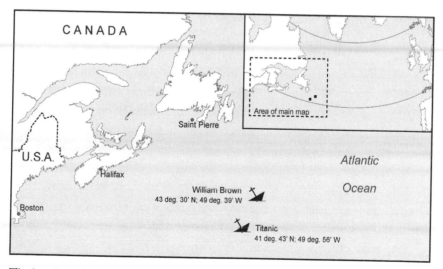

The location of the sinking of the *William Brown* in 1841, in relation to that of the *Titanic* in 1912.

What was trumpeted as justice's attempt to right a grievous wrong (and as an exercise in moral philosophy) was actually an action taken to protect the enormously profitable transatlantic shipping trade that knit together Old and New Worlds.

History's simple narrative is revealed as a complex story of a pivotal decade in the nineteenth century and the internationalism it bequeathed us all. In the 1840s the first postage stamps were issued. Newspapers were becoming a widespread and popular source of information that, mailed around the world, tied distant countries together. Steam was poised to replace wind and animal power as the force that moved goods and people around nations and the globe. The Industrial Revolution was in full advance as millions of Britons and Europeans left their homes and farms for work in the cities and factories of North America. The principal forces that defined the 1840s remained in place at least into the days of the *Titanic:* America's need for Europe's, and especially Britain's, cast-off emigrants; the conditions of the ships they travelled in; and the spirit of commerce that propelled modernity's first period of rampant globalization.

A woodblock print from 1845, titled *American Goods,* used to illustrate a popular version of the story of the *William Brown.*

Raw materials flowed from the Americas to Europe, from the cotton fields of the American South and the lumber-rich colonies of Canada. In its turn, the Old World sent to North America finished goods and expatriates, human cargo that filled the holds of merchant ships and assured profit to ship owners. The people who survived the journey then became a primary market for the finished products their former homelands were producing: good linens, fine china, scientific instruments. Simultaneously, New World emigrants harvested the raw materials such as cotton and wood that the Old World's factories and mills required.

The apparently simple tale of the *William Brown*—and the convoluted story of the cover-up that followed—is therefore also the story of the Great Migration in which more than 5 million people left Europe for the Americas. It is the story of new industry and the new attitudes that drove robber barons and staid, landed worthies as ferociously as they drove poor tenant farmers and lowly seamen. Ultimately, however, the heart of this story lies with the emigrants and the emigrant trade, with men and women who against stupendous odds braved the Atlantic crossing in leaking, wooden boats. Many died along the way; more died in the slums of North America. Those who survived the trip, and then the hard challenges that awaited them at journey's end, fashioned a new life for themselves and ultimately for us, we who inherited the world they made.

THE STORY TOLD HERE offers a historical reconstruction put together from a range of resources: old files stored in official archives, period newspapers, legal depositions, court documents, and the works of those who have written previously about this era and its events.

The surviving records suffer from the cavalier approach of nineteenth-century writers to spelling and to numbers. For instance, throughout both the official sources (depositions, legal records) and newspaper stories, the name MacAvoy is also spelled McAvoy and MacVoie; Sarah Corr is sometimes referred to as Sarah Carr; and was it Susanna, Susannah or Suzanne Edgar? For the convenience of modern readers, spellings are standardized throughout the text, except, of course, where a name is presented in an official document. There, the variant stands as written originally.

Similarly, British Foreign Office files name thirty-three persons saved to the longboat while the American trial record puts the count at thirty-two. More confusing, different sources variously record the number of persons drowned in the longboat. "Before they ended," the official trial record, *United States v. Holmes*, states, "14 male passengers and also two women" were drowned. But only six drownings are described in that record. Some European stories of the day, on the other hand, listed thirteen men and two women murdered. And while all agreed that just two women died in the longboat, whether they were thrown overboard or drowned themselves was a point of some debate. The details that history leaves us are typically contradictory and incomplete.

At this remove, there is no way to know for certain exactly how many people were drowned. Nor in the end does it matter. That so many were drowned (fourteen, fifteen, sixteen souls) was horrific to the Victorians and remains shocking today.

Our ignorance about the *William Brown* extends to the facts of the ship itself. Although we know a great deal about sailing ships of the 1840s, we know little for sure about *this* ship. No pictures of it survive. Nor are there any detailed descriptions of its rigging. Was it a brig, a barque or a brigantine? In the same vein, we have no likenesses of the survivors or the drowned, no portraits of the captain or his crew. Alas, illustrated newspapers were still a decade in the future when the ship sank in 1841.

Because the record is incomplete and sometimes contradictory, the whole hangs on my interpretation of these records, my re-creation of what is not quite known based on what is. Those seeking more information or specific references are referred to the endnotes and the bibliography.

The hope is that my guesswork may someday cause someone to realize the importance of a forgotten text, journal, diary or report now buried in a library or in an ancestor's sea trunk sitting forgotten in a corner of some attic. If that occurs, we will know with certainty the events that appear here as informed conjecture.

THE SECOND STRIKE

O N THE EVENING OF 19 APRIL 1841, the American sailing ship
William Brown was making ten knots under full sail when at
around 8:45 P.M.—survivors disagreed about the exact moment—
it scraped a floating pan of ice several hundred miles off the Newfoundland
coast. Ten minutes later, maybe fifteen, it struck an iceberg. With that
second strike, the ship's world ended, destroyed in a collision that owed
everything to the choices that had brought it to that place.

Since departing Liverpool for Philadelphia on 13 March with a complement of seventeen crew and sixty-five passengers (a child died in the
first weeks of the journey), the *William Brown* had sailed a mostly west-
erly heading against seas that fought her every day, the ship's speed
reduced by the labour of climbing the high waves that contrary gales pro-
duce. "In the fore part of my voyage I had it very stormy for about 22 or 23
days," Captain George Harris later testified.

The emigrant passengers, mostly Irish with a smattering of Scottish,
were lodged amidships in a cargo space converted into a communal dor-
mitory with racks of wooden bunks stacked two or three berths high, one
berth per family. Single women, strangers at the beginning of the voyage,
were put together to save space, sometimes two or three in the same bunk.

The sounds and smells of emigrant quarters on ships like the 650-ton
William Brown conspired to dull the senses. It was hard to tell sometimes
which sense bore the worst assault. It wasn't simply the stink of sixty-four
unwashed bodies jammed into an unventilated hold for more than a
month. To that was added the stench of the curtained privy, whose bucket

was often upended in heavy swells. Then there was the tang of past cargoes that had worked its way into the very timbers of the ship over its sixteen years on the North Atlantic run. There was as well a whiff of the barnyard from the animals—chickens and pigs—carried as food for the journey. Finally, beneath it all, were the smells of vomit, wet wood, damp clothes and the occasional rotting timber. The only comfort was that what the emigrants had known—cheap overcrowded boarding rooms and sod houses with smoky cook stoves—rarely smelled much better.

In a storm, however, the horrendous *sound* of the ship against the sea, and of the wind itself, dominated every other sense. "Thunder is no more than a dog's bark compared with the tremendous roar of the wind and sea," a nineteenth-century North Atlantic traveller wrote. "We had scarcely turned in when a sea struck her, making her reel most awfully. It came down the scuttle like a millstream, washing some of us nearly out of our beds. Two of our boxes broke from their lashings and rolled about from side to side, strewing their contents as they went." The chaos was absolute, the fear as close and chilling as the water that came through the hatches and rippled along the deck. "It was an anxious time: females shrieking, the water almost floating our things and the pails, can, etc, knocking about. It is impossible to convey an idea of such an awful sight. We had very little sleep this night."

For the *William Brown*, it had been like that for weeks until, on 19 April, crew and passengers were granted a respite. All that day and into the night, the ship charged forward in a southwesterly direction. For the first time in weeks, she was aided rather than impeded by the strong seas and the brisk winds that characterize the North Atlantic in the last weeks of winter and the first days of spring. When the winds are favourable and the seas kindly, there is on board a ship—any ship—a sense of well-being. The seas seem to invite it and its sailors onward. There was, therefore, little sense of danger among the *William Brown*'s crew or passengers as they entered the ice fields.

Toward 9 P.M., near the end of the first hour of the first watch, the night began to turn hazy. The stars, which moments before had glittered in the chilly air, were gradually obscured by first a light mist and then by almost a fog of moisture rising from ice fields nearby but still not visible. If any aboard were Londoners, they might have experienced a moment of

Crowded conditions of emigrant quarters on a ship similar to the *William Brown*. From the *Illustrated London News*, 10 May 1861, courtesy British Newspaper Library

nostalgia for those Thames nights when a cold front pulled moisture from the river, holding the supersaturated air over the land. Then, the air turned opaque and vision was even more obscured. It was as if all who sailed upon the ship suddenly had developed cataracts.

One of the crew, Charlie Smith, was working on the foredeck when he heard a seaman at the bow sing out, "Bear off, bear away!" Like Smith, the seaman was a member of the first watch that had come on duty at 8 P.M. when second mate Walter Parker, the watch commander, set his men to repairing some of the havoc that weeks of stormy weather had caused. Torn sails needed mending; worn lines needed to be replaced or respliced. Deck fittings loosened by the storms required attention. There was work enough for them all.

On hearing the warning, Smith looked over and saw a pan of ice almost dead ahead. In his turn, he called to the helmsman, "Bear off, bear away!" Joseph Stetson was at the wheel and maybe he heard the warning, maybe not. Sometimes it is hard to hear words shouted above the sounds of a ship rushing through heavy seas. But if he did not, then Parker did, ordering Stetson to put the helm hard over, the ship away. Stetson tried to change course, but, by then, they were almost upon the ice.

Nineteenth-century sailing ships were not racing vessels built for manoeuvrability. In the best of circumstances, it took time and effort to turn them even a few degrees. There is the inertia of the vessel, its tonnage propelled forward and held in balance by sails trimmed just so. To change direction means pushing the weight of the vessel against that of the sea through which it is travelling. It is hard enough to change direction when sails are reefed and speed therefore reduced, the motion of mass through the water diminished. With all sails unfurled, the ship heading more generally with the wind than against it, a quick course change requires more than a turn of the wheel. Sailors must be called to loose the lines that hold the sails taut, breaking the balance of tensions that propel the vessel forward, if the rudder is to take full control.

The first blow was glancing, the ship sliding across ice rather than colliding directly against it. It must have felt like scraping over a sandbar near low tide, the keel chafing against but not stalling upon the ground. The hull is slowed by friction as the vessel seeks a way past. In the North Atlantic, hundreds of miles from shore, there are no sandbars, but in April there *are* icebergs riding the cold currents that flow down from cold northern waters to the Gulf Stream. Some ride above the sea, large as tenement buildings. Others are submariners, cruising below the sea with at most their peaks just visible above the waves. The ice pauses, its southern run stalled where the Gulf Stream's relative heat holds them in thrall as it speeds their dissolution. When this happens, the sky is filled with haze or fog, a condition that should have alerted the sailors on watch aboard the *William Brown*.

Decades later, passengers on the *Titanic* described the sound of ice against a ship's hull precisely. What each heard depended on his or her location: amidships and below in steerage, in the crew's forward cabins, or lodged in first-class quarters on the upper decks with a porthole and a view of the sea. George Hander, a honeymooner travelling with his new bride, called it "a sort of rumbling, scraping noise." Lady Cosmo Duff Gordon in first class said there was a sound "as though somebody had drawn a giant finger along the side of the ship." It was, Mrs. J. Stuart White said, as if the ship had rolled over "a thousand marbles."

Aboard the *William Brown*, the sound was less because the impact was light, the sound of rolling over a hundred marbles rather than a thousand. As such, it was just one more odd sound, one more jolt on a voyage that had been filled with the noise of a ship continuously pummelled by early spring storms and their heavy seas. Those who heard or felt the encounter paid scant attention to it. Ships at sea are noisy beasts, wooden ships the loudest of all. There is the groan of timbers protesting against the push of the sea, the rush of the wake and the sound of the waves themselves; sometimes they brush quietly against the hull, but at others they fall with a loud crash upon the deck. Sails flap loudly until hauled taut by ropes crying through pulley blocks that moan as if the strain of it all were just too much to bear. The rigging creaks as it pulls against the tension of stretched canvas sail.

Amidst all this, the noise of the ship scraping the ice pan would be easy to miss. Only the first mate, Francis Rhodes, later said he noticed it, describing a "violent shock" that roused him from his bunk: "I immediately ran on deck and found the ship had struck an iceberg." The helmsman, Stetson, or Parker, the second mate, told him they had sailed against a pan of ice, not an iceberg, and the danger was already past. Assured there was no immediate problem, Rhodes then returned to his cabin for a change of clothes. The implication was that he intended to return to the bridge and take charge.

The problem of history, of remembered events recalled long past their time, is that people say one thing in the hours or days after a disaster, and say something else months or years later. In reconstructing this story, it has been necessary to navigate the shifting truths of survivors who told and retold their stories to each other and to friends, to officials and to lawyers, and especially to themselves. For example, when talking about that night, Rhodes afterward always insisted he was roused by the first strike and then went below to change into warmer clothes. He presented himself as an able ship's officer who did as much as any man could. But almost surely what he remembered was actually the second strike that *was* violent and universally felt.

If the first blow was as harsh as Rhodes remembered, then the sailors off watch, and probably the passengers, too, would have marked it. As first officer, Rhodes's quarters, and those of the captain, were aft, where the sea's motion is less intrusive and the berths, therefore, more comfortable. The crew's quarters, on the other hand, were a small crowded area between decks in the bow of the ship, where motion is exaggerated: every lift and drop of the hull against the waves is amplified. Had the first strike been a violent shock, the hammocks in which the sailors rested would have swung in an unnatural syncopation rather than the casual sway of a steady boat in harmony with a rollicking sea. As for the passengers sleeping on wooden bunks nailed into the ribs of the ship's central hold, a violent shock would have dumped them to the deck.

But none of the off-watch sailors and none of the passengers remembered the first strike. It seems unlikely that Rhodes, alone among all the crew and passengers, felt it. And had Rhodes believed the ship was in danger—and a violent collision with ice is the very definition of danger—there were actions he would have taken immediately. He would have ordered the ship's sails reduced and sent a seaman to check the holds for leaks. He would have notified the captain, because it was his job to do so when the vessel's seaworthiness was affected. To do less would have been negligent, and Rhodes was ever after at pains to assert his competence and care.

ON THE *William Brown*, there were two communities: that of the crew and that of the steerage. While the worlds of sailor and passenger were necessarily distinct, there was perhaps a shared sense of class that joined them. But what most distinguished them was this: the passengers were on a single voyage, whereas the sailors perpetually voyaged. They were only at home between destinations, men never really here or there across the span of their careers.

As importantly, perhaps, the ship's crew existed within a strict hierarchy that was almost military: captain, first mate, second mate, common sailors and, lastly, the cook and steward who served them. Another less formal hierarchy placed the experienced helmsman above the young deckhand, the truly able seaman above the neophyte on his first voyage.

The order of the passengers jammed together in the central hold was less structured. On this ship, as on others sailing westward across the Atlantic in the 1840s, most were Irish travelling to the New World where family members, earlier emigrants, had already established themselves. We know the stories of some but not all of them. Nineteen-year-old Bridget McGee was on her way to Philadelphia where her father had a stable. With her was an uncle who was to work for her father, helping to expand his business. Biddy Nugent's mother ran a lodging house in Philadelphia, a business sufficiently prosperous to permit her to bring over both her seventeen-year-old daughter and her brother, Biddy's

Uncle John. Mrs. Anderson and her three daughters were on their way to join her husband, a physician who had prospered in Cincinnati.

Also on board were extended families—brothers and sisters and nephews and cousins—making their way together. Rather than sending one or two relatives to establish a beachhead in the New World, they chose to scrimp and save until they had the passage monies for everyone at once. There were twelve in the Luden family, for example, all heading for Philadelphia from Colonel Stewart's County Tyrone estate in Ireland. The Carrs, also from County Tyrone, included five children, both parents, and an assortment of nieces and nephews.

Of course, not all the passengers were equal. In the holds of emigrant ships as in the drawing rooms of higher society, some always stand before the rest. On this voyage, Margaret Edgar held a special place. Most of the emigrants turned to her as a voice of reason when a problem or dispute arose. Even Captain Harris was solicitous. When he wished to ask after below-deck life, he sought out Mrs. Edgar. It was not simply her age, forty-two years, that set her apart; that she was a Scottish woman travelling with mostly Irish emigrants added to her status. In those days the Irish were dismissed in both England and America either as drunken and shiftless if amusing paddies or as seditious radicals to be restrained by the law.

THE BATTLE OF THE STREETS.

The cities that British emigrants fled were as crowded as the ships that carried them to North America. This drawing titled *Battle of the Streets* illustrated an article on the destruction of mews and lanes in London and the crowding of the poor that resulted. From *Punch* 1845, vol. 5, 64

AFTER THE FIRST STRIKE, the sailors of the first watch returned to the business of sailing. The rush of adrenaline that had energized the few who had seen the ice pan soon receded like a tide, leaving tiredness in its wake. Then as now, sailors generally stood four-hour watches, except between the hours of 4 and 8 P.M. when two-hour watches, called "dog watches," are covered by different complements of men.

Splitting what otherwise would be a full, four-hour shift permits the crew's hours of duty gradually to rotate through the day. But to make the system work, the men of the first dog watch also stand the four-hour first watch that begins at 8 P.M. and ends at midnight. They work a shift and a half in an eight-hour period, disorienting and tiring no matter how fine the day.

The sailors who had come on deck that night at 8 P.M., therefore, were already tired, having had only a two-hour rest following their two-hour watch, and had four more hours of service to look forward to. Sailing in the days before electronics was hard work at any time, but in the Atlantic at the end of winter, when storms and high waves dominate the sky and the sea, it could be brutal and wearing. Arduous as it was during the day, at night it was harder still.

Nineteenth-century sailors had nothing but the light of stars and the moon, and the very limited range of human senses, to guide them. In the dark, they worked as much by hearing and feel as by sight, by the sound of the ship in the water and the tension or slack on a line. The shallow beating of a sail that a moment ago had been perfectly concave meant that the wind had shifted and that the sailors would have to reshape the canvas to the new direction.

A short time after the strike, Captain Harris appeared on the quarterdeck. In the 1840s, a ship captain quite literally had the power of life and death over his crew. If he decided to punish a sailor (for swearing or drunkenness, perhaps) by keelhauling or by flogging, it was his right. Should he decide to hang a man for a more serious offence, he could do that, too. So when Captain Harris came on deck, everyone walked a little more briskly, paid a little more attention to the task at hand.

Perhaps that is why the captain decided to visit the deck that night, to enjoy the respectful company of his men. Most captains liked to observe the men of the various watches, and it is pleasing to accept the deferential report of a subordinate. Or, perhaps, Harris was on deck that night because it is customary for the captain to be present during the most dangerous parts of a voyage, and the waters they were sailing were ones where icebergs were frequent in the spring. But if so, it is odd that he did not order any precautionary measures. In harsh weather or uncertain waters, it was common practice to reduce sail at nightfall and set an extra watch. When sailing into a perilous region, it was prudent seamanship to send crewmen up the masts and into the bow, positions from which danger might be spotted a little sooner. On entering ice fields, it was wise to take the sea's temperature.

From the seventeenth into the twentieth century, ship captains in the North Atlantic in the spring used a thermometer to take the temperature of the water at regular intervals. If the temperature dropped, there was a likelihood that icebergs were near. In the days before the chronometer and the sextant, the thermometer was an indispensable navigational tool for those who sailed northern waters. This practice enabled Ben Franklin, when he was postmaster general of the United States, to draw the first map of the Gulf Stream. He asked ship captains to keep records of their daily speed and water temperature as they sailed to and from Britain. The map he made from this information detailed the current that carried

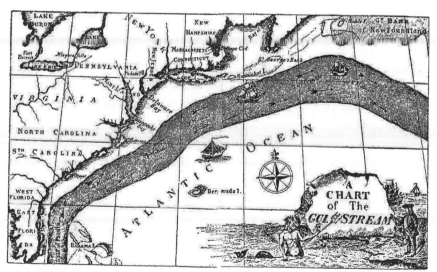

Ben Franklin's map of the Gulf Stream based on sea temperatures, 1786.

ships on the North Atlantic run and that acted as a barrier and catchment for the ice that yearly flowed south from cold arctic waters.

Neither Captain Harris nor anyone else ever suggested he came on deck because he felt the glancing blow of the first strike. Indeed, afterward, he never mentioned having any knowledge of it. Nor is this surprising. To have witnessed the strike and taken no precautions would have amounted to worse than poor judgment. To admit to such failure might have lost the man his command. So Harris insisted he simply was taking the air on the weather deck when the second strike caught him unaware.

Curiously, just one sailor, Charlie Smith, later testified that the only action taken after the first strike was that Parker ordered a modest sail change of the type made several times a watch. Men were sent to lower the fore topmast sail and then the smaller fore topgallant that hung high on the foremost mast. To do this, they climbed the lines to the appropriate boom, slid out along its length, and then gathered in and lashed the sail to the spar on which they sat. The process was time consuming and arduous, but the letting in and taking out of sails was a task that sailors might perform several times on any single watch.

After the first strike, the air developed a sharp, almost crystalline feel, as if the night itself were a hard-edged, physical presence. Shortly before 9 P.M. came the second strike. The *William Brown* hit its iceberg, colliding with an impact that reverberated throughout the hull. At that moment, all the sounds of the boat, of the water and wind and wooden planks flexing, were silenced. And, of course, the feel of the vessel was irrevocably altered as mass and momentum were transformed into the energy of a collision that crushed the forward planks—port *and* starboard—in a single blow.

"She struck very heavy," Walter Parker said, "which drove me from my feet and stopped the headway of the ship." A passenger, Mary Corr, recalled, "The shock was so great as to throw me over a box in which I kept provisions." "The shock was so violent that we thought the ship was broken in two," said Bridget McGee, another of the women in steerage. *This* was the "violent shock" Rhodes later remembered incorrectly as the first strike.

When a boat drops in a heartbeat from full speed to stopped, when the sound of a strike shudders down the keel through the ribs and up the spars that hold the sails, the only question is whether the effect is mortal. Parker rushed to ascertain the damage and begin whatever repairs he could. "We found two feet of water in the hold immediately—we pumped and sounded and found she was making water rapidly."

Afterward, Captain Harris claimed he took charge at once. "The first indication I had of the ice was when she struck. I immediately called all hands to shorten sails, and commenced pumping the ship when one of the men came aft and informed me the ship's bows were stove in. Then one of the men and I went to the forecastle and found the ship's bows were stove in. There was a sheet of water coming in on both sides of the hull as large as a man's body, so that it was impossible to get down to stop the leak."

To confuse matters further, Rhodes later insisted that *he* was the one who took charge of the vessel, personally surveying the damage before reporting to the captain: "On going to the forepeak, I found the planks stove in and the ship filling with water. I then proposed to Captain Harris to shorten sail, which was accordingly done, and on sounding the pumps found she had two feet of water in the hold."

And maybe it happened that way. Maybe Captain Harris, his first mate and the watch commander's crewman *all* inspected the damage, all came to the same conclusions and all ordered the pumps manned and the sails shortened. More probably, each remembered what he wanted to and reordered events to fit his own purpose.

Despite the claims of the captain and first mate, it was almost certainly Parker, whose watch it was, who sent a man to check the damage and ordered sailors to man the pumps. These were leather bellows on a wooden base. Large, clumsy and inefficient, they were designed to clear the bilges after a storm and to remove the water that constantly trickled in through crevices in the caulking. No matter how well fitted the boat, there was always seepage as the vessel turned across the waves, as small spaces opened when wooden planks expanded, contracted or twisted under the battering of large waves.

What those nineteenth-century pumps could not do was move large volumes of water at a rapid rate when the bow—port and starboard—was hugely holed. They could not stem the full onrush of the sea. To be fair, the huge, power-driven pumps on modern ships could not have saved the *William Brown* either. The damage was too great.

Parker then ordered the sails shortened, sending men up the masts to drop sails still full with the wind, still driving the ship onto the ice. He next called general quarters, summoning all hands to service. By all accounts, it was at least ten minutes after the second strike until he did that, however. Ten minutes seems a short enough time to a man sitting on a firm chair in a comfortable office on dry land. After an iceberg has smashed starboard and port planks forward on a cold, hazy night in the mid-Atlantic, ten minutes is forever.

In hindsight, it should have been obvious from the violence of the second strike that the ship was mortally wounded. But this was not, after all, the first time in her sixteen years on the North Atlantic run that the *William Brown* had struck something. Nor was it the first in the captain's career—or Parker's, or Rhodes's—that a vessel they were serving on was damaged. They were seasoned sailors who had spent their working lives on ships whose rough wooden planks, caulked with oakum and covered with pitch, took a fearful pounding from wind, sea and storm. Scarcely a voyage took place in which one or another hull repair was not required. This may explain why Parker did not immediately summon the off-watch crew. He had been knocked off his feet before, time and again had seen damage that could be mitigated by jury-rigged repairs and good seamanship.

Had only a few planks been damaged, it would have been easy enough to fix them. To stem the flow, the hole would have been stuffed with spare sailcloth until a wooden patch could be fashioned to reinforce the surrounding planks from inside the hull. Had the planks been stove in on just one side of the vessel, a spare sail coated with tar would have been frapped over the wound from outside. Carried down and across the keel before being lashed to the opposite side, the covering would have been held in place over the hole by the pressure of the sea itself. Then, from inside the hull, the ship's carpenter would have reinforced the covering by nailing in place spare planks carried against such an occasion. These and other tricks were part of a sailor's knowledge.

If nothing else, a temporary hull patch would have offered the possibility that the pumps might at least slow the onrush of water even if they could not clear the hold. The time gained would have permitted the crew and passengers to prepare for the ship's dissolution. But both port *and* starboard planks were stove in. *Two* waterfalls, not one, were pouring in through the vessel's sides. The pumps were insufficient to cope with even half the volume of the incoming flood. After years of almost constant sailing across the North Atlantic—from Philadelphia to London, Liverpool to Boston, New York to London, and then back, perhaps, to Quebec City—the life of the *William Brown* was coming to an end.

THE LAST WATCH

CAPTAIN HARRIS QUICKLY DECIDED that there was no time for repairs, for consideration or recrimination. "Finding it was impossible to free the ship with pumps," he said, "I then immediately gave orders to get the boats out to save as many souls as we possibly could." Harris knew that lowering the boats at once doomed at least half the ship's complement.

The *William Brown* carried no lifeboats, only two open tenders secured on deck. Together, they would not serve even half the passengers and crew. Auxiliary craft sufficient to carry a ship's roster in the event of a disaster were as rare in the nineteenth century as maritime catastrophes themselves were frequent. The first purpose-built lifeboats, ones with positive buoyancy, were purchased for the ss *Great Britain*, launched in 1843. The *Great Britain* was a new kind of steamship whose lifeboats were an experiment added to its already radical design. Once the ship's safety had been established, however, its complement of lifeboats was reduced from the six sufficient to save all passengers and crew to only four.

The sole hope for the *William Brown*'s sailors and passengers lay in the ship's two tenders: an open longboat designed to carry goods and cargo in harbour, and a smaller jolly boat used to ferry passengers in harbour. Both lacked the buoyancy, decking, freeboard and keel that would have suited them for service as ocean-going craft. During the voyage, both boats had been periodically filled with seawater to prevent their planks and caulking from drying out. After an hour or less, the seawater was drained by removing the plug from the bilge hole in the bottom of the boat. It was a minor ritual of ship's maintenance, a nod to the havoc that fickle Neptune could wreak.

A LARGE SAILING SHIP is a scene of controlled chaos. Work on deck is co-ordinated with work aloft as different crews handle different lines and sails. If the ship is holed, the number of simultaneous tasks increases. Not only must everything be done at once, but each task—reducing sail, manning the pumps, preparing the boats—is itself a complex job requiring a number of sailors working together. To launch the jolly boat and the longboat, for example, each was first freed from its lashings and its canvas cover removed. The materials stored in them—they were a handy place to keep spare lumber, blocks and lines—were thrown on deck or overboard. Provisions—water and food—were gathered and placed on board. Then the boats were raised by tackle so that they could be swung out over the water, free of the deck. On the *William Brown*, this required cutting away the railing that ringed the deck as it was so high that swinging the boats over it proved to be impossible.

According to Walter Parker, "After Captain Harris ordered the boats to be cleared away the longboat was cleared away and put over the side. I cleared the jolly boat, and after this the jolly boat then was lowered down with four men besides myself and a Miss Lafferty in her. After the boat was lowered, the rest of the crew came down by the boat tackle falls, by which we hoist up the boat, and a few minutes after the men were in the boat I took it alongside the ship and took Captain Harris. Then the boats were made fast to each other—I recollect nothing about the longboat from the time she was taken out of the blocks. I do not remember who were in the longboat."

It all sounds expeditious, a simple set of procedures. But it was two hours, by Rhodes's count, between the moment of the second strike and the moment the auxiliary craft rowed away.

When Captain Harris gave the order to abandon ship, he gave it not to the passengers but to a crew whose first (and second) thoughts were for their own safety. Having clewed the sails and lashed the wheel so it would hold a straight course without a helmsman, the sailors prepared to escape with little thought for the passengers, who were left to tend for themselves.

James "Jack" Black was among the first emigrants to come on deck. A thirty-two-year-old Edinburgh native, he was in bed with his wife, Ellen, when the *William Brown* struck the iceberg. "I went on deck and inquired of the Captain if there was any danger, who at first said 'no,' but afterward told me the vessel was going down." There was no sense in denial. All around them, sailors were busy preparing the jolly boat and longboat.

Black rushed to inform his fellow emigrants of the disaster. "It was a quarter hour after that shock that Jack Black called down that the ship was sinking," said Bridget McGee. Another passenger, young Owen Carr, agreed. "Jack Black went up on deck and presently he halloed for his wife to come and fetch a blanket with her for the ship was sinking."

While some passengers took the time first to dress and then pray, Ellen Black immediately climbed the companionway to the deck with nothing but a blanket over her nightclothes. "The seamen were crying out to keep the pumps going," she said. "I took a hand and assisted at the pumps until I was exhausted." Having offered at least token assistance— she tired quickly—Ellen Black and her husband made for the longboat as the sailors swung it over the side.

Several other passengers also rushed on deck after Black's warning, and then, in the words of Mary Corr, a sailor "came down and told us the vessel was sinking and to do the best we could for ourselves." From the start, the sole thought of crew and passengers alike was personal salvation. The best any could hope for was a few minutes' head start in the race for seats in the two boats.

"The vessel has been split," thought twenty-two-year-old Julie McCadden. "I told the two girls who shared my bunk to get up and get dressed." As they grabbed warm clothes from their footlockers, she, too, went to find the captain and "ask if the vessel was in danger."

"Yes," replied Captain Harris, "the ship is going to be lost."

"What are you going to do for us, then?" she asked.

"Nothing," Captain Harris replied. "You must all do the best as you can for yourselves."

Hearing that, she wasted no time. McCadden was the first to grab a seat in the longboat, even before it was slung over the side. Like an empress in a palanquin, she sat immobile as the boat was first hoisted and then lowered to hang in the air beside the ship. "When I got into the boat there were two sailors keeping her to the side of the ship," McCadden later said. "One of them told me to get back to the ship, but I refused."

Seventeen-year-old Susannah Edgar was no less decisive. Leaving the bunk she shared with a sister and cousin, she "immediately went on deck and joined the crew occupied in taking down sails and lowering the boat." While she was probably less than adept, she must have been welcomed as another hand on the tackle blocks, because one of the crew then helped her to the bow of the longboat once it was ready for loading.

Few of the passengers had her pluck. The majority remained below until well after Jack Black's warning. Some waited a brief time and then went on deck to investigate before hurrying back to gather their families and belongings. Others fled in haste, taking nothing with them. Those who took time to put on warmer clothes and gather a few precious items took too long. They were left on deck as the jolly boat and the longboat were lowered. The ones who made it into the boats had not paused for anything.

The sailors on watch were dressed already, of course. Those off watch were sleeping in their clothes—common practice on an unheated ship—with perhaps their jackets bundled under their heads as pillows. Unlike the passengers, the crew did not travel with treasures they could not easily leave behind. Their few mementos—a gold earring, a cross or perhaps a saint's medallion—they wore. And so, as the passengers were being told the ship was sinking, the sailors were already staking out their places in the boats. They made sure there were small casks of water aboard, that some food had been provisioned. They knew that in the middle of the ocean, survival meant a seat in a boat, any boat, and that provisions were as necessary as physical space.

The *William Brown's* sailors were irritated when a passenger commandeered a seat in the captain's jolly boat before it could be lowered away. James Patrick's sister-in-law, Eliza Lafferty, spied the chance and took it, despite the insistence of sailors that she join her fellow emigrants in their rush to the larger longboat. She refused, however, and because no one was willing to manhandle her away, she became the only emigrant in the jolly boat, whose complement ultimately included Captain Harris, second mate Walter Parker and seven common sailors.

By the time Mary Corr arrived on deck, the boats were being swung overboard, cleared of the deck and readied for the open sea. With her was a younger cousin she had been caring for. Corr went on deck to find the infant's mother, whom she left kneeling on deck with the child in her arms, surrounded by her husband and other children. Mary Corr made for the longboat. The child and its parents did not survive the night.

Others were more fortunate. Young Owen Carr was tumbled into the longboat almost by accident. "When I went on deck they were cutting the boats from the side of the ship. I went down again to get some clothes for I was nearly naked. When I came up the longboat was going over the side of the vessel. I tried to get in but fell out, when Julie McCadden pushed me in again."

Not everyone's entry into the boat was so haphazard. Margaret Edgar and her family received treatment befitting the dowager of the lower decks. The Maryland-born cook, Henry Murray, and seaman Charlie Smith helped Mrs. Edgar into the longboat. Only her daughter, Susannah, and, of course, Julie McCadden, made it into the boat before the older woman. After helping Mrs. Edgar, the two men handed down another of her daughters, her namesake, nineteen-year-old Margaret. "Get to the forepart of the boat," Smith told the women. "There you'll be out of the way."

Most were treated with less courtesy. In general, the crew either ignored the passengers—leaving each to his or her own initiative—or actively discouraged their attempts to gain a seat. Bridget McGee later gave the most complete account of these events from the perspective of a passenger. Other witnesses who saw things that she did not added details to the story, but McGee was a natural reporter whose statement was calm, complete and unadorned.

"There was a good many on deck before me," she said. "When I went on deck, the sailors were busy getting out the longboat and jolly boat. There was no water in the steerage when I left it. I heard them pumping as soon as the ship struck. I saw Holmes as soon as I got on deck. He was throwing wood and things from the longboat over the side, before they launched the boat. The cook and Jack Stetson were helping him. The jolly boat was hanging out of the bow. The sailors were getting her ready to put her into the water. I waited until the longboat was got out, and went into it. Some of the other passengers were in before me."

Alexander Holmes was a Swedish-born sailor in Parker's watch, one of those who had stood the first dog watch and then returned to the deck, two hours later, for what turned out to be the ship's final watch. At sea since his tenth birthday, the twenty-six-year-old had a reputation for being a respectful seaman, a competent if uninspired fellow who followed commands without complaint. In the world of nineteenth-century sailing ships, this was high praise indeed. Sailors were not supposed to think or question but simply to obey. They were told never to get "above" themselves, to be content with their lot. If that meant life as an anonymous member of one or another country's maritime fleet, there were far worse lives to be lived in the burgeoning cities ashore.

Holmes was the one responsible for preparing the longboat, while Murray, the cook, cut away the ship's railing with a hatchet so the boat could be swung out and lowered away. Murray had served aboard the *William Brown* since 1839, and though he was not a sailor, he knew what needed to be done. While Murray chopped away, Holmes took off the boat's canvas cover, tossed aside the spare parts stored within and grabbed a small wooden cask of water kept on deck for the use of the watch. Portable and easily moved, it was refilled daily from larger barrels stored in the hold below.

"The longboat was then launched by Holmes and other sailors," said Bridget McGee. "The boat was not nearly full at that time. There were men and women in her when I got in. Bridget Nugent was in when I got in. James Black and his wife came in after me. There were others in but I don't know who they were.

"Holmes ordered Bridget Nugent and me to go on board the ship again. He took hold of Bridget by the shoulders when he told her to go on board the ship. I heard her interceding with him. She told him he might pull her about as much as he pleased, but she would not get out [of the longboat]. I also told him I would not leave the boat and go back to the sinking ship."

Holmes gave up when Smith said to him, "They're women, after all. Leave them alone." Smith then ordered the young women to move forward to be out of the way. What did it matter if *these* two were saved rather than others? Space in the boats was insufficient to save all the *William Brown*'s passengers and crew. That is why there were no lifeboat drills in those days, no on-board rehearsals against the event of disaster. Why remind people that, if the ship sank, most would drown?

It did not matter if Bridget or Biddy or Julie held a seat in the long-boat or died on the sinking ship. Whether the Blacks or the Patricks or the Corrs lived or died was irrelevant. Some would die, and who might live was a matter of guile, gall and chance. What *did* matter was the longboat itself. The sailors feared that too many passengers fighting for too few seats might swamp it and thus endanger them all. That was the reason why Holmes had tried to lighten the boat's load, and thus improve its chances, by ordering the two young women back to the canted deck of the slowly sinking *William Brown*. Holmes's argument with McGee and Nugent was replayed elsewhere, and for the same reason. Other sailors worried about the boat's capacity and they, too, sought to convince this or that passenger that he or she should return to the now wallowing ship.

It is hard to blame the sailors for their attempts to discourage the passengers, who were by then crawling over each other in a desperate effort to gain a seat. Passengers were "jumping into the boat as it was being lowered down, which the crew tried to prevent them from doing, but could not," Holmes said. "The instant it was lowered into the water," Rhodes remembered with a shudder, "a number of passengers jumped from the rail into the boat which was then dropped astern" to prevent this. Some made it, but many did not.

In 1841 there were not even the lithographs that a decade later would fill the pages of illustrated dailies in cities like New York, Paris and London. A sense of the details of disaster, of the confusion that reigned as some were saved while others had to watch from the sinking deck of a holed sailing ship did not come until later in the century. In January 1873, however, when the *Northfleet* was struck by a steamer off the coast of Dungeness, Scotland, the disaster was immortalized by an artist at the *Illustrated London News*. There were only 142 seats in its auxiliary vessels, enough for perhaps a third of the 412 passengers bound for Tasmania.

Among the *Northfleet*'s survivors was the captain's wife. Although Captain Knowles placed her and other women in the bosun's lifeboat, he stayed on his ship in an attempt to save as many of his passengers as pos-sible. It was this gesture of duty, familial care and personal sacrifice that the newspaper artist immortalized. The longboat, overfull and rocking in the

The chaos of a sinking ship is captured in this lithograph, *The Captain's Farewell from the Northfleet*. From the *Illustrated London News*, 1 February 1873, courtesy British Newspaper Library

waves, pulls away from the dying ship, whose captain stands on deck to share the fate of the 300 men, women and children remaining in his charge.

The lithograph is dark, the faces difficult to discern. And yet it is this very lack of clarity that best conveys the sense of uncertainty and confusion that inevitably marks the emotions of those saved as they look upon friends and families who minutes later will be drowned.

As the *William Brown*'s longboat filled and then became overfull, Francis Rhodes ordered his sailors to haul away from the ship and the remaining passengers seeking a seat on board. "The passengers kept clinging to the side of the ship in order to get into it," James Black said. The sailors "were obliged to push her off, and she was hauled about 14 yards from the vessel." That was far enough to keep away the passengers who, leaping for the boat, had fallen into the cold water. Near naked, they rapidly succumbed to hypothermia. If well dressed, their warm clothes weighed heavily, dragging them quickly under the waves.

The longboat, rigged only for rowing, was 22½ feet long, almost 3 feet deep and 6 feet wide at the beam. It could hold perhaps twenty or so passengers. In the end, it carried more than forty people from the sinking ship to the perilous safety of the ocean. The smaller yawl-rigged jolly boat, whose dimensions are not known, held ten people from the ship.

The wonder is not that thirty-one men, women and children were abandoned to their deaths on the sinking ship but that more than thirty passengers, the officers and all the seventeen crew survived its loss. The operative rule in 1841 was not "women and children first" but "every man jack for himself."

The story was much the same when the *Titanic* sank in 1912. Only one of eighteen lifeboats—some no more than 60 per cent full—returned to pick up surviving passengers who had fled the sinking deck for the sea. In Boat Number Five, a lady begged the steward in charge of the vessel to not go back. "Why should we all lose our lives in a useless attempt to save others from the ship?" she asked. In Boat Number Two, passengers urged the ship's officer on board to not return to look for survivors. In Boat Number Six, on the other hand, a first-class passenger, Mrs. J. J. Brown, begged the ship's officer in charge to return to the scene. Even though the boat was less than half full, he refused, painting "a vivid picture of swimmers grappling at the boat, of No. 6 swamping and capsizing. The women still pleaded, while the cries grew fainter. In boat after boat, the story was the same: a timid suggestion, a stronger refusal, nothing done."

If there were any impulses to heroism among the crew of the *William Brown*, they were dampened by the captain's example. He made no orders to his crew to care for the passengers or to see to their safety, even though the passengers were his responsibility. If Captain Harris seemed indifferent, then why should the sailors concern themselves with the emigrants' fate?

To be fair, the axiom that "a captain should go down with the ship," like the master of the *Northfleet*, was one whose currency had yet to be fully struck. In the 1840s, navigation was no simple matter. Only the captain, and perhaps the mate, knew the art of navigation, and thus the best way to salvation; therefore, nobody in the longboat or jolly boat thought the captain should give up his place. They needed him. All knew the captain's job was to steer survivors away from the sinking ship and toward the nearest shore.

After giving the order to abandon ship, Harris rushed to his cabin to check what the ship's last position was—probably calculated from a sun sight taken in the late afternoon—and to ascertain the direction of the nearest port. He grabbed several charts, his quadrant and two handheld compasses, but he did not save the ship's log, useful as it would have been at a future inquiry.

Still, Harris's departure was a tad precipitous, even by the standards of the day. The rule for nineteenth-century military vessels also held, in 1841, for merchant craft. "Both in the revolutionary Navy and the Royal Navy of France, the captain, by law, was required to be the last man to leave his ship. It was not just the tradition of the sea, a code of honour; it was a matter of discipline. In no other way could order be preserved in a situation of extreme distress."

Whether the ship was French or English, Dutch or American, orders for sailors from a firm, unquestioned commander were considered to be a necessary balance to the sometimes self-serving inclination of lesser souls. All assumed that the captain's presence in the lifeboat would increase the chances of everyone's survival. But the assumption also was that the captain would not leave his ship until he had assured as orderly a departure as possible by his crew and passengers.

As THE WOMEN WERE DEFENDING their longboat seats, even as Owen Carr was being unceremoniously dumped head over heels into the longboat by McCadden, Captain Harris was securing himself in the jolly boat as it prepared to pull away. He therefore did not see Holmes, the sailor who had tried to convince McGee and Nugent to give up their seats, leaving his own. The longboat had lowered away and, while still tethered to the dying ship, was standing off, away from its sides, when Holmes saw Margaret Edgar's youngest daughter, Isabella, on deck. She was crying out to her mother and sisters, who were settled in the bow of the longboat.

"I had been sick from the time we left Liverpool until the day we struck, and had not been on deck before," Isabella Edgar recalled. "When the ship struck I had nothing on but my nightclothes; I put on my dress in the steerage, and helped my mother to the side of the ship, where someone helped her into the boat." One sailor told Isabella to crawl into the longboat at the bow, but "the cook pulled me back and told me to go with him to the stern, that they would swing the boat round there; I fell down on deck in going there." So it was that her mother and sisters left her behind.

Certainly, the young woman was a piteous sight, but she was only one of more than thirty emigrants remaining on board. "The passengers on the ship were shrieking, and calling on the captain to take them off," said Bridget McGee. Some prayed. Others cried or shouted to friends and relatives who had gone to the longboat without them. Charles Conlin was safe, for example, but all his relatives were left on the ship. Ann Bradley made it into the boat, but her sister was left behind. And eleven-year-old Owen Carr left five brothers and sisters on deck.

When Mrs. Margaret Edgar pleaded, "Oh Sir! Someone! Save my daughter for pity's sake!" Holmes told the other sailors in the longboat to take them nearer the ship. No, Charlie Smith responded, it would be foolish and dangerous. The longboat could be crushed by a roll of the

The longboat of the *William Brown* from a woodblock print in *The Highwaymen and Pirates' Own Book*, by H.K. Brooke, published in 1845.

larger, dying, vessel, or sucked down in her death roll. It is safe, Holmes insisted, again urging Smith and the others to row them alongside the sinking ship.

After his mates brought the longboat close, Holmes grabbed the boat tackle falls that had lowered the longboat into the sea and hauled himself back aboard the *William Brown*. People on deck begged him to aid them. Mrs. Anderson, whose husband was a prosperous Cincinnati physician, offered him "as much money as you can earn in a year if only you will take me." She was travelling with her three daughters, but at that moment bargained only for herself. It was young Isabella Edgar whom Holmes had decided to rescue, however. "Money is not the object," Holmes told the woman. "It is lives I wish to save." Mrs. Anderson was left behind.

Henry Murray, still on board, helped Holmes to manoeuvre Isabella onto his back. Her arm around his neck, Holmes swung back overboard to climb down to the longboat as the girl shouted, "I'm coming, Mother, I'm coming!" The longboat was so crowded that when they returned to it, Isabella had to sprawl across her sister Susannah and Jane Johnston Edgar's shoulders. Murray followed Holmes from the ship to the longboat. Both struggled to find seats for themselves.

Later, Isabella Edgar was matter-of-fact about her salvation. "The cook picked me up, lifted me on Holmes's shoulders, and he carried me down by the rope into the boat. I held on by one hand, to his neck, and he swung down by the rope, holding it in one of his hands."

The sailors in the longboat, however, understood what she apparently did not; Holmes's rescue was a dangerous and perhaps foolhardy act. Even a year later, there was admiration for the audacity of the rescue in Parker's retelling of the deed: "I saw Holmes myself take a sick woman down by the tackle falls and put her in the boat. There was great danger in this, both of him and the female . . . He brought in the last passenger who was this woman."

In this selfless act, Holmes put himself at multiple risk. First, he gave up his seat in the longboat and risked the likelihood that another might claim it. Second, clambering up the side of a sinking vessel is a dangerous affair. Had he fallen either while climbing up or returning with the young woman on his back, the chance of being saved by his fellows was exceedingly slim. Third, had the *William Brown* begun its death roll while he was aboard, or before he returned, the longboat would have abandoned him in a minute. Finally, at any moment, Rhodes, who was in command of the longboat, might have decided that prudence dictated he cast off and pull away from the ship. After all, passengers were still attempting to climb aboard and she was already unwieldy in the rolling seas. Holmes's crazy act was, Rhodes must have thought, endangering them all.

Like most acts of heroism, Holmes's was neither rational nor sensible. At the time he surprised his fellow sailors, and, in retrospect, almost surely surprised himself, too. Why give up his seat in the longboat to save one among the many passengers left on deck? Even if he saved this young woman, the others were sure to drown. There was no good reason for him to aid her rather than another. This is not to say that Holmes didn't know the Edgar women, who had earned a few pence washing and mending his clothes. But they had done the same for other members of the crew, like Charlie Smith, and he did not leap from the longboat to save the daughter of his occasional laundress. Holmes did. Why he did this is anybody's guess. Perhaps he simply felt he had to do *something*, save *some*one, and Margaret Edgar's cries made Isabella an obvious goal. Maybe Holmes saved her for no other reason than that he could. He was twenty-six years of age, a young man in love with his strength. It is an age in which one can take pleasure in a physically arduous, demanding feat for its own sake.

The last of the crew to leave the *William Brown* was the black South Carolinian, Joseph L. Marshall. While only a steward, he had stayed on deck as long as possible—longer than any officer or sailor—to help as many passengers as he could. After Holmes and Murray left the deck, Marshall knew time had run out for him, too. He jumped into the sea, now rising toward the ship's deck, and swam toward the nearer of the two auxiliary craft, the jolly boat. The water was freezing and the waves made swimming difficult. When he reached the boat, however, Captain Harris refused him entry. "We are full enough," he said. "Swim to Mr. Rhodes in the longboat." The others in the small boat did not protest. Harris was the captain and it was his to say who entered his craft and who did not. Marshall then swam to the already overfull longboat. There, he was accepted if not welcomed, hauled into the centre of the craft and tumbled among the crew and passengers who together now waited for the ship to sink.

After Isabella's rescue—the only one of the night— the longboat pulled away. In the bow were the Edgars and most of the single women, who were soon cold and wet from the rain and the rolling ocean swells that broke against the boat. But at least for a time they were safe and out of the way of the oarlocks amidships where the sailors had congregated. They rowed for the warmth that exercise returns and to keep the boat's nose forward into the sea. It was the safest position, permitting the boat to meet the ocean's swells rather than be caught by them broadside, increasing the risk of a capsize. At the stern were the married couples, the Blacks and the Patricks, and any other emigrants who had managed to clamber aboard.

Until the *William Brown* finally sank, the jolly boat and the longboat rowed together, waiting like theatregoers for a tragedy's last act. Parker later recalled the type of minor detail that remains after a disaster—a small fact to hide the greater horror behind it—that the longboat was tethered to the ship's stern by a 10-fathom line. The jolly boat was tied to the longboat by another line, forming a two-boat train. Rhodes asked Captain Harris for more rope; he was worried the longboat would be upset if not sunk by the whirlpool that a sinking ship creates, pulling everything close by into its centre, flotsam and small boats alike.

The length of the tether was calculated so that the two boats were far enough away from the *William Brown* that other passengers could not swim to their side, demanding entry. But until the last moment, those on the boats were not ready to sever their ties completely; sentiment kept them attached to the floundering ship. Without it, they were indeed shipwrecked. And that was a state, inevitable though it was, they were unwilling to recognize until the ship sank and forced it upon them.

The passengers abandoned on the ship kept up a continuous cry to those who had found seats in the longboat and to the captain in his jolly boat. For some of the survivors, this was the most heart-rending time of all. "As the passengers on the ship were pleading and calling out, the mate on the longboat said to them, head turned away, 'Poor souls! You're only going down a short time before we do.' " Rhodes did not shout this as poor comfort but said it softly, in the voice we reserve for private prayers. He was both participant and observer, anticipating the deaths that they were about to meet and, he believed, his own as well.

The longboat's sailors waited until the last moment before severing the line that held it to the *William Brown*. They almost waited too long. When Rhodes finally gave the order, Holmes took his knife and struck at the rope, missing as the boat rocked with the waves. He grabbed the line to haul the boat in a bit and put tension on the rope to make it easier to cut. He missed again. On the third attempt, he succeeded in cutting the line, and the longboat was freed from the ship. At that instant, the passengers on deck knew their lives were forfeit.

Both boats rowed a good distance away from the sinking ship to watch in silence as the now bow-heavy vessel seemed almost to welcome its own death. The *William Brown* dove, front end first, like some vast marine creature too long in the air. Its aft-deck remained above the waves until the very last as below-deck air flowed back and up, forced out by the flood of seawater gushing into the broken hull.

Air pockets exploded underwater, bursting through hawser pipes, open hatches and portals not closed against the pressure of the sea. Even at a safe distance from the dying vessel, the survivors in the two boats must have heard this just as, almost surely, they heard the rush of seawater into the hull drown the last farewells of those they had left on board. First, there was mass and presence, and then, eerily, there was nothing but a trace of the moment on the surface of the sea. The ship was gone.

"In a minute nothing was to be seen except one water cask, which was [already] over when we cleared the boats," said Walter Parker. "I saw no passengers. It was a thing impossible: I heard crying on board the ship, but just before she went down it was perfectly silent."

Some people could not look away. Others, like Rhodes, could not look back. Survivors of the *Titanic* reported similar reactions when their ship sank beside its April iceberg in the same North Atlantic waters. Col. Gracie Lightholler, for example, always remembered the sight of the poorest passengers, kept below decks until finally they were released in the ship's last minutes. In collapsible Lifeboat C, Bruce Ismay, president of the White Star Line that owned the *Titanic*, "bent low over his oar— he couldn't bear to see her go down." And in Lifeboat One, businessman C. E. Henry Stengel turned his back, saying, "I cannot look any longer."

The official records of the sinking of both the *William Brown* and the *Titanic* minimize the horror and bathos that attend such moments. Captain Harris later remembered events this way, for example: "After as many got into the boats as could, I veered the boats astern of the ship by a line, and at 20 minutes past 12 o'clock, the ship pitched and went down head foremost, and as she pitched her masts went out of her. For about two minutes previous to the ship sinking, I did not hear a soul speak; previous to this they were calling to me to take them out of the ship, but my boats were overloaded."

How did Captain Harris know the minute and hour in a small boat without a lantern in the dark of a clouded night? Was his precision real, or merely a false certainty ordered up after the fact? Perhaps he reckoned the time from the passage of the moon through the haze that surrounded the small boats as his ship, their home, disappeared forever. Or, perhaps, he just chose an hour and minute that from then on were emblazoned on his memory to set that moment aside from all others in his life.

ALONE IN THE NORTH ATLANTIC

ISOLATED IF NOT TRULY ALONE on the wide, wide sea, the *William Brown*'s survivors could console themselves with the experiences of others who had lived to tell the tale of shipwreck at sea. These sailors and their emigrant passengers were not the first and certainly would not be the last to be sunk by an iceberg in the spring.

There was in the nineteenth century a very public lore concerning shipwrecks: the frequency of such incidents, ways to avoid them and, if all else failed, codes of behaviour that in theory should guide those who found themselves adrift on the sea. Because the stories that were told were those of survivors, the message—implicit and hopeful—was that survival was a likely outcome.

Tales of shipwrecks were as popular then as are detective stories and science fiction today. After all, these were common events, and the accounts of those who survived them had a sense of immediacy, and of practicality, that at this remove it is easy to forget. There were stories and adventures from every ocean, covering a gamut of experiences. Because the North Atlantic was so well travelled, however, the tales of its wrecks were more numerous. Not surprisingly, many of these described collisions with icebergs and the way people survived to be rescued.

In April 1805, to take one well-reported example, the ship *Jupiter* was sailing home to Boston from England with seventy-two passengers and a load of goods when it sank in the ice fields of the North Atlantic. On board, the scion of an important Boston family, John Tappan, was returning from a British buying trip when, "On April 6 the vessel encountered fields of ice so extensive that it was impossible to escape them. At midnight, the ship struck upon a piece of ice that had penetrated its starboard bow. Immediately, the *Jupiter*'s two auxiliary craft were launched, thirty-nine people embarking in the longboat and eight in the jolly boat. The ship went down with twenty-seven souls on board."

It was not bad luck but demon rum that was responsible for the sinking. "At midnight the first mate was so intoxicated that he fell upon deck and the captain being upon the bowsprit, looking out for islands of ice to direct the men, there was no one to steer the ship aright, and she struck the ice."

Once struck, the *Jupiter* filled with water and "the boats were got out, and all but twenty-seven sprang into them." Among those who did not spring fast enough were the heads of several large emigrant families who found it difficult to rush for a safety that required them to abandon their loved ones in the process.

A portrait of John Tappan, survivor of the wreck of the *Jupiter* in 1805.

"One man with his wife and nine children were among those who were lost." Not every family head remained on board to die with his or her family: "Another man lost his mother, brother, sister, and two nephews," a polite way of saying he left them behind as he scrambled for a seat in the longboat.

Tappan acquitted himself "very handsomely," as they said in those days, on the jolly boat. Although he was only a passenger, he used his pocket knife to fashion a fork-shaped spear from an extra oar. With it, he caught fish to feed his fellow survivors. Since the jolly boat and the longboat with its larger share of survivors remained together for their three days at sea, Tappan's fishing expertise fed the others, too. It helped, of course, that the *Jupiter* was wrecked in one of the world's richest fishing grounds. The Grand Banks was and, despite more than a century of overfishing, remains fecund with edible sea life of every kind.

Tappan distinguished himself in other ways, too. When a ship finally hove into view after "three days and nights, suffering much from fatigue and cold," it was plucky John who raised a large silk handkerchief on an oar to attract their rescuer's attention. Boston matriarch Sarah Tappan told her other children that Providence had saved their brother, John, from the wreck of the *Jupiter*. He was spared, she lectured, as a lesson for them all.

A portrait of Sarah Tappan, mother of shipwreck survivor John Tappan.

The story of the *Jupiter* was not unusual. Every year, a score or more ships were lost in the rush to commerce. Hundreds of people died when ships sailed from harbours to which they would never return. Hundreds more survived to be found by passing ships, their exploits of endurance detailed in newspapers and in privately published family histories.

THE AGE WAS RIFE with tales of those who had survived wrecks after long passages in small boats. By 1841 everyone knew about the *Essex*, sunk in 1820 in the mid-Pacific by a giant whale that twice rammed the whaling ship, staving in its bow on both sides. When the ship was struck, its three small, open whaling boats were hunting the pod whose largest male attacked the ship. Returning to the *Essex*, the whalers salvaged food, water and a few tools from the sinking vessel before setting off for the coast of South America. It was their bad fortune to be wrecked in one of the most desolate parts of any ocean, where the probability of rescue by a passing ship was remote. For ninety days the *Essex*'s crew endured intense privation—exposure, hunger and especially thirst—on a journey that became a legend.

That the survivors in two of the whaling boats eventually were forced to resort to cannibalism, then called the "custom of the sea," gave the tale an added horror. But the story of the *Essex*, published in 1821 by one of its crewmen, Owen Chase, had as a central theme the importance of the solidarity and community that had sustained those who survived. Sailing together offered practical as well as emotional support. Several times when one or another boat sprang a leak, the others assisted with repairs. Difficult as the trip was, Chase insisted, it was made possible by the community of survivors. None would have made it had each boat set off on its own.

Everyone also knew the story of the *Medusa*, a French ship wrecked off the coast of West Africa in 1816. A popular book by two of the survivors about the disaster, translated into English from the original French, was published in 1818 as the *Narrative of a Voyage to Senegal in 1816*. This was not a tale of shared endurance, however, but of ignominious betrayal. If the *Essex* endured because its crew stayed together, the *Medusa* was the story of what happened when some sought to survive at the expense of others.

When it was obvious there were not enough auxiliary craft for the 240 passengers and 160 crew, the *Medusa*'s officers had the sailors build a crude raft from the ship's timbers. Loaded with 150 people—mostly sailors, soldiers and French emigrants bound for Senegal—the raft was soon abandoned by the officers and survivors in the boats, leaving its passengers to fend for themselves. After two weeks at sea, only fifteen persons, dehydrated and starving, were left alive when rescuers came upon the raft adrift off the African coast.

Eventually, and despite official attempts at a cover-up, the story of the *Medusa* became an international *cause célèbre*, a cautionary tale about what happens when officers attempt to save themselves at the expense of passengers and seamen. The most dramatic symbol of the story's importance is Théodore Géricault's huge canvas, *The Raft of the Medusa*. In exquisite detail, it shows the raft's survivors the moment before their salvation. Among the dead and dying, one man, supported by a compatriot, stands on a barrel, waving a shirt at a distant ship as the sea swells around the raft, its makeshift sail in tatters. So great was the story's attraction (and so dramatic the painting) that more than fifty thousand Londoners paid to see the work when it was put on exhibit there. The painting still draws thousands of visitors, year by year, to the Louvre.

FOR THOSE SHIPWRECKED on the North Atlantic, the chance of rescue was very real. Given the heavy traffic, it was the rare voyage on which a ship did not spy another at sea, noting its time and position in the log even if they did not heave to and send boats back and forth for an exchange of news, letters and conversation.

Many of these mid-ocean meetings were later reported in the shipping news that by 1841 had become a constant feature of the daily and weekly newspapers springing up in cities on both sides of the Atlantic. An example from the *New York Herald* of 11 October 1841 is typical. The abbreviated sentences and shortened phrases reflected the terse style of the naval logbook rather than the verbose narratives of the journalists of the day: "Ship Lowell Remmes, from Macao 20th May and Anjier, 27th June, with a valuable cargo of teas and silks to Cary & Co. Saw in the southern part of Macassar Straights ship Hamilton from Canton for New York. Ship Vespucian was signalized off St. Nicholas Point 26th June. No date, lat. 15 30, long. 83, spoke Br. whale ship May, from Liverpool for Calcutta, out 90 days. Off St. Helena, passed Br. Ship Orlean, from Canton for Liverpool."

Immigrants read the shipping news to keep track of the voyages of relatives and friends. Ship owners read these short notices, too, hoping to hear of their investment's safe passage. Equally interested were the merchants who prospered selling the cargoes that were hauled in a ship's hold. Ship chandlers were concerned about the fate of their customers and the business that maritime wreckage might bring to their stores. A notice that the ship *Romulus* "experienced a gale of wind, split foresail and done other damage at latitude 40°30' and longitude 69°" would bring them hurrying to the docks to offer their services for the ship's repair.

The papers of the day were quick to report the demastings, groundings and sinkings that occurred with astonishing regularity. Rarely did a month go by without the Montreal, Boston, New York and Philadelphia newspapers carrying the headline: DREADFUL SHIPWRECK AND LOSS OF LIFE. On 11 October 1841, for example, just months after the *William Brown* sank, the *New York Herald* carried a dispatch under that banner, a story copied from the *Quebec Gazette* about the "loss of the bark, Amanda, Captain Davis, from Limerick, which came on shore at Little Metis Point at five o'clock on the 26th, last. She had forty passengers and a crew of eighteen. The captain, two seamen, and two apprentices were among those saved." The emigrant agent, whose job it was to sign up passengers for these ships, "kindly favored us," the *Gazette* reported, "with a list of the passengers and crew." The final paragraph is a stark, summary statistic: total crew lost 29; total passengers lost, 112.

Other stories, and there were many, detailed the rescue of those whose ships were lost in a gale or the ice flows of the North Atlantic. The form was the same, however, with the names of survivors, and often of those drowned, reported "for the interest of the reader."

Shipping notices also served another and quite different purpose. They warned outward-bound captains like George Harris of the dangers they might encounter at sea. For this reason, from early February into May, reports of icebergs in the North Atlantic were as common in the nineteenth century as are stories of the progress of hurricanes and tornadoes today. Thus, for example, the *New York Herald*'s shipping page reported on 15 April 1842, the year after the *William Brown* sank, that the packet ship *Albany*, homeward bound from Le Havre, at "lat. 42° lon. 47°, saw large islands of ice; same time, spoke bark Frederick Warren of and for Boston, from Bangor, Wales, 41 days out. In lat. 44°44' and from lon. 48°30' to 49°11' passed between icebergs—the weather being clear, they were as far north and south as we could see."

THE WRECK OF THE *William Brown* was only one dot on a busy map of shipwrecks in the North Atlantic in the spring of each year. Over the decades of the nineteenth century, the situation worsened year by year, as ever more emigrant ships plied the North Atlantic. In a seven-year period beginning in the mid-1840s, at least sixty-one passenger-carrying ships were wrecked with the loss of sixteen hundred lives. Between 1854 and 1869, Lloyd's Register calculated the worldwide loss of sailing ships at ten thousand vessels.

Brian Hill of the Institute of Marine Dynamics in St. John's, Newfoundland, has plotted hundreds of reports by ship captains of iceberg sightings and collisions in the North Atlantic from the early sixteenth century to the present day. While voluminous, his records are less than encyclopedic. He lists only those collisions and sinkings for which an exact latitude and longitude are known. Excluded, therefore, are the "many, many tragic incidents that occurred when the vessel was caught in the pack ice and crushed." Those ships were listed simply as "lost at sea." Still, his list of published iceberg sightings and ice-related ship sinkings is

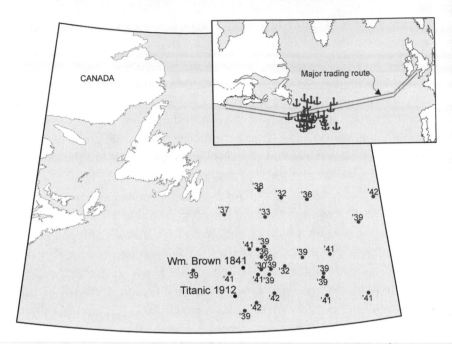

A map of ships sunk by icebergs in the North Atlantic, 1830–42. Only ships whose exact location at point of collision is known are plotted. Data courtesy Brian Hill

sufficient to give an idea of the damage that resulted from the migration of icebergs, year by year.

The map printed here based on Hill's data has no listings for 1840, an exceptionally mild year in which the ice did not descend into the shipping lanes. Included for reference is the location of the *Titanic*'s death in 1912. The encounters between ships and ice are clustered in a relatively narrow band along the established sea route along which ships sailed back and forth between Europe and North America. Each year, the warm Gulf Stream shifted as it flowed north from the Caribbean and east from Canada as it turned toward England. One year, it would flow a few degrees to the north, closer to Labrador and then southern Greenland; the next year, a few degrees to the south. When the stream was to the north and the weather mild, the number of iceberg incidents was comparatively few. In other years, like 1841, when the winter was harsher and the stream a few degrees to the south, accidents and sightings were frequent.

Then and now, ships that sail eastward from the New World to the

Old are aided by the Gulf Stream's swift current, propelled by favourable and relatively constant winds that run together along the shortest path between North America and northern Europe. This fact has been known since the first European cod boats worked the Grand Banks in the early sixteenth century. Indeed, it was the difference in sailing times east and west that first prompted Ben Franklin to map the Gulf Stream in the eighteenth century.

A top-class sailing packet in the late 1830s took as long as forty-eight days to travel the North Atlantic from England to the United States— but only thirty-six days to sail in the opposite direction.

Ships sailing eastward from the United States and Canada followed a slightly more southerly course than those voyaging westward from Great Britain. Europe-bound ships tended to stay within the Gulf Stream, whose current gave them a few extra knots of speed. Those heading for North America sailed a bit to the north to avoid travelling against the full force of the current, even though the more northerly course put them at a slightly greater risk of encountering ice. Despite the carnage that resulted, it was not until after the *Titanic's* sinking in 1912 that ship owners finally shifted the accepted North Atlantic route a degree or so to the south in order that vessels would be able to sail below the path of the dangerous spring ice flows.

THROUGHOUT LATE WINTER and early spring, hundreds of ships carried passengers and cargo between North America and Europe, especially between England and the United States. The trade was too profitable, the demand for service too great, to halt in these months because of danger. A cautious captain might choose to sail a few degrees south of the fastest and most efficient route, but that cost time—a few days or perhaps a week—and it was speed that captains and their employers, the ship owners, sought. The sooner a ship was unloaded and its fees collected, the more quickly it could pick up new cargo and return to paying work.

Ships sailing the North Atlantic in the spring were likely to encounter icebergs, but not all that did so were wrecked, of course. Most ships survived by taking simple precautions. Whenever ships encountered icebergs, intelligent captains reduced their speed and proceeded with caution. On the same day that the *William Brown* was rushing toward disaster, the packet ship *United States* was returning from Europe to its home port when it encountered the same ice flows. Travelling slowly under minimum sail, it cautiously manoeuvred to find safe passage into clear seas. So, too, did the *Great Western*, perhaps the most famous ship of its day.

The first steamship to regularly cross the Atlantic, the *Great Western* is in nautical terms the grandparent of luxury liners like the *Titanic*. It was the first of three ships designed for the Great Western Railway by the remarkably named Isambard Kingdom Brunel. Launched in 1838, the 236-foot wooden ship was powered by paddle wheels driven by four boilers feeding two-stroke engines. A steamship could not be becalmed and did not have to tack with the changing winds, instead steaming directly, and thus more swiftly, across the sea.

On its maiden voyage, the *Great Western* took only fifteen days to travel from Bristol to New York. Passengers paid for the privilege of speed, of course. In the early 1840s a one-way ticket on the *Great Western* cost thirty-five guineas, a very large sum in those days. By contrast, travel on ships like the *William Brown* cost a passenger less than ten pounds.

As the commander of a steam-powered luxury ship, the *Great Western's* captain, James Hosken, was something of a celebrity. He was the future, a captain whose ship was at least a generation ahead of more common craft. His notes on the North Atlantic ice fields that both his ship and the *William Brown* encountered in April 1841 are, therefore, of special interest. Captains often provided information about the waters they travelled for the newspapers. Their letters were usually published without change or correction. Captain Hosken's was written for the *London Standard* and then almost immediately reprinted in the *Times* in London on 17 May 1841. The headline, EXTRAORDINARY FIELDS OF ICE, was set in capital letters for effect. "The first iceberg we saw was in latitude 43° longitude 40°30', and the last in latitude 42°20', longitude 40°. I am quite sure there was an unbroken field of that extent, and from what I heard from Captain Bailly, of the American packet-ship United States, I have no doubt the field ice extended, with very little break, to latitude 40°30', where Captain Bailly fell in with it on the morning of the 19th."

When the *William Brown* sank, it was riding the northern edge of the Gulf Stream in a search for friendlier currents and favourable winds. The *Great Western* was headed in the opposite direction, travelling *with* the Gulf Stream's currents and thus a little to the south of the other ship. Still, the conditions they encountered were similar. But where the *William Brown* was sailing at maximum speed, the *Great Western* manoeuvred cautiously from the start. "On Sunday, April 13, the ship steering west, at 6 P.M. first saw one iceberg on the starboard bow, at 7:30 P.M. passed it; at that time four or five others in sight; at 9:15 P.M. passed several small pieces of ice—slowed engines. A few minutes after the ship was surrounded with light field ice which appeared similar to a field I ran through on the 11th of February 1839; this induced me to go slowly, with the hope of getting through, as I had done on that occasion; but by 9:30, finding it became closely packed, and much thicker, prudence dictated our escape by the same channel we had entered."

Throughout his traverse of the ice fields, Captain Hosken regularly took the temperature of the sea in an attempt to chart the ice and its expanse. "The temperature of the water, when within two miles of the first iceberg seen, fell suddenly from 50 degrees to 36 degrees; air 40 degrees to 36 degrees," he wrote, summarizing his logs. "When in the ice the water was 25 degrees, air 28 degrees."

Taking the sea's temperature was a hoary but useful practice that continued into the twentieth century. As historian M. L. Hansen put it, in the early years, "Many a skipper of the North Atlantic ventured out to sea with nothing but experience, a collection of [nautical] proverbs, and a thermometer with which to locate the Gulf Stream." When the temperature dropped, the captain would order a special watch to look for the ice the thermometer warned was ahead.

Ships that found themselves caught in ice-filled waters had a range of options. Sometimes they set out the longboat to guide them through the field of ice. At other times, they picked their way at slow speed. Even if a submerged iceberg was encountered, a slow enough speed would minimize the damage that resulted from the impact. Captain Hosken proved this nicely when the *Great Western*'s 1,321-ton wooden hull was several times lifted a few degrees when a spinning paddle wheel rested on the ice, slipping forward through the floes rather than being ruined by a collision.

To SEE A FIELD OF ICE upon the sea, small growlers and large icebergs heavily dotting miles of water, is a wondrous sight. As they float together in the cold northern currents or sit, dissolving, on the edge of the Gulf Stream, they seem more than the refuse of inanimate glaciers. Perhaps that is why the language we use to describe icebergs in their journey from creation to dissolution is biological—we speak of them being "calved," for example—rather than geologic. They are simply too mobile, too active, to be considered as insentient things. Like whales, icebergs travel in packs along a well-defined route; like whales, they cruise the cold Atlantic waters until they reach the warmth of the Gulf Stream as it bends south of Newfoundland. Whales, however, repeat a migratory path again and again, generation to generation without end. Icebergs, on the other hand, are born of northern glaciers and migrate to their final waters only to die.

Most of the icebergs produced in the Northern Hemisphere are calved and die out of sight of humans and their ships. Of the more than ten thousand icebergs calved in the Atlantic in an average year, fewer than five hundred typically survive to pass the Newfoundland coast at 49° N latitude. Those most likely to reach southern waters originate in western Greenland, whose glaciers calve perhaps three quarters of the annual population. Fewer than one in ten reaches the Gulf Stream and its shipping lanes.

Of all Greenland's glaciers, the most prolific is Jakobshavn, which calves perhaps thirteen hundred icebergs a year, more than 20 per cent of the Arctic's annual total. Almost certainly, this was the birthplace of the iceberg that sank the *William Brown* and the ice field that mired the *Great Western*.

Once icebergs separate from the glacier's body, they travel into the open sea and are carried by currents into Baffin Bay, where they may spend two or three years slowly shrinking in the frigid but not frozen water until they become light enough to travel. They shrink at an average rate of perhaps two metres (six feet) a day, solid mass transformed into liquid when the temperature is between 0 and 4 degrees Celsius (32 to 39 degrees Fahrenheit). When an iceberg has lost perhaps 90 per cent of its original mass, what remains is carried south by the North Atlantic's cold currents: the Belle Isle, the Labrador and the St. Lawrence. These, in turn, stall where they meet the easterly flowing waters of the Gulf Stream, in whose warm waters the rate of decay is increased. Mass is shed more rapidly as the icebergs grow smaller, shattering into smaller and smaller blocks of ice until finally, at one with the sea, they disappear.

The parade of icebergs from Baffin Bay to the Gulf Stream was an annual event. So, too, were ship sinkings and ship damage from vessels that collided with them. Only after the *Titanic* sank in 1912 were scientists like G.I. Taylor commissioned to map the cold airs and the broad life of the currents in this region.

DESPITE THE INSISTENCE of the newspaper headlines announcing "Extraordinary Fields of Ice," those that blocked the passage of the *Great Western* and the *United States*—and wrecked the *William Brown*—were in fact quite ordinary. In 1841 the extent of the annual ice was approximately 271,535 square kilometres (104,850 square miles). Compared to the mild winter of 1840, when the ice covered only 122,845 square kilometres (47,435 square miles), 1841 seems to have been a harsh winter. But between 1810 and 1830, the average flows of ice were more than 317,000 square kilometres

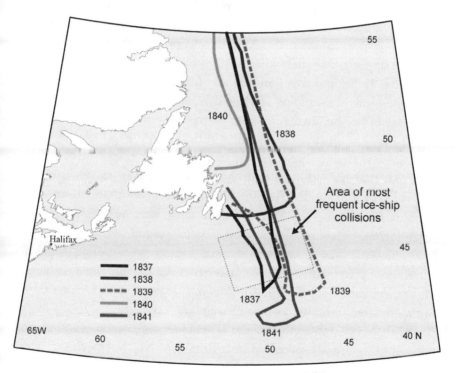

A map of the extent of ice flows, 1837–41. Except in extremely mild years like 1840, icebergs descended into the shipping lanes of the North Atlantic. Data courtesy Brian Hill

(122,400 square miles), and from 1830 to 1850 they averaged 261,145 square kilometres (100,835 square miles). In the greater history of ice flows, therefore, 1841 was merely average.

In other words, the captain of the *William Brown* should have expected to encounter icebergs. And with reasonable precautions, the ship should have been able to sail carefully past the ice. Moreover, if the ship was wrecked, the chances of rescue were actually very good.

In spite of Francis Rhodes's pessimism, there was, therefore, ample reason for optimism. Passengers and crew alike might have been cold and grief-stricken, but the situation was by no means hopeless. After all, the survivors of the *Jupiter* had been rescued after only three uncomfortable but not particularly dangerous days. Thirty years later, when the *William Brown* went down, the number of ships on the North Atlantic run had increased more than ten-fold, so there was that much greater a likelihood of rescue.

By 1840 the shipping lanes of the North Atlantic were busy with ships voyaging along them throughout the year. On 15 April 1842, a *New York Herald* story counted the American ships in harbour in New York City: "It appears that there are seventy [tall] ships, thirty-four barques, ninety-five brigs, and two hundred and fifty schooners in this city, and sixty-one of all classes lying at Brooklyn, making in round numbers an aggregate of five hundred vessels in the waters of the southern district of New York." The situation was similar in Boston and Philadelphia, where other ships waited for crew and cargo. Nor was this the entire American fleet, only that portion in harbour. Many more were at sea, as were hundreds of vessels plying the Atlantic under the flags of other nations.

Not all of the New York-berthed ships were scheduled for the Atlantic run, of course. Some were coastal vessels heading north for Massachusetts, Maine or Nova Scotia. Others were sailing south to Charleston, Savannah, and perhaps even to Cuba and the Caribbean. Still others were bound for Latin America, Hawaii or the China coast. But many were committed to the rich emigrant trade that annually transported thousands of people like the *William Brown*'s passengers from the ports of Europe, and especially Great Britain, to North America.

It was the sea that linked Old and New Worlds, its North Atlantic shipping lanes the route along which goods and people flowed. It was ships that carried emigrants to the New World and carried their letters home. And, later, these ships transported the relatives that emigrants had left behind, family members enticed by letters pleading with them to leave the inhospitable tenant farms and city slums of Europe for the open farmlands and burgeoning towns of North America.

Along with emigrants and the mail, ships carried American raw materials to European manufacturers, and then European products to North American markets. It was this commerce that powered economies on both sides of the Atlantic, creating the jobs that lured emigrants from London, Dublin, Limerick and Edinburgh to Philadelphia, Boston, Montreal and Ottawa. Little wonder, then, that just about everyone was interested in the sea and the ships that sailed it. By 1840 it would have been hard to find a town or village on either side of the Atlantic that did not rely upon the maritime trade in one way or another.

THE *WILLIAM BROWN*'S SURVIVORS could hope for and perhaps even expect to see a rescue ship in the coming days. While they waited, both the jolly boat and longboat were fortunately well provisioned. The jolly boat had five gallons of water, twenty-five to thirty pounds of biscuit and six pounds of meat. The longboat had six gallons of water, seventy-five pounds of biscuit, eight to ten pounds of meat and some oatmeal, which became soaked with rainwater.

Most important, perhaps, the survivors in these two vessels had each other, evidence of a greater society that could be called upon in need. "You are not going to leave, are you sir?" Rhodes asked Captain Harris as their boats stood away from the *William Brown* just before she sank. Captain Harris promised only that they would stay together during that first night.

AT SEA

WHEN THE SEAMEN severed the rope that held the two boats
to the *William Brown,* they severed their ties with each other
as well. Before, they were part of the ship, linked to it and its
history by the lines that held them to the *William Brown* and thus to each
other. Afterward, the jolly boat and the longboat were independent,
pulling away from each other if not yet too far. They became just neigh-
bours upon the open sea.

In the enormity of the disaster, in the moments after the *William
Brown*'s sinking, there was little to say. The night was overcast and the
winds mostly silent as sailors in the two boats sculled through the
night, keeping a distance of perhaps a quarter mile between them.
Amidst the ice and steep rolling seas, it was good seamanship and common sense to keep a certain distance apart, especially from the longboat's
point of view. Too close together and they might collide as one or the
other slipped on the crest of a wave or turned to avoid a pan of ice. And
while the smaller and less laden jolly boat was fairly manoeuvrable, the
longboat was not.

Moreover, as Rhodes and his crew had discovered, the longboat's
rudder was damaged. Rhodes tried to use an oar to steer, but its blade
was too narrow and the result too unsteady to permit him to hold his boat
on course. Still, he sat in the stern near the useless tiller as if he could
steer the boat with its long arm. To converse with his men, he would
move to the boat's centre where they manned the oars, then return to
the stern.

Rhodes knew the yawl-rigged jolly boat would do better on its own. Yet as long as the two boats were within sight of each other, he was reassured by the captain's presence. Not only would the boats be able to assist each other, but as long as they travelled in tandem, the captain would remain in charge. Rhodes did not want sole command of a situation that struck him as hopeless. The first mate was desperate to have his superior make the hard choices their situation would require.

"Captain Harris was about to leave them but Mr. Rhodes requested him to stay by them until morning, which he did," Biddy Nugent said. Other passengers remembered both the exchange and Rhodes's relief when the captain agreed to stand by the longboat, at least until dawn. Nor was Rhodes alone. Sailors and passengers alike were glad to have the boats together. As long as Captain Harris remained nearby, none felt as if they were wholly abandoned, alone at sea.

"The boats were not continually together that night," Bridget McGee said. "They would get off a short distance and then row up. No part of me was wet but my feet. They [the crew] said nothing, only when they wanted the passengers to bail they told them to get up and bail. They could bail with the passengers sitting up. There were seats for those who rowed. The sailors took turns at rowing. There was no dispute during the night, but all were silent."

The longboat was so crowded that when sailors changed places to relieve each other at the oars, passengers had to shift as well. Because there were not enough seats, many of the emigrants sat not on the thwarts but on the wet floor of the boat, snuggled beneath the gunwales and away from the wind and out of the sailors' immediate sight.

Neither bailing nor rowing was regarded as a chore. The limited exercise provided a modicum of warmth against the cold that pervaded the air and seeped into their bodies, deep into the bone, sapping strength and will alike. Most knew instinctively that what today we call hypothermia was, in the short term, their most dangerous enemy. Numbing and exhausting, it brings progressive drowsiness as the body's functions slow until finally unconsciousness and then death's long sleep arrives.

In the bow were the Edgars, Margaret and her daughters, as well as other single women who had gathered around them as the longboat had filled with people. In the stern were the two married couples—the Blacks and the Patricks—and those others taken aboard just before the longboat pulled away from the *William Brown*. Between these groups, the sailors congregated around the oarlocks.

Crew and emigrants alike were half-dressed, wet and miserable in the chill rain that already seemed interminable. "Some of the passengers had little or no clothing on them, the women their nightdress, the men their shirts and trousers," the trial record later said. "The sailors succeeded in saving some of their own clothes, which they distributed among the passengers." The most scantily clad survivors, the women who had fled in their nightclothes with only a shawl for modesty, were in the greatest danger from the cold. To protect them, several sailors shared their extra clothes and sometimes the clothes they wore on their backs. The Edgars were well taken care of. One sailor gave Mrs. Edgar a jacket; another gave a blanket to her daughter. "Every care and attention was paid to us," Isabella asserted. Holmes gave his jacket to another woman who, ill dressed, was shivering from the cold.

"I was up to my waist in water," complained one of the women. Another's shoes were submerged. The women in the bow suffered the most because it was there that the waves first broke.

"For the first night, I was in the middle of the boat lying on the side," young Owen Carr said. "Not much water came on me, only the rain. The plug was about the middle of the boat. It was not as big as my fist but about the size of a chair post. For the first night I was near the plug, but could not reach it with my hand. I could touch it with my toes. There was little water there. Some came in at the plug and some was the rain. Can't tell how the plug was fixed." This was the bailing plug, the wooden peg used to stopper the hole that was drilled into the boat to allow water to drain out. At sea, if the plug became dislodged, water would flow into the boat that all were working so hard at bailing.

Another passenger, Ann Bradley, recalled, "They first fixed the plug in the bottom of the boat after the ship went down that first night." Whether she meant the plug was checked and set, or that it had come loose and was then replaced, is unclear. But Julie McCadden knew when the plug was first displaced by the inflow of water over her feet. "On Monday night I felt some water coming into the boat very fast. I called Holmes and put his hand down to the place, and told him the boat was beginning to leak. I pulled some rags out of my pocket, rolled them up and put them down to the place. Holmes looked for the plug, and when he could not find it he took an axe and made a new one. After that for an hour no water came in at that place. I think I heard them say afterwards that first night that the plug was coming out again."

There was little conversation in the longboat in the early hours of what would have been the ship's second watch. Some of the emigrants prayed quietly, while others sat in stoic silence. Many wept silently so as to keep from imposing their grief upon others. All struggled to understand how their world had changed, to see themselves in these new circumstances.

That night, those who had survived the sinking did not want to think about the future. Even if they were rescued, what would they do without money in North American cities already teeming with Europe's poor? It was all very well for those like Bridget McGee, who was travelling to stay with family members who were already well established. But for those without American connections, there was now no capital to start a small business, no tools with which to follow a trade. Capital and tools had sunk with the ship, and along with them the emigrants' once confident dreams.

The only comfort for most was that they were alive. There was food in the boats and drinkable water all around in the form of ice. Also, their ship had sunk in well-travelled shipping lanes of the North Atlantic. They were about 400 kilometres (250 miles) from Newfoundland, and every day they pulled toward land would be another day in which they might be rescued. Others had survived similar circumstances and so, the optimistic presumed, would they.

DAWN DOES NOT RUSH upon the day in the North Atlantic in the month of April. It comes almost reluctantly, as winter gives way to spring. Even the false dawn that gladdens the hearts of sailors who stand the early morning watch arrives slowly, almost hesitantly.

That first morning, sailors and passengers dozed fitfully until the world lightened, revealing an archipelago of ice that in other circumstances would have been a wondrous sight. Until they were rescued, this frozen land floating unanchored upon the water would be their companion. "I saw some ice about after the ship went down," Bridget McGee said, "but I don't know if it was on Monday or Tuesday. It was an iceberg at a great distance. It seemed to reach to the tip of the sky. There were small pieces of floating ice which the sailors broke with the oars."

To Bridget McGee and her companions, the big iceberg, and the floes that surrounded it, must have seemed malignant, weapons of a fate that had deprived them and their friends of their dreams and loved ones. It is difficult to say how far away that icy mountain was from the boats. On the sea's undifferentiated horizon, an object's distance is as hard to calculate as its height. If what Bridget McGee saw was the iceberg that stove in the hull of the *William Brown*—and it is not clear that this was the one—they had drifted some distance in the ocean currents throughout the night's hours, 16 or 24 kilometres (10 or 15 miles) at a guess. And while the iceberg seemed mountainous to Bridget McGee, she was from Ireland, where smaller hills dominate the landscape, not the thrusting peaks of the world's younger ranges.

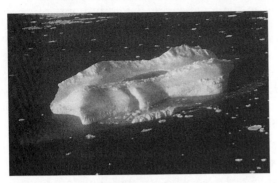

A saddle-shaped iceberg surrounded by its melt, as seen from the air. The *William Brown*'s longboat would have been dwarfed by icebergs like this, and perhaps the ship as well. Courtesy United States Coast Guard

Probably what she saw was a saddle-shaped iceberg with peaks at either end. Viewed at sea level from a slow, rocking boat, an iceberg can indeed seem mountainous. Toward the end of their journey, the huge towering icebergs, eroded by the warm sea, come to look like this, their high peaks diminished. Around them float smaller pieces that have broken away from the main body, splinters that have calved from the iceberg as it in turn was once separated from the glacier that gave it birth.

AS THEY PULLED THEIR OARS through the debris of melting ice, the sailors must have thought that at least death would not come from thirst. Some grabbed shards of ice to suck upon. Certainly it was tastier than the brackish water stored in the cask that Holmes had brought aboard. Passengers nearest to the gunwales who could dip their hands into the sea grabbed some ice from time to time as well. Others, fearful of attracting the seamen's attention, did without.

During the night, Captain Harris had considered the critical choice that was his and his alone to make. Should he keep the boats together and risk the death of all? Or should he increase the chance that at least some would survive by splitting their company in two? For Rhodes and his companions in the longboat, the hope and expectation was that the two parties would seek survival together, as had those in the whaling boats of the *Essex*. But because the longboat could neither sail nor steer, that would mean standing together for hours, days or weeks in wait for a passing ship. Would that ship see them, however? And if it did, would it stop to help?

Weighed against Captain Harris's duty to his crew and passengers was the fact that the jolly boat could probably manage to reach Newfoundland on its own. The longboat surely would not. Of course, there was also his reputation to consider. Captain Harris did not want to be remembered as the man who had abandoned passengers and crew in a longboat that could not be steered. Surviving only to be condemned, like the captain of the *Medusa*, would mean calumny and disgrace. Still, he might have thought that would be better than death.

At about 6 A.M., Captain Harris ordered his crew to row toward the longboat. The sky was slowly lightening as the rays of the sun bent around the horizon, outlining the sea and its ice floes. He had made his decision. It was time for action.

The swells rolled around the two boats as they held within shouting distance of each other. With captain and first mate in the sterns, the boats needed to stay close enough for them to hear each other but far enough away so that their oarsmen could manoeuvre in safety. This was not the time for one or the other to be holed by ice or rolled onto its companion by a freakish wave.

"Good morning, Captain," Rhodes shouted. "A hard business, sir." The mate was always uncomfortable before his captain, conscious of the differences in class and rank that separated them. Further, Rhodes was desperate not only for them to stay together but for the jolly boat to take some of his passengers and thus reduce the weight under which the longboat laboured. Nor was he alone. Passengers were clamouring for a transfer to the jolly boat, too.

"Good morning, Captain," interrupted James Patrick. "Will you allow my wife and I to come aboard?" "No," Harris replied. "We are already full and it would not do, more weight and we will find it hard to make way." "But my wife's sister, Mrs. Lafferty, is in your boat," Patrick shouted to the captain. "Let us stay together, our family," Mrs. Patrick pleaded.

Harris looked at Mrs. Patrick and the baby she cradled, then looked again at his vessel, how it sat upon the sea. He calculated how his boat would handle with a few hundred extra pounds on board. "I'm sorry, Madam. It can't be done."

"I know you, too, are burdened," Rhodes ventured, adding his weight to the Patricks' request. "But, Captain, we are overfull. Without a rudder we can scarcely manoeuvre, and the boat is so full the men can barely handle their oars. We are too many, and so crowded that if it become stormy we will be obliged to draw lots. I mean to say..."

And here Captain Harris cut him off. "Say no more. I know what you mean. I know what you'll have to do. But don't speak of that now. Let it be the last resort. You must do the best you can. Pull for Newfoundland and the shore. It is 200 miles [320 kilometres] distant, north by west. I'll give you charts, a compass and this quadrant to seek your position as you can."

He might as well have commanded the longboat to make for Heaven as to head for the coast of Newfoundland. "They could not put the boat to any point, for safety," according to second mate Walter Parker. From his favoured seat in the jolly boat, he saw that the longboat "was going around like a tub; she was like her own mistress; they could not keep her head any one way, even for a minute."

Ending the discussion, Captain Harris told his first mate the decision was made. The jolly boat would sail alone for Newfoundland. The longboat might attempt to follow, but Harris and Rhodes knew, as did everyone else, that it quickly would fall behind.

Rhodes then asked if the ship had been insured. A strange question at this time, but precisely the type that pops unbidden to mind when hope seems destined to die. Captain Harris must have been surprised at the question. His answer, laconic and bemused, was, "Does it matter, now?" And really, it did not.

After ordering his sailors in the longboat to "all follow the mate's order, and to do nothing without his consent," Harris called upon each crewman to individually acknowledge this instruction. Parker said, "I recollect Captain Harris giving his advice to the men to obey Mr. Rhodes the same as if he, Captain Harris, was in the boat; then Holmes made his answer, as the rest of them, that he would obey."

The crew of the longboat now laboured under a double burden. They were bound first by their personal oaths and second by the laws of the sea. In the nineteenth century a man *was* his word, only as good as the promises he kept. Here, each had given his vow to the captain to accept Rhodes's leadership without question. But Captain Harris's instruction was important for a second reason. A seaman who disobeyed a captain's explicit order faced corporal punishment or worse. Insubordination—questioning a superior's command, or drunkenness, for example—could earn the lash or keelhauling. To *refuse* an order was mutiny, pure and simple, and in those days mutiny was a capital offence. The offender could be immediately shot or hanged from a yardarm, on the captain's order. When Captain Harris made each seaman individually promise to acknowledge Rhodes as their *captain*, he knew they would be doubly bound by both personal oaths and the impersonal laws of the sea.

"Give me your names so that I may carry a record of you all," Captain Harris then ordered the longboat's passengers and crew. One after another, the emigrants called out their names, which Harris wrote down on a sheet of paper he had brought from the ship. Then the seamen shouted their names across the water, some punctuated by grunts of effort as they hauled at the oars to keep the longboat within speaking distance.

Passengers and crew alike must have taken the captain's name-taking to mean that he believed they would not survive. Why else ask for their names? All had heard Rhodes tell Captain Harris that if the jolly boat would not take on some of the longboat's load, he would have to lighten the boat some other way, perhaps by lottery, if the seas grew heavy. And so, as the captain wrote down their names, the passengers must have looked at each other and wondered who would be the first to be sacrificed when the winds blew up and the sea grew boisterous. Given the stormy weather that had filled their passage from Liverpool, none doubted the seas would freshen again in coming days.

During the night, Captain Harris also had considered the sum of ship's stores saved for both boats. If he had wished to give hope to the passengers of the longboat, he might have given Rhodes a pound or two of the jolly boat's meat or some of the biscuit that he carried. But Harris reserved for his boat a proportionately larger share of the food and water. He could not have said more clearly in words what he did in deed.

Harris gave Rhodes a chart, a quadrant and, some said, his watch—the longboat already had a compass—and advised him once more to row toward Newfoundland. Then he hoisted sail and was off. "I could not see them ten minutes after I left them," Harris said, "the weather was so foggy. At the time I left them they were all tranquil and sad—they were all crowded up together like sheep in a pen, they could not steer the boat, they could not use the oars, I could not take them in tow, could hardly pull my own." For the next week, his concern was not the longboat and its passengers but the salvation of the jolly boat as it struggled toward a far shore.

As HARRIS SAILED NORTHWEST toward Newfoundland, the longboat pulled slowly behind him in the same direction. At first the winds were out of the south, helping them along. At mid-morning, however, the winds turned and were freshening out of the northwest. Now the sailors pulled into the seas, into the waves that rolled down upon the bow of the boat, drenching all who sat there. Water poured over the gunwale each time the boat took a wave. The male passengers bailed as much as they could, but it was not enough.

Rhodes suggested putting out a sea anchor or a drogue. A sea anchor is a line set with weights, often a small anchor, dropped from the bow to hold a boat forward into the wind and waves. A drogue (or "drag") is usually a heavy line (or one with weights) streamed from the stern to slow the boat and keep it steady in high following seas.

"When the wind changed to northward," Joseph Stetson said, "we lay the boat to with a drag, and then consulted together and concluded that it would be best to get to the southward and westward, as there would be no use in trying to get to Newfoundland." And so the longboat came about, abandoning any hope of Newfoundland. The turn was timed so they would not be caught broadside by an errant wave. Then the longboat headed back to the centre of the warm Gulf Stream, rowing toward where they so recently had been. To steady the boat's motion, the sailors tied several oars together and streamed them aft on the longest line they had, calming the boat's motion with this tail.

Some of the sailors attempted to fashion a makeshift sail. They thought a shirt or jacket—even better a blanket—raised on oars set in the front of the longboat would steady the passage as it was propelled forward through following seas. But without a working rudder, the longboat rolled dangerously as the wind and the waves each pushed it at slightly different angles. The makeshift sail was quickly struck, and the men went back to rowing. None worried about the loss of speed that accompanied the striking of the makeshift sail. With the sea behind them, they were making perhaps three knots an hour, even with the drag streaming off the stern; more than enough for a boat with no place to go.

Rhodes provided little leadership either to the sailors under his command or to the passengers in his charge. Indeed, he seems to have been incapable of developing a plan to make the most of their chances of survival. He did not set watches or instruct his men to preserve their food stores by rationing. Nor did he suggest they increase them by making a fishing spear from an extra oar. He set no rotation so that crew and passengers—those who rowed and those who bailed—would have clear duties and clear times of rest. He had a chart, a compass and a quadrant, but nobody reported his consulting them. He knew too well where he was and saw no hope in precise navigation. And anyway, he was a poor navigator at the best of times, barely able to take a sun sight and log the resulting position.

"The mate asked one of the men if he knew navigation," recalled Sarah Corr. When a sailor replied that he did, Rhodes said, "Then I give up all charge of the boat." But the sailor refused to take over, and Rhodes made the offer open to all. "I would give up my command to any man who might better master this ship," he said several times to his men that day. "Who will take us forward?"

Nobody took up his offer. How could they? Each had sworn an oath to the captain that he would follow Rhodes, not Holmes or Smith or another sailor. And even if a sailor had agreed to take charge, it is unlikely that the others would willingly have followed him as long as Rhodes was able. For better or worse, the longboat was Rhodes's responsibility.

Because the first mate was unwilling or unable to take control, the crew handled their duties in an idiosyncratic, haphazard fashion. Each man took a turn at the oars when he wished to, or when another was ready to yield his place. Those who bailed did so until they were tired and willing for another to take over. The sailors shared their clothes and the boat's stores with this or that passenger as each saw fit. "Holmes took off his oil cloth jacket and covered my head with it," young Margaret Edgar said. "He cut up his oilcloth pants and spread them over Julie McCadden. After this, he had nothing on but his shirt and pantaloons." Holmes then gave her a sea biscuit and some water. There were other spontaneous acts of sharing. This or that seaman leaned to one or another passenger and, as the spirit moved, offered a biscuit or a small cup of water from the ship's stores, or a jacket he thought he might do without.

Sea biscuits were a staple aboard nineteenth-century sailing ships. Commercially baked on shore, they were stored below decks in canvas bags and offered up at meals. They became food for vermin and home for insects long before they were ever served to the passengers and crew. The best way to eat one was to break it open and put a piece of fresh fish (if available) on the biscuit's surface to draw out the worms and maggots. Their absence did not make the dry biscuits more palatable or more nutritious, but the tracks they left aerated the biscuits, making them crumbly and easier to eat.

AROUND FOUR THAT AFTERNOON, at what should have been the beginning of the first dog watch, Rhodes moved from the stern to the middle of the boat to talk to his sailors. The weather had turned colder and the rain was hard, sometimes turning to hail or sleet. "We cannot continue like this," he told his crew. "It will be impossible for the boat to live should she come to blow any more heavily." It was time to consider how to lighten the boat, how to divest themselves of at least some of the burdensome weight the passengers represented.

Later, Rhodes claimed that the passengers had heard him talk to his crew and that none had protested. Perhaps they thought he was proposing a lottery. All had listened to him tell the captain that one might be necessary; all knew that in extremes sailors drew lots to see who would be required to die so at least some might survive. The *Essex* survivors had drawn lots twice: once to see who would die, and a second time to choose the sailor who would kill the man who had pulled the shortest straw. Or, perhaps, the passengers who heard Rhodes consult his men were simply afraid to protest, afraid to draw attention to themselves.

Whatever the reason, the sailors were not yet ready to undertake the murder of their charges. "There is no need yet, Mr. Rhodes," one sailor said. "Let it be and perhaps the sea will turn kindly," said another. "Perhaps a ship will come along for rescue." They still hoped, even if Rhodes did not. And so the first time he broached the subject, the crew themselves turned it down not as loathsome but precipitous.

But no ship found them that afternoon, and as night fell, the seas were anything but kind. The longboat was again surrounded by ice. The rain pelted down. Constant bailing barely held the level of water in the bottom of the boat. In the gathering darkness, nobody could tell if the water was from the waves, the rain or a leak. In the early evening, some of the sailors decided the boat was too heavy and the seas were sufficiently severe that something had to be done.

At Rhodes's urging—and it could *only* have been with his permission—several seamen decided to dispatch a passenger or two. "At about seven o'clock, we spoke to each other and took hold of one or two of the passengers, but they resisted and fearing they would be too strong, we stopped," Joseph Stetson said.

Perhaps it was Owen Riley. Maybe it was Jack Black. Whoever it was shook them off. "God's wounds," the man cried. "Let me be. This isn't the way. You don't just take a man and shove him into the sea." In an overfull boat in a freshening sea, a brawl would have been disastrous, shipping water as the struggle rocked it, perhaps enough to swamp the boat. The sailors agreed to leave off for the time being.

The seamen were not eager to murder their male passengers, so when this attempt failed, they gave up and returned to their rowing. Rhodes sat in the stern and brooded over the hard fate that had brought him to his unlucky command.

By about ten o'clock that night, the rain was falling steadily and the boat was filling with water in spite of the efforts of the passengers and sailors to keep it dry. At that moment, Rhodes, who had taken a turn at bailing, gave it up, exclaiming, "This won't do. Help me, God. Men, go to work." Not one passenger protested. When later asked to describe his reaction, young Owen Carr replied, "I made myself small." In this he was not alone.

At first, none of the sailors responded to Rhodes's order. The seas were not much higher than they had been at seven o'clock and the danger was little greater. Then "Some of the passengers cried out, about the same time, 'The boat is sinking.' 'The plug's out.' 'God have mercy on our souls.'" Panic took hold. Exhausted and frustrated, Rhodes and the other crewmen did not hear the caution that "The plug's out," only the warning that "The boat is sinking."

"I consulted with the ship's company," Rhodes claimed, "asking them what it would be best to do and stating that if they did not lighten her, they would all be lost. I said it would be better that a few should be saved that all should not perish but I did not order them to their work. I did tell the men that whatever was necessary to be done must be done immediately, or the boat would swamp."

"That night I heard some of the passengers say the boat was sinking," Jane Johnston Edgar recalled. "I said to Isabella we should all be lost. She said we must trust to the Almighty. I then heard the mate say this work [bailing] would not do, and tell the men to go to work or they would all be lost. I felt the boat move backwards and forwards as the men got up on their feet. They sat down again and the boat was still. The mate called them up again and said they must fall to work or all would perish."

Neither Rhodes nor the sailors asked themselves why the boat was sinking. It seemed to them self-evident: the boat was too heavily laden. At that moment, Rhodes's sole, dominating thought was that if only the boat could be lightened, it might be more seaworthy. "Men, you must go to work, or we shall all perish," is what both passengers and crew remembered Rhodes saying.

IN SPITE OF RHODES'S STATEMENT that morning to his captain about the necessity of drawing lots, he never proposed it that evening. Nor did he consult the passengers about what to do. In the end, sailors Charlie Smith, Alexander William Holmes, Joseph Stetson and the cook, Henry Murray, simply approached a male passenger, tapped him on the shoulder or grabbed his arms, told him it was time, and then pushed or threw him overboard into the sea. There was no order to it, no animus; no personal scores being settled.

Owen Riley, a married man sailing to join his wife, was the first to die. He protested when the sailors ordered him to stand up and prepare himself, pleading with Mrs. Edgar to intercede on his behalf. "Please, Ma'am, tell them this isn't the way. I have a wife in Philadelphia." He called out, too, to Julie McCadden, who, when she realized what was happening, shouted to the others, "Good God, are they going to drown the man?" That was perhaps the strongest protest that night from the passengers, most of whom, like Owen Carr, worked hard to made themselves small. Some covered themselves with blankets so they would not see or be seen. Most looked away.

Detail from a woodblock showing the longboat of the *William Brown* in *The Highwaymen and Pirates' Own Book*, by H.K. Brooke, published in 1845

Next, the sailors dispatched a Scotsman, James Todd, who put up no resistance. They then came to James MacAvoy. "Please," he asked, "give me a moment to make my peace with God." Now that the work had begun, the sailors were not willing to wait, but Henry Murray was a God-fearing man who insisted on giving MacAvoy a final moment of prayer. And pray he did, for perhaps five minutes. "Lord, be merciful to me, a sinner," he concluded. Then, as the sailors stood by in case his courage failed, MacAvoy buttoned his coat, nodded to them and jumped overboard without their help.

George Duffy was next. He begged them to spare him for the sake of the wife and children in America awaiting his arrival. When that failed, he asked, "Let me live so that I may watch over my niece, who travels with us here." The sailors shook their heads, grabbed his arms and threw him over. His niece, Bridget McGee, watched in fury as he drowned. In retrospect, it is impossible to know if she was angrier with the sailors who killed her uncle or with him for attempting to use her as an excuse.

After Duffy, they came upon affable Charlie Conlin, who asked, when Holmes stood above him, "Holmes, dear, you won't put me over, will you?" How the men knew each other is not clear, what tales or truths they shared about the *William Brown* remain unknown. Whatever they were, they were insufficient. "Charles, you must go," Holmes calmly replied, and he did.

The next to be approached was Francis Askin, who sat with his two sisters, Mary and Ellen. He reminded the sailors that Rhodes himself had talked of a lottery rather than a random slaughter. And unlike Duffy, Todd or Riley, Askin argued against the enterprise itself. "I'll not go out," he said. "You know I wrought well all the time. I'll work like a man till morning, and do what I can to keep the boat clear of water," he promised. To sweeten the offer, he announced, "I have five sovereigns and I'll give them for my life till morning, and when morning comes if God does not help us we will cast lots, and I'll go like a man if it is my turn." Beside him, Holmes quietly said, "I don't want your money, Frank." The crewmen then jettisoned Askin without prayer or other ceremony.

Askin's reminder about drawing lots and his promise to "go like a man" if he lost the draw touched a nerve. At that point the sailors became almost vicious and certainly less discriminating. It was blood lust, perhaps, which, once felt, must run its course until exhausted. The next to go, therefore, were not male passengers but Askin's two sisters, who might have survived had he been quieter and meeker. After all, these were Victorian sailors to whom women were precious and fragile, and thus deserving of their protection.

"When Holmes seized him, his sisters entreated for his life, and said that if he was thrown over they wished to be thrown over, too; that 'they wished to die the death of their brothers,'" the trial record states. "Give me only a dress to put around me," his sister Mary said after her brother had been dispatched, "and I care not now to live longer."

When Mary said she would go with her brother, the sailors did not hesitate, and said they might as well throw Ellen out, too. Ellen, the remaining sister, asked for a dress so she could meet her Maker demurely clothed. Someone gave her a wrap, and she went almost gladly, stepping into the sea on her own. What did she have to live for? A penniless emigrant woman without special skills, now without family or friends, had little to look forward to in the Americas except, perhaps, the shortened, vicious life of a prostitute.

Moving around the boat, Holmes grabbed the next man by his shoulder and asked, "Who is this?" In the starless night in which vision could not have been no more than a foot or two, murder had become like a parlour game of blind man's bluff, one in which the sailors decided who was "it."

"Why, it's James Black," one of the sailors said as the others prepared to lift him up and throw him overboard. "If you're to drown me, let my wife come, too," Black said. Ellen Black then stood up, and stood by her husband. "Let us go together," she said.

Rhodes then intervened. After setting the deadly work in motion, he had sat back, silent and uninvolved, unable to take part. "They will not live overlong at any rate," he announced. Now or later, in a day or two, the first mate believed that all were doomed. "Do not separate man and wife, let them be," Rhodes ordered. And so the sailors released the Blacks.

"After they had thrown overboard most of the men [and the two women]," Owen Carr said, "the sailors looked for more, and told the women not to hide them, as they would not leave a damned soul of them in the boat." But Holmes seems to have lost heart in the affair after Francis Askin's reminder of the lottery and the Blacks' display of courage. He stood by as the other sailors continued the work: Martin MacAvoy, Robert Hunter, John Wilson, John Welsh and then James Smith were thrown overboard in turn. "Blood-an-ouns," one of them said, "let go of me and I'll go myself."

Even young Owen Carr was tumbled into the sea by the murderous crew. Unbeknownst to them, however, he grabbed the bow of the boat and later crawled back aboard when the killing was done. He hid there, surrounded and sheltered by the women, throughout the night.

Not all the crewmen followed Rhodes's orders. Some sat quietly as the passengers were dispatched, and at least two protested the decision to arbitrarily jettison passengers who came to hand. John Messer and another sailor who was never named argued against the first mate's order, insisting that the slaughter of the emigrant passengers would not do. "I heard a splash alongside, and the whole boat was in an uproar—the work of death had commenced," said Messer. The other man and myself had both remonstrated against such cold-blooded proceedings, and said, 'If we are to die, let us die fair—let us cast lots.' 'Very well,' said the mate. 'They will throw you overboard next.'"

Rhodes was angered by Messer's insistence that lots be drawn. He knew that to do it fairly, they all would have to be included in the lottery, including himself. And so when Messer insisted on a lottery rather than a massacre, Rhodes sent two crewmen to deal with the dissenting seaman and his unnamed companion. "I then drew my sheath knife and swore that whoever should lay a hand on me should share my fate," Messer said. "The mate then called a tall Negro, one of the crew, to toss me overboard, but when he saw my knife, he went forwards again and lent the others a hand. My companion stuck close to me during the whole of the heartrending scene, determined to defend himself to the last." And so Messer and at least one other seaman refused the order; refusing, too, the order to permit themselves to be drowned. For the rest of the night, the two sat together, knives drawn against any attempt by their shipmates to attack them.

THE NEXT MORNING, at first light, the killing continued. Charlie Smith seized Biddy Nugent's uncle, John Nugent, who protested, "I have my orphaned nice to care for. Surely there has been enough. It is morning, let me live." Smith did not answer as he threw Nugent into the sea. At the same time, Joseph Stetson told Hugh Keigham to get up and help bail. When Keigham stood up, Stetson pushed him over into the sea.

Even Rhodes was appalled by these last two killings. When Keigham was thrown out, the first mate turned to Stetson and shouted, "Lord, cruel, cruel!" This seems a strange sentiment for the man who the night before had ordered his men to slaughter their charges. For their parts, Stetson and Smith were probably surprised by Rhodes's newfound sensibility. After all, they must have reasoned, fairness demanded consistency. Were they not simply finishing the work their superior had directed the night before?

But the situation had changed. Hours earlier, the sailors could not see the faces of the men and women whom they threw into the sea. In daylight, they had to look at their victims. The panic over the boat filling with water was gone, and the sailors discovered that the bailing plug had become dislodged. *That* was why the boat was filling with water.

What is unclear is whether it was the displaced bailing plug that led to the cry that the boat was sinking or whether the plug came out in the turmoil of throwing the passengers overboard. Julie McCadden later said it was "in the confusion of throwing the passengers out that the plug came out." But several others heard the warning—"The plug is out" —at the same time they heard the shout that the boat was sinking.

What seems most likely is that the plug was not wholly dislodged but loosened, so that water came in around it but not in torrents. After all, it was a makeshift plug carved by Holmes during the longboat's first hours at sea. If it had been wholly displaced, water would have entered at a rapid rate and the boat surely would have swamped.

Whatever had happened to the plug, the sailors had reset it firmly well before the final two murders of Keigham and Nugent. When they were thrown overboard, the longboat was relatively dry and riding nicely in the sea. It could easily have rowed into the day with both men alive and on board.

After the last two murders, those who remained "looked very distressed," as Susannah Edgar put it with understatement. Rhodes's mental state was worse than that of his charges, however. He was paralysed by guilt or remorse over the deaths he had ordered the previous evening. From the start, he had believed the occupants of the longboat to be doomed. Now he had to live with the knowledge that, whatever else might happen, passengers in his care had been drowned on his watch and on his orders. He settled into what today might be called a dysfunctional stupor.

It fell to Alexander Holmes to take effective command. "The mate asked the men what he should do. Holmes said we ought not to steer for Newfoundland, as we would never reach it, but to go south, as it would be warmer, and we might meet a vessel. The mate said he would do as Holmes wanted. He would give up all to Holmes." The young sailor, at least, had not lost hope.

There seems to have been little animosity toward Holmes for his part in the drownings of the night before. After all, he had not ordered them. Nor had he carried it to the extremes of that morning's killings. He had been polite in his work, if deadly. And now, relieved of Rhodes's orders, Holmes's first act was to reassure the remaining emigrants and to prepare for their possible rescue. He told them that they had sufficient food and water to sustain them for days. When passengers asked if the drownings would continue, he promised they would not. "No," said Holmes, "no more shall be thrown over. If any more are lost, we will all be lost together."

The passengers believed him and were reassured. After all, Holmes had returned to the *William Brown* to rescue Isabella Edgar, the only rescue of that first, horrible night. And now it was the Swedish sailor who gave them hope. "Holmes told us to keep our hearts up," Susannah Edgar said. For their part, the sailors accepted him as honest, strong, competent and without animosity toward anyone. None had thought him a leader, but all respected his skills. Besides, nobody else stepped forward. There was nobody *but* Holmes to turn to.

An hour after the last two drownings, after taking *de facto* command, Holmes took a quilt left by a passenger whom he had helped drown and "tried to raise it to make a sail, but the wind was too strong. He then stood up and said that he saw the mast of a vessel, and afterwards, got to work to raise a shawl on the end of the oar." Like Joseph Tappan in the *Jupiter*'s yawl, like the survivors of the *Medusa* upon their raft, he raised a makeshift flag in the hope of signalling the still distant vessel.

John Messer later insisted that he was the first to see the *Crescent* slowly working its way through the ice fields. When he sang out, Rhodes supposedly replied, "By God, Jack, you're a lucky fellow, you have saved your life." Perhaps. But by all accounts, so boisterous a comment was beyond Rhodes's emotional state at the time, unless, of course, the sight of another ship magically had roused him from his stupor. Whoever first sang out the *Crescent*—Holmes or Messer—it was Holmes who took command of the longboat in the minutes before its rescue and who raised the shawl on the oar as a signal.

"The great distance of the *Crescent* rendered it almost impossible that Holmes' signal should be seen. The second mate of the vessel happened, however, to be aloft, watching for ice; and as soon as the ship, responding to the signal, put about, the voice of exultant joy and gratitude burst forth from the wretched assemblage on the long-boat. Some were crawling up the side of the boat to see the approaching vessel, and others, who had seemed congealed, now stood erect: 'Lie Down,' said Holmes, 'every soul

SHIPWRECK OF THE MEDUSE.

C. Hullmandel's Lithography.

A tattered, makeshift signal flag is raised by survivors on the raft in an engraving titled *Shipwreck of the Meduse*. Courtesy Bibliothèque Nationale de France

of you, and be still. If they make so many of us on board, they will steer off another way and pretend they have not seen us.'"

While both law and custom demanded that ships rescue those whom they found adrift and in distress, the law in those days was often ignored. Everyone knew the story of the *Peggy*, shipwrecked in 1765. Famous for the cannibalism that kept some of her survivors alive—they had been eighteen days without food—the ship's crew had watched in helpless frustration as first one and then another ship sailed close, only to deliberately turn away from their longboat. That ships had similarly ignored the castaways of other vessels, adrift in boats, was common knowledge.

The wonder is that anyone was ever rescued. It was no easy thing to inch up to a frail survival craft as it skittered to and fro on the waves of a heaving sea. It took time to hoist weakened and dehydrated passengers to the larger ship, time lost on voyages already too long for most captains and their crews. Worse, should a captain stop and rescue castaways, they then became his responsibility. He had to provide them with food, clothing and care until the ship made port. Because many ships carried barely enough bad food and brackish water for their own use, this meant rationing and added costs.

In short, stopping to save the shipwrecked survivors of another ship was a time-consuming, expensive business, especially when the number of survivors was, as they were in this case, large. Rescue meant short rations for everyone aboard if those saved from the sea were not to die of starvation. The cost cut into the rescuing ship's profits, and it was profit that drove the trade and goaded captains to sail as fast as possible across the Atlantic. Thus, while the *Crescent* was obliged by law and custom to help the survivors of the *William Brown*, there was no guarantee that she would.

Captain George Ball, master of the American ship *Crescent*, was not one to shirk his duty, however. He was a decent man and a careful captain, who, the night before had mounted a full watch, including a man in the bow and another up the mast, to assure safe passage through the ice-filled waters. He had early reduced sail as another precaution, remaining in charge and on deck as his ship travelled through the false dawn and then first light. Once the longboat was spied—visible when it rode to the crest, disappearing in the troughs—he ordered the *Crescent* to its rescue.

To those in the longboat, it must have seemed to take forever as the *Crescent* tacked, first here and then there, moving slowly toward them. Finally, she drew parallel and then alongside the longboat. Only then did Holmes lower his makeshift signal. He used the oar to fend off the ice floes that surrounded them as they came alongside the *Crescent*. By that time, the ship's crew would have seen how populous the longboat was, but to abandon it then would have been too cruel.

Some of the survivors, like Messer and Holmes, were still strong and able, and they climbed the *Crescent's* lines unaided. Others, however, too weak to make the trip unassisted, were hauled up by ropes thrown to them from the deck. While this transfer was being made, the longboat was caught between the ship and one of the growlers that surrounded both the longboat and its rescuer. The damage, while serious, was not enough to sink the boat at the moment of its salvation.

Captain Ball had the longboat hauled aboard and secured to the deck. It was wood, after all, and if nothing else could be broken up and used as fuel. The longboat's provisions were carried aboard as well. In their thirty-three hours at sea, few of the *William Brown's* passengers or crew had been interested in eating. The meat and sea biscuit and even the water-soaked oatmeal would be needed so that the *Crescent's* cook could feed everyone in the coming weeks.

Noting the weakness of most of the passengers and their state of relative undress, Captain Ball saw to their needs as best he could. At his request, the *Crescent's* sailors contributed coats and shirts for the emigrants, some of whom still wore only the nightclothes they had on when Jack Black first shouted to them that the *William Brown* was sinking. The men of the *Crescent* responded without hesitation, sharing clothing from their sea chests with those who needed them.

The survivors accepted these gifts without comment and with little outward emotion. They were tired, exhausted, hungry and in shock. After preparing for death, it is not easy to adjust to the idea of a future measured not in hours or days but in years and decades. A similar, almost eerie, silence held sway on the deck of the *Carpathia* when it rescued the *Titanic's* survivors. "Everyone noticed it, everyone had a different explanation," W.A. Lord wrote in his book *A Night to Remember*.

Like the survivors of the *Titanic*, those of the *William Brown* would have to live with the memory of the friends and relatives and countrymen whom they had abandoned in the rush for their own salvation. All remembered the last lamentations of those they had left behind.

More critically, the longboat survivors were rescued the morning after the deliberate drowning of at least thirteen of their number, and less than three hours after the last two had been killed. The emigrants knew they had watched without protest the murder of their friends and relations when what had been really needed was for somebody—anybody—to check the bailing plug. The price of rescue by the *Crescent* was the knowledge that each would sacrifice anybody without a murmur of complaint if that would provide even one additional hour of uncertain life. No wonder none of them cheered when brought aboard the rescuing ship.

John Messer was an exception. Like Holmes, he had remained relatively strong and alert throughout the ordeal. As importantly, he had refused Rhodes's order to get rid of passengers and had fought back when his fellow sailors had turned on him. He was not a man to let bygones be bygones and would not quickly forgive those who had attempted to drown him the night before. "So strong was my indignation against the Negro [who thought to try to throw me over]," Messer said, "that upon reaching the *Crescent*'s deck I seized a heaver [a heavy iron implement] and threw it at his head." He missed.

THE *CRESCENT*

AFTER RESCUING the longboat survivors, the *Crescent* spent several days of cautious manoeuvring under reduced sail before it managed to get clear of the ice floes that surrounded her. Then Captain Ball ordered all sail raised and headed for Le Havre. With the Gulf Stream behind and strong winds to aid her, the *Crescent* fairly flew on the eastward course to Europe. To the emigrants it must have seemed as if Fate itself—and Neptune, too—had conspired against them. In the course of just two days, their ship had sunk and they had witnessed the deaths of relatives and friends as they sat helpless in a small, open boat floating through shards of dying icebergs. Now, they were safe, at least for the moment, but that safety came on a ship that was retracing with speed the miles at sea that the *William Brown* had laboured to achieve.

Gone was their sense of security aboard a sailing ship. Some worried the whole thing might happen again. This time they were not paying passengers but flotsam retrieved from the sea, charity cases less valuable than the damaged longboat that now sat in hastily fashioned blocks on the ship's deck. Why wouldn't they be abandoned if Captain Ball's ship needed to save its own?

Throughout the days of the *Crescent*'s voyage, the emigrant survivors continued in their state of shock and bereavement. They suffered from the effects of their exposure, of hours in damp air and cold rain without protective clothing. Warm now, and at least temporarily secure, they had time to mourn their drowned companions and to worry about their own uncertain futures. They had lost all their worldly possessions. Worse, they

A field of ice similar to the one that, after rescuing the longboat survivors, the *Crescent* sailed carefully through in search of open seas. Courtesy United States Coast Guard

had lost the relatives and friends with whom they had hoped to build a new life. It was bad enough to be penniless; it was far worse to be without family. Now they were forced to consider how to make a life alone.

What were they going to do once they arrived in Le Havre? Where were they to go from there? Who would pay their passage home, or for a second try at emigration? Wherever they ended up, what life might they expect? There were no jobs to return to in Ireland and England and Scotland, no shops to reopen. The land they had lived on had gone to others to work. If life had not been impossibly hard, they would not have left in the first place. And so, together, they wondered how any might raise the money to seek again the America whose promise had recently seemed so close.

Almost certainly there was anger as well as anguish. The survivors now realized that all the longboat's passengers might have lived if only Rhodes had not panicked, if only his courage had lasted that first night of his command. And though they had not murdered their compatriots in the longboat, they were not blameless, either. All had scrambled over others to gain a seat in the longboat, fought past their friends and abandoned their relatives in the struggle to get off the sinking *William Brown*. Each had thought first of himself or herself. Later, in the lifeboat, none had protested when Rhodes had ordered the drowning of their companions.

A good lawyer might have fought for compensation for the emigrants had their tragedy happened on land. But at sea, the law said that one was in God's able hands and that to hold merchants responsible for His acts would be unreasonable, even blasphemous. Further, to offer compensation to passengers who were the victims of a maritime disaster would make the transatlantic trade less profitable. Ship owners faced with even the possibility of passenger lawsuits would be forced to raise their freight and passenger rates to prohibitive levels. To encumber the commerce of the sea would endanger the economy of nations like the United States and Great Britain. Even today, the American *Death on the High Seas Act* limits compensation for the wrongful death of a seaman on the high seas to "pecuniary" loss, the monies the deceased was earning at the time of death.

In 1834, Lloyd's Register of British and Foreign Shipping established a system of insurance that "removed from commerce the tragedy of individual ruin which had hitherto attended the loss of a ship and its cargo." But the "tragedy" resulting from a shipwreck attached only to the ship owner and his or her loss, not to passengers. In the larger economic scheme, they were more expendable than the crockery and fine lace that ships like the *Crescent* and the *William Brown* carried from Europe's factories and mills to the Americas. Since the emigrants had paid their fares before embarking, their loss at sea would not affect the ship owners' financial returns. If some died, there were so many that the deaths of a few scarcely mattered. One newspaper displayed the spirit of the age when, in reporting another shipwreck, it stated that "twenty souls and 240 emigrants perished." There were souls and then there were emigrants. The first were to be mourned and the second merely counted.

Had a titled Englishmen been aboard the *William Brown*, or the scion of an important Boston (or Philadelphia) family, the situation might have been different. People of breeding and men of commerce were treated in a way that emigrants, especially Irish emigrants, were not. In the mid-nineteenth century, more than fifty thousand emigrants left Great Britain for the Americas; by 1850 more than a hundred thousand would sail from Europe's ports each year.

They were pushed onto the ships by a host of causes, and their departure was widely considered as good riddance, especially the Irish, who were regarded as, if not subhuman, then still clearly inferior to the true-bred Englishman or woman.

The science of the day assured legislators and ship owners alike that the Irish were less intelligent, less in control of their faculties than were their betters. Like the Africans bought and sold in the slave trade, the Irish had demonstrable limits. They were a people with smaller brains but with the brawn that God gave to working animals. One answer to the perennial "Irish Question" was to send these boisterous, troublesome, almost humans to the New World, where they might be of some use. And if they did not survive the journey, who cared?

This cartoon, titled *The Wild Irish in the West*, shows how people then regarded the Irish as an inferior race, just as they did the Africans in the slave trade. From *Punch*, 19 May 1860

THE SAILORS RESCUED from the longboat enjoyed a busman's holiday. After all, they lived not in one country or another but on board ships and, over a full career, most would serve on half-a-dozen vessels, maybe more, furling sails and hauling lines for any captain who would have them. Once on board the *Crescent*, they were in a very real sense at home, though this time they travelled not as working sailors but as supercargo. There were no watches for them to stand, no repairs that required their skills. The *Crescent*'s sailors turned in and turned out, watch upon watch, while the *William Brown*'s crew lolled below and sometimes above deck. If they came up for a constitutional or a gam (a chat) with their counterparts, they did so without responsibility. For perhaps the only time in their working lives, Rhodes, Holmes, Messer, Stetson and the rest were passengers, living the lives of those they had so recently first served and later drowned.

As they sailed eastward, the *William Brown*'s former crew must have discussed and then discussed again the events that had taken place in the longboat. John Messer remained angry and would not be mollified. He certainly had words with Murray, the cook, who had attempted to throw him overboard. For his part, Rhodes perhaps relived in his nightmares his order to drown the emigrant passengers a few hours before the longboat was rescued. Maybe he remonstrated with Joseph Stetson about the two passengers he had thrown overboard the morning they were rescued. But who could have guessed that rescue was so close at hand? The crew had a lot to talk about.

Alexander Holmes may be forgiven if in discussion with his fellows he saw himself as a hero. He would not have boasted; that was not his way. But when he thought of his own actions, it must have been with self-satisfaction. At the least, Holmes must have assumed that he would be complimented for returning to the *William Brown* to save young Isabella Edgar.

Captain Ball was aware of the currents of argument and complaint that swept among his passengers. The shipwrecked sailors talked to his crew; his crew talked to him. And as master of the rescuing vessel, it was standard procedure for him to interview Francis Rhodes, the man in command of the longboat, at the earliest opportunity. Only one existing record testifies to their discussions. From it, we know that after all the survivors were brought aboard, and after the *Crescent* had cleared the ice, Captain Ball took Rhodes aside and asked him to report on the events that had brought him and his charges to their sorry, abandoned state.

Rhodes recognized an opportunity when it presented itself. He did not mention that the *William Brown* struck an iceberg while under full sail in an area known for ice. To admit that they had ignored basic precautions would have impugned his captain's seamanship, and unless he said that he had protested his master's order, his own seamanship as well. And he knew that Captain Ball would not be impressed with a first mate who was quick to blame his own captain.

Rhodes also did not report that after the first strike, the glancing blow, he visited the helm and then left without giving orders to reduce sail or to add to the watch. Nor did he admit to having been so discouraged that he repeatedly offered his command of the longboat to any who would take it. Instead, he put the best possible face upon what had happened on the *William Brown* and then in the longboat, on the drowning of his charges the night before the rescue. Francis Rhodes had not survived the sinking of his ship only to drown in the seas of self-incrimination.

In this first, God-given opportunity to tell his story, Rhodes presented himself as an active and experienced seaman. It was he who sensed danger with the first strike (immediately changing his clothes) and who took charge after the second. And in this telling, he, first mate Francis Rhodes, ably assisted in the disembarkation and then commanded the longboat with confidence and knowledge guided by experience.

When in command, he had been man enough, democratic enough, to consult his seamen about the terrible choice they together faced: should everyone share the same watery fate or should some be drowned so that at least a few might survive? None had doubted that unless something was done, the longboat would be swamped, he told Captain Ball. He had raised the issue with Captain Harris prior to the jolly boat's departure, he said. Everyone had heard him tell the captain that the longboat with its heavy load could not endure. "I know what you mean," Captain Harris had responded. And for Rhodes, that was enough to justify the murders.

Rhodes pointed out to Captain Ball that the longboat, which now sat on the *Crescent*'s deck, was stove in. Did this not prove how dangerous the waters had been? True, the damage had happened as the longboat was pushed against the *Crescent*, not on the open water. But still, the damage was there, on deck, for him to see. If only because his was the business of ship's command, Captain Ball would have been loath to second-guess or doubt either Captain Harris or his first mate. He was, therefore, not disposed to ask if Harris had placed an extra watch on deck or shortened sail. He did not ask if Harris had taken the sea's temperature when the night air turned foggy, the very scent of ice in the air. He simply assumed that Harris had.

Captain Ball accepted Rhodes's story exactly as the first mate presented it and then did his best to help the man to write a satisfactory report, coaching its presentation as if it were his own. Later, in fact, Rhodes's telling was presented as the result of an independent investigation, one carried out by an impartial authority, Captain George Ball, master of the *Crescent*.

The perspective is Rhodes's; there is no doubt about that. But the style is practised and professional, not that of a mate whose job is to pass on orders and supervise the ship while the captain is occupied otherwise. To ensure a sense of dispassionate inquiry, Captain Ball asked some of the *William Brown*'s survivors to sign it as well. The sailors who had drowned the sixteen passengers were willing to do so, of course, as were one or two passengers. Those who disagreed with Rhodes's version of events, John Messer, for example, and Bridget McGee, were simply omitted from any mention.

ON 2 MAY, while the *Crescent* was still at least a week from France, her lookout spied a ship on the horizon. Captain Ball ordered his men to sail an intercept course. Any chance meeting at sea was an opportunity for news, and if help was needed, it was usually given. As they approached the *Ville de Lyon*, an American sailing ship, the *Crescent*'s sailors reduced sail and then hove to, holding their place just off the wind as Ball signalled the other vessel that he would like to come aboard. This was common practice when ships met offshore. They would sail close enough for an easy meeting but not so close the two vessels might collide. With sails reduced, the captains shouted across the sea that separated them. If they decided to meet, one would lower his jolly boat and be rowed to the other by his seamen. After boarding the *Ville de Lyon*, Captain Ball told his counterpart, Captain Stoddard, about the situation.

It must have been an interesting conversation. Certainly, Ball told Stoddard the highlights of the sinking of the *William Brown*, the events on the longboat and the rescue, as we know from Stoddard's report when he reached Le Havre. Captain Ball asked for any stores that the other ship might be able to part with, as his extra passengers had depleted the *Crescent*'s larder. The emergency provisions retrieved from the *William Brown*'s longboat already had been consumed. The *Crescent* was also low on fuel, as the additional cooking required had used up those stores. The shortage of fuel was so dire that Ball had ordered his own longboat dismantled and its wood used for the cooking fire. He could have ordered the *William Brown*'s damaged boat to be broken up, but he wanted to keep it as evidence for the inquiry that he expected to be called. And, some later said, it was the better boat despite its damage, better timbered and easy enough to repair.

Captain Stoddard rose to the occasion, offering Captain Ball what stores he could spare. He also agreed to share the burden by taking aboard some of the survivors. The question was who to send? Surviving emigrants or the remnants of the *William Brown*'s crew? If the rescued passengers were shipped on the faster *Ville de Lyon,* their version of what happened on the *William Brown* and the longboat would be the first that officials would hear. Their stories might be angry and intemperate. If crew members involved in the drownings were sent, however, the first word to officials would come from those who, like Rhodes, would put a good face to the longboat drownings.

In the end, the *Ville de Lyon* carried ten of the *William Brown*'s seamen and a copy of Captain Ball's report. Transferred to the faster ship were Charlie Smith, Joseph Stetson and the 22-year-old-cook Henry Murray. Alexander Holmes was sent as well. These sailors could be trusted to put the face of necessity upon their actions in the longboat. To leaven the mix, several others were included: a young Swede, Isaac Freeman, who spoke little English; James Norton, another adolescent sailor; William Miller, a sixteen-year-old Dane; and the African-American steward, Joseph Marshall. Also dispatched were John Messer and the unnamed sailor who stood with him against the drownings.

THE *VILLE DE LYON* reached Le Havre on 10 May, two days before the *Crescent.* As he entered the harbour, Captain Stoddard sent a letter to the United States Consul, Rubin G. Beasley, informing him of the ship-wrecked sailors he carried and of the general course of events that had brought them to his ship. With his letter, he sent a copy of Captain Ball's "investigation" based on the interview with Rhodes. Stoddard's message was carried to shore by a small, fast cutter. In those days, local vessels would race to reach incoming ships, collect the news they carried—often news-papers, but in some cases personal reports—and rush it to the docks. If the incoming ship was damaged and repairs were required, or if there was an urgent need for stores, the information would be conveyed to chandlers whose representatives would wait at the dock, order books in hand.

On reaching a foreign port, a ship flew a signal flag to announce its arrival, anchoring in the harbour until a berth could be arranged. And, of course, then as now, an inbound ship had to endure a visit from what today we call customs and immigration. Contraband, if present, would be confiscated. If there was disease on the ship, the vessel might be quarantined or sent away. And if untoward events had occurred during a voyage, the appropriate officials would be notified.

Like his counterpart on the *Crescent*, Captain Stoddard was a careful man who was well aware of the potential for scandal of the news he carried. The demise of seamen and passengers in shipwrecks was a common enough occurrence, but drowning them *after* they had been saved certainly was not. That was ... shocking. At the least, a public outcry might damage the very profitable trade in emigrants. At worst, it could lead to new regulations that would limit the captain's authority and make expensive luxuries—lifeboats, for example—a requirement on all ships.

In the late 1830s tales of shipwreck had become so frequent that the flood of emigrants diminished for a year or two. Bad as things might be at home, when travel was perceived as too risky, people chose to stay where they were. As a result, the profits of every maritime business had fallen. The economics of the shipping trade demanded a full cargo hold of raw goods on the eastern voyage and a full hold of finished goods, topped off by paying emigrants, on the return trip. Anything capable of endangering that business needed to be handled cautiously.

Rubin Beasley was a practical, experienced consul who understood at once the problems that the story of the *William Brown* presented. He was there to promote trade and to represent the interests of the United States; anything that threatened either of these was his concern. Beasley was the first official to be informed because Captain Stoddard was an American citizen in command of an American vessel, and because the *William Brown* had been an American ship bound for Philadelphia. But because the passengers drowned in the longboat were British subjects, albeit mostly Irish, his younger and less experienced counterpart, British Consul A. Gilbert Gordon, would become involved as well. This was no real obstacle, however. Beasley knew that Gordon admired him greatly and was a respectful junior who deferred to his senior whenever they met.

Ambassadors are political appointees, representatives not only of a nation but also and more particularly of an administration. Their work takes place at a level of representation beyond that of working consular officials like Beasley and Gordon, who handle the daily activities of international relations. While ambassadors come and go, consuls and consular officials often spend years in a post. Their job is not policy but practice. Rubin Beasley had served his country for twenty years in Le Havre and had handled scores, perhaps hundreds, of shipping incidents.

There is no record of the consuls' first meeting, but knowing what happened later permits a reconstruction that catches its sense if not the precise words. In the normal course of events, Beasley, as the senior representative, would ask Gordon to attend him at the American consulate. But almost certainly this time the older man went to his British counterpart's chambers, a sign that an important and urgent matter had arisen. First, they would have chatted about social affairs, as good manners demanded, until Gordon finally asked what pressing affair of state brought the United States consul to his chambers.

Beasley informed Gordon that there had been an unfortunate incident, a matter of some delicacy that demanded their attention. He then gave Captain Stoddard's letter and the Ball/Rhodes report to Gordon. The British consul understood immediately that the lamentable affair might be used by riffraff and radicals in a manner that could adversely affect trade between their two nations, and the emigration of British subjects to American shores. He therefore agreed without hesitation when Beasley suggested they begin a joint investigation.

"In consequence of this representation," the British Foreign Office files report, "application was made to [French] civil authorities for arrestation of these men" from the *William Brown*. This was nothing but a formality. In the 1840s France claimed no legal jurisdiction over events occurring on the "high seas," defined as anything out of sight of land. The affairs of British or American sailors were no concern of theirs as long as they did not involve French citizens. Most nations had a similar position.

Le Havre was an international harbour with ships from both the Americas and Europe stopping for provisions, repairs and cargo. Honouring requests from foreign consuls was part of the French port's service. It happened all the time. The previous August, for example, a

British sailor, James Dixon, had been reported killed aboard a ship from Montevideo when it arrived in Le Havre. At Gordon's request, the captain and both the first and second mates were taken into custody and questioned about the murder. Upset by the homicide of a British sailor on the foreign vessel, Gordon had the second mate, a British subject named Langley, held by the French until he could receive instructions from Britain's Foreign Secretary, Lord Palmerston. After reviewing Gordon's report and consulting with legal experts, Palmerston ordered the consul to have Langley returned to London, where the magistrates of the Thames police were prepared to take him into custody. That was how it worked. Modern legal niceties, the rigmarole of extradition hearings and refugee pleas, were things of the future.

When the *Ville de Lyon* docked, port officials and their constables were on hand to take the *William Brown*'s crewmen into custody. Beasley arranged for them to be delivered to the American consulate the next day to make formal depositions. From the start, however, the issue was more the protection of the emigrant trade than an investigation of the sinking of the *William Brown* and the drownings on its longboat.

Both Britain and the United States were desperate to preserve the emigrant trade. The population of Great Britain was booming, and while industrialization sucked up much of the population, it could not absorb it all. Moreover, the centres of new industry were in England—London, Manchester and Liverpool—and not in Ireland, whose population was exploding but whose industries could not absorb the growth. Thousands of Irish men and women were pouring into England's largest, already overcrowded, cities. The squalor they created was impossible and their political agitation intolerable. Nobody doubted the Irish would continue to leave their homeland. The question was whether they would go into already overcrowded British cities or to North America with its vast hunger for labour. Better, the British government believed, that the Irish go overseas rather than remain a bother at home.

But potential emigrants in Britain and Europe were nervous about the transoceanic voyage and its dangers. Too many people had died on coffin ships with rotting timbers, or had arrived near death from cholera or typhus or malnutrition from the swill they were fed. In Great Britain and North America, emigrants and potential emigrants were agitating for regulations regarding ship safety, the quality of ship food, the duty of sailors and the comfort of passengers. Beasley and Gordon both knew, albeit from their own distinct national perspectives, that the longboat's murders might well fuel those arguments. Any inquiry would have to be carefully crafted to appease the Irish emigrant communities in the United States and to calm those contemplating the voyage in Great Britain. To make the situation even more complex, wealthy and politically powerful shipping lobbies on both sides of the Atlantic were opposed to new and expensive shipping regulations.

While both consuls saw the potential of the *William Brown* for scandal, their assessment of the importance of the situation differed. Gordon regarded the whole affair as melancholy and lamentable, but no more than business as usual. Another ship had been lost at sea. That some survivors had been drowned to lighten the longboat in an effort to preserve at least a few of those saved from the *William Brown* was tragic but understandable. The whole, he believed, could be easily handled. It would be weeks before he understood his error.

For his part, Beasley recognized that the sinking of the *William Brown* and the subsequent events in the longboat presented a different problem from other shipwrecks he had handled. For one thing, the murders in the longboat were too numerous to go unanswered. A range of issues surrounding the status of emigrants and the condition of the ships that carried them across the Atlantic might come to a head with this case. He realized what Gordon did not: because the ship was American and the emigrants killed were British, his country's interest and those of Britain were not the same. If an example was to be made in the case of the *William Brown*, one that would speak to the emigrant trade, he knew his masters in Washington and Gordon's in London would each want to claim jurisdiction. From the start, therefore, Beasley worked to make sure that any precedent, any judgment, would be American and not British.

As soon as the sailors were taken into custody, Beasley set up a private hearing through the local board of police. Without informing Gordon, he interviewed the *William Brown*'s sailors the day before official depositions were to be taken by the joint U.S.-British investigation. The sessions were brief and informal. No secretary was present to record the unsworn statements. Beasley simply wanted to get the lay of the land and to remove any potential problems before he presided with his British counterpart at the official, recorded, hearing.

What he heard disturbed him greatly. The events on the longboat might be construed, as the Rhodes/Ball report said, as sad and tragic but necessary—were it not for John Messer and his companion's scathing condemnation of both the drownings and of Rhodes's command. Messer insisted that Rhodes should have held a lottery and that the failure to do so offended any reasonable sense of justice. He condemned his fellows for following the first mate's orders, especially when he became their target.

Months later, Messer told a Boston newspaper that "the American Consul, when made acquainted with the facts, advised me and my companion to remain and give our evidence against the mate and the crew but we declined, upon the grounds that we conceived the testimony of the passengers sufficient. As he was not very urgent, we were liberated after an examination before the Board of Police."

Beasley immediately understood that if Messer made an official statement, it would give the lie to the general picture of competent seamanship in difficult conditions that the Rhodes/Ball report promoted. He suggested Messer and his friend testify so that nobody could accuse him of suppressing their testimony, but he did not order them to stay and in fact freed them to go. He did not inform Gordon about the two witnesses thus liberated.

Having ensured that the most damning testimony would not be heard, Beasley set about squelching the rumours that had begun to circulate as soon as the *Ville de Lyon* arrived in port. Its sailors quickly carried the story of the *William Brown* to pubs and rooming houses, to brothels and gaming dens. The tale of sixteen passengers saved from yet another wreck only to be drowned by their own ship's sailors was worth a drink or two from dockside hangers-on, from sailors waiting for a berth. As the tale was told and retold, it naturally grew in the telling.

Soon townspeople were talking about the vicious seamen who had hacked off the hands of the poor passengers who desperately clung to the longboat in hopes of rescue. Nor were the rumours confined to the French port. The story travelled like cholera, carried by the seamen of a dozen nations who shipped out daily for a score of ports in Europe, Great Britain and the Americas.

Who leaked the Rhodes/Ball report to the *Journal de Havre*? Since the story was published on 11 May, the *Journal*'s editors must have received a copy the very day the *Ville de Lyon* docked. The report might have come from Captain Stoddard, but there was no reason for him to involve himself in the affair and good reason for him to stand off from what promised to be a messy fray. Rhodes and Captain Ball could not have supplied it, because they were still at sea. And Consul Gordon surely did not do it, as he truly did not understand the report's implications. Therefore, it was must have been Beasley who gave the report to local journalists. It seemed definitive, the official statement of an investigation by Captain Ball, rescuer of the survivors of the *William Brown*. Originally set in a single column of narrow eight-point type, the Rhodes/Ball report is presented here in a more readable format to give an idea of how official it appears to be.

DREADFUL SHIPWRECK
(from the *Havre Journal*.)

The following is an account of the loss of the ship William Brown of Philadelphia, Captain George L. Harris, which left Liverpool on 15th March, having 17 for the ship's crew, and 66 steerage passengers, freighted for Philadelphia:

At sea, on board the ship Crescent, April 28, 1841: The passage was very rough, accompanied by squalls and loss of sails. On the night of 19 April, in lat. 43 30 N., and 49 39 W. long., making all sail in the open sea, and running 10 knots an hour, the larboard side of the vessel struck upon an iceberg which stove her in. At 10 minutes past nine we struck upon another. I then proposed to the captain to take in sail as quickly as possible, which we did and, sounding the pump, found two feet water in the hold. On going below I found that the vessel was rapidly making water.

All hands set to work to disengage the boats, and at 11 o'clock they were alongside. I descended into the long-boat with eight of the crew and 33 of the passengers; the captain, lieutenant, a lady, and five sailors, embarked in the jolly-boat and we fastened the boats together. At midnight the vessel sank, carrying with her 33 persons. We remained alongside each other until 5 o'clock in the morning. Captain Harris then informed us of his intention of leaving us, and making the best of his way to Newfoundland, and advised me to do the same.

My boat being full and heavy, I could not manage it; to pursue that route was impossible; I therefore directed my course south. In the afternoon we fell in with a large quantity of ice. Throughout the night the wind blew with violence from the north in squalls, with rain and hail, and a very heavy sea.

Finding that the boat was literally surrounded by small and large masses of ice and that the water was gaining upon her, I thought it improbable she could hold out, unless relieved of some of her weight. I then consulted the sailors, and we were all of the opinion that it was necessary to throw overboard those who were nearly dead, until we had room enough to work the boat and take to our oars. The weather becoming worse, it was almost impossible to keep the boat afloat and disengage it from the ice.

At daybreak we were still surrounded by icebergs. On counting the passengers 16 were missing, and the rest were in a desperate state, and almost stiff from cold.

At 6 o'clock in the morning we perceived to the westward a sail steering an easterly course. We exorted every effort to approach it. The captain being aloft in order to steer his ship through the ice, saw our boat, and, notwithstanding the danger to his own ship, made sail for us. On Thursday morning at 7 o'clock we were alongside of her, and before she had received us all on board was struck by the ice, which stove in the boat. We, however succeeded in saving her.

Banks and islands of ice were in sight as far as the eye could reach. I then ascertained that it was the Crescent of Portsmouth (New Hampshire), Captain G. T. Ball, bound from New York to Havre. We met the kindest reception on board, and assistance in the way of food and clothing was lavished upon us.

(Signed by the crew saved in the boat and two passengers)
Francis Rhodes, mate
Joseph Stretton, sailor
Alexander Williams, ditto
———— Lemarchal, steward
H. Murray, cook
Charles Smith, sailor
James Northon, ditto
Isaac Freeman, ditto
William Miller, ditto
James Patrick, passenger
James Black, ditto
The above is a correct statement of the loss of the William Brown, which I have been able to learn from the mate and passengers.
G. T. Ball, Captain of the Crescent.

That many of the facts were not correct—sixty-five, not sixty-six passengers departed from Liverpool, for example, and the *William Brown* left port on 19 March, not four days earlier—did not matter to those who read the report reprinted in the newspaper. Even the location given, lat. 43°30' N and 49°39' W was wrong, but it was close enough so that readers would appreciate that the events took place in dangerous waters in the spring of the year when icebergs accumulated along the edges of the warm Gulf Stream. In this telling, it is Rhodes who proposes to the captain that sails be reduced, Rhodes who goes below himself to check the damage. Finally, it is Rhodes who directs the departure of passengers and crew after the captain decides the ship cannot be saved. The order that Rhodes imposed upon the event is one no other participant witnessed.

The report passes quickly over Captain Harris's decision to leave the longboat behind and take the jolly boat toward Newfoundland. It does not mention the longboat's damaged rudder, and thus the limits of its steering, blaming the weather and the ice for the longboat's inability to follow the captain to Newfoundland. Nor does the report mention Captain Harris's repeated refusals to take aboard some of the longboat's passengers in response to Rhodes's lament that the longboat was too loaded to endure.

Most importantly, perhaps, the report downplays Rhodes's role in the murder of the passengers. Indeed, according to it, no actual murders occurred because those thrown overboard "were nearly dead." The implication was that the truncation of the last minutes of those flickering lives for the greater good made harsh good sense. There is here the sharing and solidarity, the communality of people in dire circumstance that Victorian audiences admired. And as in any good Victorian tale, the survivors were saved in the nick of time when hope itself had almost disappeared.

The final, official-sounding touch is Captain Ball's affirmation—"the above is a correct statement." More authority is conferred by the signatures of eight sailors—including that of Stetson (incorrectly named Stretton), the man who had thrown the last two passengers overboard the morning the longboat was rescued—and, for good measure, those of two passengers. How was anyone to know that the most important signatures—those of Messer, for example, or the caustic Bridget McGee—had not been appended to the report?

As *JOURNAL DE HAVRE* READERS were digesting this news, French authorities were delivering the *William Brown*'s sailors, minus Messer and his longboat companion, from their place of detention to the consul's offices. Beasley and Gordon were ensconced in comfortable chairs behind an imposing table. A secretary sat nearby, sharp quills and a full bottle of ink at the ready, prepared to summarize for the record the seamen's formal statements. The sailors were brought forward one at a time to stand, cap in hand, to answer questions. They were, after all, seamen to be controlled and directed, not businessmen or officers who had to be treated with respect. Nor, of course, did they expect fine treatment. They knew their place.

A summary of their statements is preserved in British Foreign Office records in a leather-bound book that contains official correspondence between consul A. Gilbert Gordon in Le Havre and his London masters for the years 1840–41. The book's rag paper is in good condition, the inked words faded but wholly legible. What is preserved is not verbatim testimony, however, but summaries of depositions that in most but not all cases were signed by the literate or marked with an "X." The statements are all in a single, uniform handwriting—that of the consul's secretary—and signed, at the end, by each consul as well.

"There is a suspicious formalism about these statements," the great legal historian A. W. Brian Simpson wrote in his review of these depositions. *Of course.* No one was asked to relate everything that he or she remembered or wished to say. Nor was anyone asked to point a finger, lay blame or otherwise criticize the judgment of the ship's officers. The point of the exercise was not simply to gather facts but also, and, more importantly, to control the story. The sameness of the statements suggests that provocative points were left out and that contradictory facts were obscured.

THE DEPOSITIONS BEGAN with the sailors who directly participated in the drownings, assuring that the best face possible would be put on the longboat murders. Charles Smith, a British seaman from Sheerneys (presumably present-day Sheerness), was the first sailor called. Because Smith was a British national, Gordon would have started the questioning. Smith described the *William Brown*'s first strike and remembered an order to reduce sail—the fore topmast steering sail and the fore topgallant—just before they ran against some more ice. It was he who first told the consuls that the longboat "had no rudder" and so could not be steered, a complication that they did not want to hear about. Smith said that he heard Captain Harris tell Rhodes they were "perhaps 200 miles" from land and that "he would make for it, and so should we. And then he said good-by, and was gone."

When asked about the night of the murders, Smith stated that the boat required constant bailing and that on the night of the drownings, "It was gaining fast upon them, by the incipient rains. The Mate told some of the passengers that the boat was filling, and that he should be obliged to throw some of them overboard, and then said the same to the crew, asking them if they were willing to do it, as it was the only means they had of saving the lives of a part. That they commenced throwing some of the people overboard at about 9 or 10 o'clock at night as he believes, save one or two of whom resisted, but after saying a prayer expressed themselves willing to submit. That two of the female passengers were sisters of one of the men thrown overboard, one of whom voluntarily jumped after him and the other expressed her willingness to go with the others."

Smith went on to say that at daylight "they attempted to set a sail" and then saw the *Crescent* on the horizon "only two hours after two of the passengers, who were however almost dead, had been thrown overboard." When asked how the men thrown overboard had been chosen, Smith said simply "that those who were thrown overboard were the first who presented themselves." He added that those drowned were mostly accepting of their fate, "save one or two who resisted." In many respects, however, his statement supported Rhodes's report and testimony.

The consuls then heard from Alexander William Holmes, erroneously referred to in the official records as Alexander Williams. That is also how his name was written in the Rhodes/Ball statement, giving reason to believe the consuls and their secretary cribbed from that report in the summaries of their interviews. If Holmes tried to correct the consuls, speaking English with a strong Swedish accent, neither they nor their secretary listened to him.

At least regarding the voyage and the sinking, Holmes's deposition was similar to Smith's. Then he turned to the night in the longboat, "when it came on to blow very hard, raining very heavily and snowing, and as they could not bail the boat out or keep her free the Mate stated to the crew that it would be necessary to throw some overboard, having told the captain before he quitted them that if it came on to blow hard, that they would be obliged to do so, and that he is sure that some of the passengers heard him say so. That on the mate relating this they consulted how they should act, and at last commenced throwing some of the passengers overboard, several of whom tried to hold on, and it became necessary to use force to accomplish it. That they threw fourteen of them overboard when they hoped to be able to save the others, but at daylight one of the women found the plug hole and they got the boat light and were able to manage better." He added that two others of the passengers, one of whom he believed was already dead, and the other nearly so, were thrown overboard the next morning.

Holmes's deposition goes on to say that the morning after the drownings, some of the crew were "also so much frozen as to be unable to move, and that he believes that if they had not fallen in with the *Crescent* the next morning they would have been obliged to throw them overboard likewise."

It seems unbelievable that anyone could be so self-effacing, so modest, that he would not include in an official statement any mention of his own acts of heroism and leadership. And yet, in this document, neither his return to the *William Brown* to save Isabella Edgar nor his taking command of the lifeboat the morning after the murders is mentioned. The details of these come from other depositions, not his. It seems equally unlikely that Holmes would have dismissed so easily the murders of the last two men—in which he took no part—the morning after the bailing plug had been reset. After all, John Nugent was alive enough to stand up before being pushed overboard.

These errors of omission, and perhaps commission, point to a careful editing of the depositions to support the consuls' official vision, one based on the Rhodes/Ball report. More damning is the deposition's final line: "(Signed) The mark X of Alexander Williams." If the deposition had been read to him before signing, Holmes certainly would have corrected the erroneous representation of his name. The likelihood is that the consul's secretary simply put the deposition before him and told him to sign it without review. Holmes made his mark but had no idea what his statement said.

At this remove, all we know from later events is that Rubin Beasley, at least, was aware of Holmes's rescue of Isabella Edgar and also of his taking command of the longboat. We can only speculate, however, whether the consul learned these details from Messer and his friend the day before or from a part of Holmes's statement that was not recorded.

THE REST OF THE *William Brown*'s sailors brought to Le Havre by the *Ville de Lyon* were no problem for the consuls. The first was twenty-eight year-old Isaac Freeman, another Swedish sailor. "Speaking English imperfectly," the record says, he "stated that the mate gave orders to the crew to throw some of the passengers of the *William Brown* overboard and that he was obliged to assist in doing it." Twenty-two-year-old James Norton from Tipperary, Ireland, "stated in effect the same as Charles Smith and Alexander Williams did."

Levity arose with the next sailor, sixteen-year-old William Miller, who had joined the crew in Liverpool. A Dane from Alberg, his English was better than Freeman's, but not by much. His only contribution was a complaint: "The oatmeal was stored in the stern of the boat, on the top of the bread [i.e., sea biscuit], and was wet clear through." That his greatest concern was for the state of the oatmeal...well, he was just a lad, after all.

Joseph Marshall, the ship's steward, was another case entirely. He was an African-American born in Beaufort, South Carolina, and at thirty-seven years of age the oldest crew member. He was not involved in the drownings, so his testimony was brief. Most importantly, he was the last crewman to leave the ship because he stayed on board to help others. "He only succeeded in saving his life," the record states, "by jumping overboard and swimming to the jolly boat and afterwards got on board the longboat." That Captain Harris refused Marshall permission to come aboard the jolly boat, sending him to swim the icy waters to the longboat, was a harsh condemnation of Harris's humanity, even in those times. But if there was questioning from the consuls on this point, it was not recorded.

The last person deposed that first day was Henry Murray. The African-American cook from Georgetown, Maryland, had served aboard the *William Brown* since December 1839. His contribution was summarized in a single sentence: "That he the deponent assisted in throwing the passengers overboard till the boat was sufficiently lightened, when they discontinued, and they were enabled to bale out the water." Whatever he really said, the secretary did not record it.

With Murray's testimony, the hearings adjourned for the day.

WHAT MUST RUBIN BEASLEY have thought after the last deposition was taken that day? When he leaked the Rhodes/Ball report to the *Journal de Havre,* he must have been confident it would defuse what promised to be a difficult case. The report presented the story as a lamentable but understandable series of events. Both on the *William Brown* itself and later, in the longboat, the survivors had faced a hard choice in a hard situation: some had to die that the rest might live. But the depositions offered by both Smith and Holmes pointed directly to Rhodes, and secondarily the captain, as those who should answer for these deaths. "The mate stated to the crew that it would be necessary to throw some overboard," Smith's deposition read. Rhodes had warned Captain Harris this might be necessary, and the captain had implied his permission.

More important, perhaps, Holmes made it clear that the people drowned in the longboat were not comatose, not near death as Rhodes and Smith claimed. "It became necessary to use force to accomplish it," Holmes stated. Especially problematic were the deaths of the two women that, from the perspective of public sensibility, were nearly impossible to explain away.

Worst of all, these sailors who had killed sixteen persons admitted that all they had to do was check the bailing plug to find the primary source of water filling the boat. Why hadn't Rhodes ordered that checked first, Beasley must have wondered. More critically, however, Beasley must have asked himself if he dared seek an answer to that question.

THE STORY

O N 12 May, the day after the first set of depositions was made, the *Crescent* arrived at Le Havre and the remaining survivors of the *William Brown's* longboat were taken into custody. The *Crescent's* arrival did not go unnoticed. Rumours about the longboat and its murders were rife throughout the port. Some said the crew had thrown women overboard first; others insisted that cruel sailors cut off the hands of passengers who, jettisoned from the longboat, had clung to the gunwales in desperation. Some said this had happened even earlier, when the *William Brown* was sinking. Stories like this grow in the telling, and this story was growing fast and circulating far.

Even a decade earlier, the story would not have spread so quickly. The fate of the longboat would have been a local, at best a European, wonder. In the early 1830s, news travelling by slow ships was a haphazard affair, carried in personal letters and small local newspapers shipped with the other cargos of the growing international mercantile fleet.

But this was 1841, and the international news story, one traded and built by newspapers around the world, was being born. News had became a commodity, something to be bought and sold, and it travelled as fast as the fastest packet ship with its bags of mail and newspapers, from Paris to London, and then from London to Boston, New York, Philadelphia or Montreal.

In this decade, too, first Great Britain and then most other countries discovered the lucrative advantages of an organized national postal service. Governments contracted with swift packet ships, initially wind-driven but later steam-powered, to carry the mails around the world. Postage stamps, prepaid, ready upon purchase for use, made the whole process possible and profitable. Great Britain issued the first postage stamps in 1840, the famous penny blacks graced with the portrait of a very young Queen Victoria. Simple to use and sufficiently inexpensive to be widely affordable, the stamps were the heart of a greater system that turned the national postal service into an immediate success. In the first year alone 67,989,600 one-penny black stamps were issued in England for letters of half an ounce or less, and 6,462,962 two-pence blue stamps for letters over half an ounce. Other countries quickly followed Britain's postal experiment, including many in the British Empire that also issued stamps with the likeness of Queen Victoria.

In the 1840s postage stamps with Queen Victoria's image, like these two shillings and six pence stamps from Queensland, quickly followed the successful introduction of postal service in Britain. Stamps courtesy John Carter

Newspapers were the loss leaders of the new postal enterprise. In Britain, those mailed within eight days of publication were carried for free. Politically, this made very good sense. It represented a subsidy of the evolving press and, thus, a mechanism by which to control the news, as the privilege could be taken away at any moment. As importantly, the widening reach of newspapers gave officials a podium from which to present their views to readers. Then as now, the doings of government—of Parliament, the courts and their officials—dominated the broadsheet pages. And so, supported by free mailings, weekly newspapers became daily publications, and some larger newspapers—the *New York Herald* and the *Times* in London, for example—developed national and sometimes international readerships.

Without planning or premeditation, a new medium had been born whose principal mission was to offer the type of information that businesses and governments increasingly demanded. In the first ten months of 1841, 85,510 newspapers were posted from London alone. They were sent to the Americas and to the continent, to individual subscribers and to subscribing newspapers around the world. Editors in Boston, New York, Quebec and Paris reprinted the stories from them at no greater cost than a byline. British newspapers were equally quick to copy stories first printed elsewhere. The downside for officialdom was a decreased ability to act imperiously. A decade earlier, the Rhodes/Ball report and the consuls' investigation would have been the definitive statement about the *William Brown*. In 1841, however, newspapers were presenting independent opinions.

The *Journal de Havre* was the first to publish the *William Brown*'s story under the headline "Dreadful Shipwreck," on 11 May, the day the first depositions were being taken. The next newspaper report was on 12 May, when the *Crescent* arrived in Le Havre. *Galignani's Messenger* published a story whose focus was the swell of rumours within the port and comments from the consuls themselves. A Paris-based, English-language newspaper founded in 1814 by Giovanni Galignani, the broadsheet had a wide circulation both in England and among English-speaking people on the continent.

Dreadful Shipwreck
(From Galignani's Messenger of Wednesday.)

We are enabled to add to the account given of the loss of the William Brown, on her passage from Liverpool to Philadelphia the following melancholy particulars, derived from a statement drawn up by some of the survivors, and remitted to Captain Ball, of the Crescent.

The ship was of Philadelphia; her company consisted of 17 persons and she had 65 steerage passengers, nearly all Irish, with a full cargo on board. She had had a rough passage out, and struck against a field of ice at 9 p.m., when going under all sails at the rate of 10 knots an hour, in lat. 43 deg. 40 min. N., and long. 43 deg. 39 min. W. by account. She stove in her larboard bow, and within two minutes struck another field of ice.

The ship soon began to fill and the captain and crew got out the boats, which were cleared away at 11; at midnight the ship went down, and the 30 passengers, who could not be taken into the boats, were drowned in her. The boats lay by each other till 5 a.m., when the captain in the cutter steered for Newfoundland.

The longboat being very heavily laden with so many persons, 42 in all, could not be managed, and was obliged to steer to the south. At night she fell in with more ice, and the wind came on to blow hard; the boat began to leak badly and shipped a good deal of water.

Finding she was likely to sink the mate consulted with the crew, and it was deemed necessary to throw overboard some of the passengers who were nearly dead. 16 were then thrown into the sea, and perished, while the rest were nearly stiff with the extreme cold. Shortly after a ship hove in sight, and the captain, who was up aloft looking out for ice, saw the boat, and steered for her at the imminent risk of his own safety. This proved to be the Crescent, and they were received with great humanity and kindness on board. At that time ice was in sight on the surface of the Atlantic as far as the eye could reach.

Out of the passengers saved 10 were women. The Journal de Havre adds to this dreadful narrative, that the first boat passenger thrown overboard was a woman! Sisters and relations were afterwards thrown over; and a young boy, who begged for a respite to say his prayers, was not allowed it, but was sent into the deep! This journal adds, that the most serious rumours are afloat as to the cause and nature of this horrible catastrophe, which, however, cannot be cleared up until the Crescent, which is daily expected, arrives with the surviving passengers.

The American Consul at Havre has interrogated the sailors of the William Brown brought by the Ville de Lyon and has had them committed to prison.

The Havre Journal states that the sailors of the William Brown have been interrogated separately as to the cause and circumstances of the dreadful catastrophe in the longboat of that ship, and that each having given the same account without any attempts at prevarication, and shown that they were driven to it by sheer necessity, the American Consul has had them set at liberty.

It appears that the boat was letting in water very fast, and that the crowd was so great that it was impossible to ascertain where the leak was. It was only after the passengers had been thrown overboard that it was found that the plug had come out, and if this had not been stopped, the boat must have sunk.

Reprinted days later by the *Times* in London, the *Messenger's* version of the Rhodes/Ball report of a "dreadful" but commonplace shipwreck made the story into a murky catastrophe. Suddenly, the sense that what had happened on the longboat was horrible but somehow acceptable disappeared. Why, "the first boat passenger thrown overboard was a woman!" Worse, a young boy was dispatched without being permitted to say his prayers!

That many details in the *Messenger's* story were incorrect is irrelevant. They put forward the sense of general indignation perfectly. It did not matter that the first person drowned was not a woman, but Owen Riley.

Nor was it important that it was James MacAvoy, not young Owen Carr, who begged for time to say his prayers. Although the report still claimed that the passengers thrown overboard were "nearly dead" from exposure, a Victorian reader might have wondered how a boy (or a man) could beg for a chance to say his prayers if he was comatose. What made this story critical was its view that out-of-control crew members had killed those whom in theory they were supposed to protect.

The real news in the *Messenger's* article was the consuls' conclusion that whatever had happened in the longboat was the result of "sheer necessity." But the point was that "the most serious rumours are afloat as to the cause and nature of this horrible catastrophe." Coming on the heels of the *Journal de Havre* report, it left open the door to future revelations.

There is still, however, a decidedly official tone to the *Messenger's* story. The problem of the bailing plug is mentioned, for example, not as an act of incompetence but as a triumphant piece of seamanship: "if this had not been stopped [by throwing people overboard so the plug became visible], the boat must have sunk." The whole points to the American consul as its unnamed source. Poor Gilbert Gordon is nowhere mentioned in the story, as if he, too, had gone down with the ship and been forgotten. According to the *Messenger*, it is Rubin Beasley who interrogated the sailors and then released them. That the official investigation was just beginning and that the rush to judgment precipitate were ignored by the reporter as well as by the American consul himself. In this light, the excuse of "sheer necessity" was not an official explanation but a diversion that Beasley came up with in an attempt to hold the expected outcry at bay.

Why did not Beasley simply admit that the incident was shocking and promise to find and punish those who were responsible? Because it was his job was to protect the interests of the United States. His duty as consul was to find a way to minimize the real failures that led to the choices that Francis Rhodes had faced. At the same time, he understood that the murders might be used as an example of the need to reform the laws relating to shipping. If that happened, he believed it should be one controlled by the United States, not by Britain. Although common interests and a common language joined the two nations, there was also between them a rivalry for maritime supremacy. And, Beasley knew,

England would be no more eager for an American precedent than his masters would be for a British one. From his first informal interview with the *William Brown*'s sailors, therefore, he worked to assure that whatever the final judgment might be, it would be one rendered under American and not British law.

ON THURSDAY, 13 MAY, the day after the *Crescent*'s arrival, the French authorities brought Francis Rhodes and the surviving passengers of the *William Brown* to the American consulate, where Rubin Beasley and Gilbert Gordon waited to question them.

The first to be called was Rhodes, the most important witness. He was in command of the longboat, and if Captain Ball was to be believed, a better than competent first mate. After Rhodes had declared his name, his rank, and his American nationality, the consuls heard, as they had from Charles Smith and Alexander Holmes, the details of the voyage. "Nothing of material consequence occurred till the nineteenth April, when at 9 P.M. during the deponent's watch below, the wind blowing from the southward and eastward, the ship being under all sail and going at the rate of ten miles an hour, felt a violent shock when immediately he ran on deck, and found the ship had struck on an iceberg. That he then went below and after dressing himself returned on deck, and about ten minutes afterward the ship again struck another iceberg, when he proposed to Captain Harris to shorten sail, which was accordingly done, and on sounding the pumps found she had two feet water in the hold."

Here was the "violent shock" of the first strike, the one nobody else but Rhodes felt, preceding the second. He then described finding the hold filling with water and the bow damaged beyond hope of repair. "Passengers jumped into the longboat as it was lowered and the jolly boat with its passengers pulled away," Rhodes said. The next morning, he told Captain Harris the longboat "was so deep in the water" that he "could not manage her and that if the weather should become bad, they should all perish, and something must be done. That Captain Harris replied, 'I know what you are going to say,' or something to that purpose, and might have added something else, but as they were at some distance from each other, and confusion being very great, he cannot repeat exactly the words he might have used.

"Captain Harris took down the names of all the passengers in the boat as well as of the crew, desiring them to avoid quarrelling and to be obedient to his [the deponent's] orders, and that he left—steering for Newfoundland." Rhodes then described how he had tried to follow the captain: "They steered their own boat as well as they could with an oar, as she had no rudder, but that around 1 P.M. the wind changed and they could no longer row in a northwesterly direction.

"With a heavy sea running, they again fell in with large quantities of large and small ice, and as the boat was taking in water fast and leaking badly, it was found impossible that she could live." That, Rhodes said, was when he consulted with the ship's company "and asked them what it would be best to do." He admitted stating that it was his opinion that, if "they did not lighten her, they would all be lost, remarking at the same time, that it was better that a few should be saved than that all should perish." He insisted that what happened hours later was a communal decision and not the sole result of his order.

This was all discussed, Rhodes continued, "in the presence and in the hearing of some of the passengers," who did not protest. "At about eleven o'clock, as near as he can suppose, they commenced throwing such of the passengers as were nearest to them overboard. Some of whom were in a state of insensibility and unable to make any resistance. And that one of them of the name of Black, who had his wife on board, was about to meet the same fate, but knowing his voice, he [Rhodes] told the men as they had not long to live not to separate man and wife, and he was saved."

There it was. Just as Harris had not given permission to kill some of the passengers but had implied he knew what would be needed, Rhodes had not "ordered" his men to kill the passengers. Instead, he had argued the necessity of lightening the boat, to sacrifice some that others might live. In the end, it was Rhodes's responsibility because Harris had made the men swear to follow the mate's orders.

The first mate had done his best, and for the consuls to challenge him was to challenge the greater order as well as Rhodes's judgment that some should die that others might survive. These were desperate actions, he implied, adding that even in these extremes he had not separated man and wife in what he believed were the last hours of everyone's lives.

And the desperate murders worked, Rhodes pointed out to the

consuls. Once lightened, "they found a plug loose in the boat which had been the cause of her making so much water, but which he supposed was occasioned by some of the lower planks being loose or started off." The implication was that the condition of the plug could not have been ascertained in the crowded boat, that only as a consequence of the crew's harsh action did they find and stop the leak.

Finally, Rhodes described how the next morning, when the fog cleared, he (and not Messer or Holmes) "perceived the ship Crescent of Portsmouth, NJ, George T. Ball Master, which bore up to them and took them all on board."

The last sailor to be called before the consuls was helmsman Joseph Stetson, a thirty-year-old American from Thomaston, Maine. Of all the witnesses, he was the one most able to speak to the first and second strikes, to the icebergs that stove in the *William Brown*. "The deponent being at the wheel at the time, saw an iceberg, which he tried to avoid, but as the ship would not obey her helm, she struck against it, and about ten minutes afterward, struck another, when they clewed down the sails and lashed the helm amidships."

Stetson next described how the next morning the captain advised them to steer for Newfoundland before recording the names of both passengers and crew. "The mate [Rhodes] also asked him [Captain Harris] what he should do with so many passengers onboard, as it was impossible the boat could live, and that he thinks he said something about drawing lots, and the captain interrupted him saying he knew what he [Rhodes] was going to say and that they must settle that among themselves, and they parted."

None of the other sailors mentioned in their depositions that Rhodes had talked of drawing lots. But the detail was passed over by the consuls, who did not recall Rhodes to ask why he had not, in fact, drawn lots. Nor were the other sailors asked to explain why they had not insisted upon it.

Stetson then described how, at around seven o'clock, "Finding the weather so bad, they spoke to each other and took hold of one or two of the passengers, but they resisted them, and fearing they would be too strong for them [the crew], they discontinued." Later, however, "the weather increasing in violence, and as no chance remained for any being saved, if the boat was not lightened, they were obliged to recommence and such persons as were nearest to them, fourteen in number, were seized and thrown overboard."

The fourteen killed "enabled them to bale out the boat." Stetson glossed over the drowning of the last two men the following morning, saying "two other passengers who afterwards became stiff and unable to move prevented them from managing the boat [and] were afterwards thrown overboard." It was not, in his telling, simply that the passengers were so many that the sailors could not bail but that those killed the morning of the rescue "prevented them from managing the boat." How the final two murdered men hindered the sailors if they were comatose was never explained.

Even though Beasley and Gordon heard the depositions together, their understanding of them differed from the start. The American consul had the advantage of having heard John Messer and his companion's version of events before the official investigation began, so he already knew, for example, that Rhodes had talked of a lottery to Captain Harris. Beasley also knew, from Messer, that Rhodes had insisted from the start that if any were to survive, some would have to be drowned, and that Rhodes's claim of unanimity was not true. Messer insisted that he had told Rhodes that if some were to die they should all draw lots, that it should be fair. Finally, Messer pointed out that the morning after the murderous night, Rhodes had given up command of the boat, and it was Alexander Holmes who reassured the passengers and raised a flag to signal the *Crescent*.

After the sailors had given their depositions, the consuls took a break. Refreshments were served, and they reviewed the evidence, preparing their questions for the surviving passengers, who would testify in the afternoon. Both agreed that the emigrants were landsmen and women who could not be expected to speak clearly to the business of the sea.

The first to be called was twenty-five-year-old James Patrick from County Tyrone in Ireland. He said that "when the longboat was lowered down, he jumped into it followed by his wife and child, and lay alongside another boat till morning, when he requested Captain Harris to allow him and his wife to come into his boat, remarking that the longboat was already too full, but he refused to receive him." He added that he heard

Rhodes ask the captain that the boats should stay together and that Harris had replied, "You need not be talking about that, I know what you mean." Patrick did not hear any conversations about the crew throwing anybody overboard, but he did hear the mate say, while they were doing it, "Don't throw Black overboard as he has his wife with him." And he mentioned the water in the boat was so deep that his wife's clothes were soaked halfway up her back. In conclusion, Patrick had "not the least doubt that if the boat had not been lightened that everyone onboard would have perished."

Next to be called was James Black, the thirty-two-year-old emigrant who had warned his companions that the ship was sinking. Black also testified that he heard Rhodes tell the captain that "he could not work the boat and that death must be the end of some of them, or something to that effect. Captain Harris replied, 'I know what you mean but I cannot help it,' and after taking down all their names pulled away and was very soon out of sight." Black said that he and Patrick did much of the bailing because many of the other passengers were too numb. Then, "at night he heard a mournful noise and found himself seized by one of the crew, who told him he must go overboard as it was necessary to lighten the boat, and that he asked him to let his wife go with him. Mr. Rhodes called out, 'Don't separate man and wife, they can't live long, and let them die together,' upon which he was released." Black, too, said that he "had no doubt that if the boat had not been lightened she would have gone down, and that all would have been lost, and that he does not attribute any blame to anyone for having done it, as he believes, it was a necessary measure."

It seems unlikely that the crew twice grabbed married men and that twice Rhodes told them not to separate man and wife. It is possible that the secretary mistakenly copied the story of one man as part of the deposition of the other. As likely, however, different members of the crew simultaneously seized both Black and Patrick. Four or five sailors were involved, and they were working semi-independently in the dark. Both Black and Patrick heard the mate say "Don't separate man and wife," and each assumed it was he and he alone who was, therefore, spared.

The last to testify that day was Mrs. Margaret Edgar, the matron of the emigrant passengers. Her statement takes up less than a page. If she had any significant insights to share with the consuls, they are not recorded in her deposition. "Although she knew that some of the passengers were being thrown overboard she did not see them, and that before they commenced doing it there was a cry that the boat was sinking." She did not mention hearing the pleas that those first men thrown overboard cried out to her. If her deposition is to believed, Mrs. Edgar saw and heard nothing untoward. She, too, stated that the deaths were necessary if any were to survive.

ON FRIDAY, 14 MAY, both Beasley and Gordon attended to other affairs, but they met in the early afternoon to draft a joint statement for the *Journal de Havre*, as reporters were pestering them for stories about the *William Brown*. The rumours were becoming troublesome, and the consuls agreed it was time to use the authority of their offices to squelch speculation. That afternoon, therefore, they wrote a letter to the editor of the *Journal de Havre*. It was common practice in the 1840s for letters from readers—and especially from officials—to be published, unedited and without comment. Gordon included a copy of their letter in the report he eventually sent to the British Foreign Office. There it remains, sandwiched between his other dispatches, detailing the "calamitous events" of the *William Brown*.

The letter from the consuls was, of course, a strong endorsement of the *William Brown*'s crew, and it expanded upon the version of events first given in the Rhodes/Ball report. That they wrote the letter before the passengers' depositions were complete was a detail that apparently concerned neither consul. There is no criticism of Captain Harris's seamanship and no mention that the *William Brown* sailed without a working rudder for its principal auxiliary craft. Harris's refusal to take on even one additional passenger is not questioned; nor is his decision to leave the longboat and sail on his own toward Newfoundland. After all, Captain Harris was missing and presumed drowned, so what was the point?

The letter emphasized the discovery of the failed bailing plug as a result of Rhodes's unflinching sacrifice of some of the passengers so that others might survive. It also supported Rhodes's claim that those who were drowned were near frozen and laid out like cordwood in the bottom of the longboat, and that none struggled or resisted. Rhodes's first attempt to convince his crew to get to work is not mentioned, nor is the

A LETTER TO THE EDITOR REGARDING THE WILLIAM BROWN

Sir—as much has been said about the unfortunate accident to the William Brown, and as a complete statement cannot as yet be laid before the public, we have decided upon communicating the principal facts. On the arrival of the Ville de Lyon with seven of the crew, it was thought right to examine them at the American Consulate, and since the arrival of the Crescent we have also interrogated the mate and several of the passengers.

From their evidence, it appears that in the morning when the boats divided between them the people who remained in them, after the ship had gone down with the 30 passengers left on board, the longboat overloaded and deprived of her rudder, must have gone down if the wind came on to blow hard. It did, in fact, get up, and towards night the sea became rough, and the boat making a great deal of water, presented the alternative of going down with all in her, or of saving her by sacrificing one part of those who were in her to save the oth-ers. 16 passengers, 14 of whom were men and two women, who happened to be nearest the crew in the middle of the boat, were thrown into the sea. The principal leak was then found, and the men were able to stop it, empty the boat of the water, and keep her afloat, which they previously could not do. This terrible sacrifice of lives commenced about 10 at night, and at 6 in the morning the Crescent came in sight. At the beginning the women were all placed in the stern and at the bows of the boat, in order that they might not impede the men in managing her, and this explains why so many of them were saved. They were all severely affected by the cold and it appears that scarcely any of the passengers that were thrown into the sea made any great resistance, most of them being previously laid at the bottom of the boat as if they were dead. Throughout the affair we have not discovered any fact capable of drawing down blame upon anyone whatever. We have the honour, &c.

(Signed) R. G. Beasley, United States Consul

Gilbert Gordon, British Consul

---

crew's first and unsuccessful attempt to throw passengers overboard. In fact, the consuls concluded that no one should be blamed for anything. In England, the *Morning Post* and the *Times* both ran the consuls' letter verbatim the following week.

THE NEXT DAY, SATURDAY, 15 MAY, Rubin Beasley and Gilbert Gordon, though they had already announced the results of their investigation, returned to taking depositions from the remaining passengers. They began with Margaret Edgar's daughters, whose statements are surprisingly short and shorn of any detail.

All of the Edgar women recalled the exchange between Captain Harris and the first mate about drawing lots if the boat was in danger. Most of them said the captain replied that he knew what Rhodes meant. All denied seeing the passengers being thrown over. Isabella heard "the noise made by some of the persons falling into the water, but not all of them." Susannah recalled that "somebody in the boat call[ed] out that the longboat was sinking" and that they seemed to be taking on water that night. All agreed that they were treated to "every kindness" by the crew, and in Susannah's words, "that the boat would have sunk if she had not been lightened."

The next witness, Ellen Black, did little more than confirm her husband James's story. He was in the longboat before her, and, after she got in, he "took me with him to the stern of the boat where I was up to my hips in water." She, too, heard the first mate say something to the captain about there being a great number in the boat, and that something must be done, and she heard the captain tell him to say nothing more about it.

She then described the events of that night. "One of the men took hold of her husband to throw him overboard, when she got up and said 'let us go together,' when Mr. Rhodes, the mate, asked who it was. And on being told it was Black he said it was improbable they can live long, do not separate man and wife, and they released him." She added, "She did not see anyone thrown overboard and that she did every thing by shutting her eyes and stopping her ears to prevent her from knowing what was going forward." And after all, Ellen Black and the others had practice not hearing the calls of their friends and travelling companions on the night before the murders, the night the *William Brown* went down. In conclusion, she agreed with the others. "She does not attribute the slightest blame to any on board and that she received the greatest attention from all the crew that they were capable of rendering to her."

Next was Julie McCadden, who said she was under the care of Mr. Owen Riley, who was going to join his wife in Philadelphia. She, too, declared she heard Rhodes talk about drawing lots and the captain tell him to say nothing more. And she certainly remembered her uncle Owen Riley's murder. Clearly, this still angered her, the manner of his selection no less than the fact of his death. "The men were just taken by the seamen as the men presented themselves in the boat." Despite Riley's drowning, she, too, ended by saying that "the crew behaved very kindly."

It is hard to believe that Julie McCadden heard not one of the fourteen or so being drowned, except Owen Riley, or that in spite of his murder, she really believed the crew behaved "very kindly." It is also unbelievable that none of the Edgar women mentioned Holmes's rescue of their youngest, especially Isabella, whose life it was that he saved.

Omissions are particularly glaring in the testimony of the next passenger, Bridget McGee, who said that she "completely covered up" her head with blankets and "did not know what was the state of the weather," something she would testify about with precision at the trial the following year. She went on to say that she "heard the cries of several of the persons thrown overboard, amongst whom was her uncle, who begged to be spared till morning, but did not see one of them [dispatched]." Finally, she stated that she believed "the passengers were kindly treated by the crew, one of whom lent her a blanket, and that she does not think that any blame can attach to them, for anything that occurred on board." Yet, later, at the trial, Bridget McGee *did* blame the sailors for the murders they committed, especially that of her uncle. It is, therefore, not surprising that alone among the passengers' depositions, hers has neither a signature nor the illiterate's "X."

The depositions from the remaining passengers were more of the same. Bridget Nugent and Mary Corr both heard Francis Rhodes talk to Captain Harris about drawing lots; both women also said the captain refused requests by the mate to transfer a few of the longboat's passengers to the jolly boat. Bridget remembered her uncle begging to be spared until the morning. Mary Corr said, "They threw many persons overboard." Both women thought they were "treated by the mate and by the crew very kindly."

Young Owen Carr's contribution was the pitiable lament that "All my friends were lost in the ship and I am alone." The depositions note Sarah Corr's memory of the crew member who "threw his waistcoat and part of his own clothes over me," as well as Matilda Patrick's anger that Captain Harris would not let her family join her sister-in-law Eliza Lafferty in the jolly boat. On all other matters, however, Mrs. Patrick was so much occupied with her child that she paid little attention and had nothing to report. She did not see any person thrown overboard, though she did hear some people scream without knowing what they said. Of course, her signed deposition acknowledged having "received as much care and assistance from the crew as they were able to afford her."

If the depositions are to be believed, few of the passengers heard anything that night but the occasional splash of a man going overboard, unless it was a man they knew.

Matilda Patrick was the last witness. After she finished her statement, the secretary gathered up the depositions and left the room. It was his duty to make copies of each statement for the records of both British and American consuls.

Gilbert Gordon's next action was to begin a letter to his superiors at the British Foreign Office who, he knew, had in all likelihood already seen a newspaper story or two about the *William Brown*, its survivors and the murders. But he still did not perceive the greater issues that swirled around the story like the vortex left in the wake of a sinking vessel.

Beasley promised his counterpart that he would send word to the French officials to release the crew and passengers. He rang for his secretary, gave the order and, as the man stoked the office fire—spring had not fully arrived in the port and there was a chill in the air—allowed himself a moment of private satisfaction. Indeed, he must have said to himself, it had all gone very well.

The signatures and official seals of United States Consul Rubin Beasley and British Consul Gilbert Gordon.

A MELANCHOLY AFFAIR

As STEAMSHIPS REPLACED SAILING SHIPS, the time it took for consuls or ambassadors to report to and receive instructions from their superiors decreased. Later, when the telegram replaced the urgent letter, the time was shortened further; and again in the twentieth century when the transatlantic telephone call made the telegram obsolete. In 1841, however, it was the letter carried by sailing ship, or perhaps a packet steamer, that linked a nation's government to its representatives in foreign lands.

For United States Consul Rubin Beasley, a single round of communication with Washington might take weeks, even months; and even though British Consul Gilbert Gordon was only across the channel from England, it took two, three, even four days for his correspondence to arrive in London, where it joined that of other consuls whose offices were scattered around the world. In London, several days might pass before a letter was read and days more for a reply to be considered, drafted, finalized and then dispatched to Le Havre. In the best of cases and in the most exigent of circumstances, therefore, it required more than a week for Gordon to report and to receive instructions.

All this explains, in part, why Gordon did not immediately inform his superiors when the *Ville de Lyon* arrived in port with the sailors from the *William Brown* and the Rhodes/Ball report. Given the distances separating the Foreign Office in London from its consulates around the world, Gordon knew that Lord Palmerston, the foreign secretary, expected his staff to take the initiative. Palmerston assumed not only that they would follow his instructions but also that, in their absence, his subordinates would act as if they could divine his intentions.

Consul Gordon waited, therefore, until he and Beasley had completed their investigation because, in his mind, there was no urgency. The story of the *William Brown* was just another maritime calamity, the drownings in the lifeboat no more than a variation on the common theme of death at sea. He even held off writing to London after the first stories appeared in continental newspapers. In the end, he waited too long.

Any delay by Gordon served Rubin Beasley, who understood the political implications. Every day that passed without Gordon reporting to London decreased the likelihood that he would receive instructions to return the survivors of the *William Brown* to England for a full inquiry before the deponents returned to their travels. And, if the sailors and surviving passengers sailed again for North America, they would be in the domain of the United States.

Beasley knew that a judicial review was inevitable. The question was whether it would take place in Britain or the United States. He wanted it to take place in his country, and for this, he needed the sailors and passengers to be released. Beasley was certain the longboat drownings would become a rallying point for Irish emigrant communities and for those who believed it was time to constrain ship captains and their sailors who were laws unto themselves at sea.

THE EVENING OF 15 MAY, after the emigrants' depositions were completed, Gordon returned to his office, sharpened his pen, and wrote a report that exonerated Francis Rhodes and justified the murders.

"My Lord," his letter began, "I have the honour to report to Your Lordship one of the most melancholy events from ship-wreck that has ever come to my knowledge.

"On the 13th of March last, the American Ship 'William Brown,' Geo. Harris Master, left Liverpool bound to Philadelphia with a crew of 17 persons, 65 steerage passengers, and a cargo of salt and crate goods.

"During the first 25 days they had very bad weather, and on the 19th of April at 9 P.M., the wind blowing from the southward and eastward, the ship being under all sail and going at the rate of ten miles an hour, struck upon a field of ice, which stove in the boat, and although the pumps were at once set going the ship began rapidly to fill. The crew immediately began to get out the longboat into which crowded the Chief Mate, 8 of the Crew, and 33 passengers; Captain Harris taking the small boat with 7 of the crew and one female passenger named Eliza Lafferty."

Gordon knew it was not his job to question Captain Harris's judgment or his decisions. To criticize the inadequate number of auxiliary craft the *William Brown* carried would stir up a political hornet's nest, and Lord Melbourne's Whig government was already in trouble. In his report, therefore, Gordon simply repeated without comment first the story of the sinking of the *William Brown* with half of its passengers, and then Captain Harris's decision to leave the overloaded longboat ("so deeply laden that the gunwale was only about 8 inches from the water") to its own salvation. "The mate observed that if the weather should become bad they must all perish," Gordon wrote, "and that something must be done, when Harris stopped him and told him to say no more on the subject, as he knew what he was going to say."

The consul closely followed the outline of the Rhodes/Ball report already published in both the *Journal de Havre* and *Galignani's Messenger.* He emphasized Rhodes's consultation with the crew, his "telling them all that they had as much to say in the business as he had, but that from the position of the boat whatever was to be done, must be done immediately, otherwise the boat would swamp." As importantly, Gordon repeated as fact the fiction that when the crew "commenced throwing overboard such of the passengers as were nearest to them," some of them "were from the severity of the weather in a state of insensibility, and unable to make any resistance in their manner."

Gordon so arranged his recitation to argue not only the necessity of the longboat killings but also their benefit. "As soon as the boat was lightened they had room to use the oars and bail her, rowing all the time, in a course to avoid the ice and it was then only that they found a plug out, which had been the cause of her making so much water." Gordon lacked the imagination to ask why Rhodes and his seamen did not look to the bailing plug *before* drowning so many passengers. The consul then skipped quickly to the rescue hours later by the *Crescent,* "Geo. Ball Master, from New York to Havre, who bore upon and took them all on board and treated them with the greatest kindness and humanity."

British Consulate
Havre 15th May 1841

My Lord,

I have the honour to report to Your Lordship one of the most melancholy events from Ship-wreck, that has ever come to my knowledge.

On the 18th of March last the American Ship "William Brown", Geo Harris Master, left Liverpool bound to Philadelphia with a Crew of 17 Persons, 65 Steerage Passengers, and a Cargo of Salt and Crate Goods. During the first 25 days they had very bad weather, and on the 19th of April at 9 P.M. the wind blowing from the Southward and Eastward, the Ship being under all sail, and going

Right Honourable
Viscount Palmerston
&. &. &.

A letter from British Consul Gilbert Gordon to Foreign Secretary Lord Palmerston, 15 May 1841.

Finally, Gordon announced, "I have, conjointly with the United States Consul, taken the declarations of all the passengers and crew, and find that in all the leading points they perfectly agree, and should Your Lordship desire it, will forward them to you."

The letter concluded with the modest statement that he had helped provide the remaining longboat survivors with clothes while "the inhabitants of Havre and of all nations raised a subscription to enable them to proceed to Philadelphia." Like any good bureaucrat who values a tidy report, Gordon appended the names of passengers drowned with the *William Brown* and the longboat, and those who survived both. Strangely, given the importance of the affair, this is the only official record of the names of the ship's complement. Unfortunately, it is not very accurate. Its names, spelling and numbers do not agree with those from other sources.

GILBERT GORDON SENT HIS LETTER to London by packet ship the next day, 16 May. The Foreign Office recorded its arrival in its correspondence logs on 19 May. Labelled "Wreck of the American ship Wm. Brown from Liverpool to Philadelphia, with Emigrants," it then was sent up the chain of ministerial command for review.

The distance between Gordon's official story and others being published in the newspapers was too great to ignore, the number of publications interested in the events of the *William Brown's* longboat too numerous. The drowning of women like the Askin sisters was not an action that Victorian society viewed lightly. In spite of the calm assurances of the American and British consuls, reporters on either side of the English Channel were unwilling to swallow the Rhodes/Ball report whole. It was inevitable that one or another paper would print more rumours and that the rest would pick that story up and run it as if it were fact. It was Gordon's bad luck that such stories were published in London before his letter arrived.

The honours for the first breach of the official line went to the *London Morning Post*. Published on 13 May, the story was reprinted in the *Times* in London four days later. This version, which raised all sorts of political implications, was the standard against which Gordon's submission was judged by his superiors. The language seems arcane, the style clumsy. But this was a passionate piece of newspaper writing that has the authentic feel of a story written in haste as the tide turned and an old-fashioned mail ship was raising sail for its run from Le Havre to London. It was what editors still call "a story with legs."

THE WILLIAM BROWN—HAVRE, May 13.—The American ship Crescent, Captain Ball, arrived here yesterday evening with the remainder of the passengers of the William Brown, who were saved in the longboat. The arrival of this vessel has confirmed all the horrid details given of the dreadful scene which took place during the night of the 20th and 21st of April. Of the 16 passengers who were thrown into the sea 14 were men and 2 women; of the 17 saved 15 are women and 2 are men. One of these men was seized for the purpose of being thrown overboard by the crew of the boat. He cried out to the mate to save him, and not to tear him from his wife. The mate told the men not to separate man and wife, if it were possible to help it. He fell into the bottom of the boat, and was saved. A boy of 12 years old was thrown overboard. He caught hold of the boat, and, favored, by the darkness of the night, crouched under the bows and was saved. All the women saved are young, except the mother of a Scotch family in Denfriesshire, who, with her five daughters and a servant girl, was saved; her name is Edgar. Her husband and son are settled in Germantown, near Philadelphia. A young woman, with her infant at the breast, succeeded in getting into the boat with her husband: they are amongst the survivors. His name is Patrick, from Cook's-town, county of Tyrone, the property of Colonel Stewart. Several persons from that gentleman's estate or neighborhood have met with a water grave. One family of the name of Leyden (16 in all) sank with the vessel; another family, named Corr—father, mother, and five children—sank at the same time; the little boy who was thrown from the boat was one of that family; he had not a soul left belonging to him. They were also from Colonel Stewart's property. A Mrs. Anderson, with three children, who was going to join her husband, a medical gentleman settled at Cincinnati, sank with the ship. Miss Anderson and a Miss Bradley were thrown into the sea from the longboat. The tales which the survivors relate are piteous—horrifying. The crew and passengers have been examined by the British and American consuls this morning, and the impression is, that the dreadful act of throwing their fellow-creatures overboard was of imperious necessity; but it is to be hoped the two consuls will give publicity to the examination, in order that the public mind may be satisfied on this point. Truly the circumstances must be made out in the clearest way to palliate such an act. We have emigrant ships sailing every week, and if it is held as law that "might is right," it had better be declared so, and that the crew are justified under extremities in throwing overboard whom, and as many, as they think right, without casting lots, or making any choice than their will.—*Morning Post.*

Two sentences into the story, every reader realized that a horrifying and perhaps criminal event had occurred. This was murder, deliberate and mean. Unlike the earlier stories in the *Journal de Havre* and *Galignani's Messenger*, the *Morning Post* piece points a finger at Francis Rhodes when it states that among those saved was a man spared by the first mate because he chose not to separate man from wife. This seems simple enough, a kind, even a magnanimous gesture, but it reveals Rhodes as the man in command, the ship's officer who controlled the killings. The carefully crafted fiction that Rhodes was but one voice in the decision to drown half the longboat's passengers was obliterated in this sentence.

There is innuendo as well in the observation that "all the women saved are young, except the mother of a Scotch family." The message between the lines was that, well, of course. Sailors liked a bit of young flesh. The reporter made it clear that it was *Irish* emigrants who were disposed of at sea, knowing that many London readers would say good riddance. To forestall this reaction, the story noted that the Patricks were from Cookstown, County Tyrone, "the property of Colonel Stewart." Although everyone knew the colonel did not "own" the people who worked his land, readers understood that landowners like Colonel Stewart controlled tenants' lives as if they owned them. In this way, the story gave import to the people killed. That they were from the property of the well-known colonel seemed to make the whole a very British affair.

Just to make sure readers realized that not all those drowned on the ship or murdered in the longboat were shiftless, wasteful, useless Irish emigrants, the story pointed out that among the drowned on the *William Brown* was Mrs. Anderson, on her way to join her physician husband in Cincinnati. In this way, the sense of outrage was extended beyond the longboat drownings to the prior deaths of those passengers for whom no lifesaving craft were available.

After that, Gilbert Gordon's official line that the deaths on the longboat were an "imperious necessity" needed to be acknowledged. This was less a matter of journalistic balance than an act of political prudence. Neither the reporter nor his paper wanted to alienate the powerful officials or shipping interests who might regard this story as an unpleasant challenge. And yet, even here, the *Morning Post* and its correspondent in Le Havre knew how to shade the piece. The unctuous "it is to be hoped the two consuls will give publicity to the examination" was a thinly veiled threat.

The heart of the story appeared in the last paragraph, which demanded that "the circumstances must be made out in the clearest way to palliate such an act [of murder]," and, finally, made a call for action to protect British emigrants. "We have emigrant ships sailing every week, and if it is held as law that 'might is right,' it had better be declared so, and that the crew are justified under extremities in throwing overboard whom, and as many, as they think right, without casting lots, or making any choice than their will." This put the cause of emigrant safety in the foreground and argued for the right of passengers to at least an equal chance of survival as the crew in the event of a disaster at sea. It denied the excuse of "imperious necessity" and condemned the failure of the crew (and especially of Rhodes) to at least cast lots, to share with the passengers the dangers of the sea.

To a nineteenth-century reader, the point was clear: drowned emigrants had been sacrificed like cattle—without human rights or dignity—to improve the situation of the sailors. The story raised the stakes to include the emigrant trade itself. Who would sail to the Americas if he or she knew they might be sacrificed upon the whim of a sailor, mate or sea captain?

British officials were in a bind. England was committed to the emigrant trade as a way of dispensing with its surplus citizens but at the same time the government was committed to shipping interests whose revenues were crucial to the nation. And officials did not like being made to appear ignorant or foolish by a newspaper story. The newspapers had overtaken Gordon's report and threatened to make the story a major political embarrassment.

BEASLEY AND GORDON's joint letter of 14 May to the editor of the *Journal de Havre* did not begin to repair the damage. Indeed, its refusal to assign any blame may have made the whole seem more suspicious to readers. And, as Rubin Beasley thought it might, the issue had become one of American sailors killing British subjects. More generally at issue was whether or not those subjects travelled with any more rights than the chickens and cattle shipped on board to feed them. Most galling for Lord

Palmerston, perhaps, was that he had to read about these events in the *Morning Post* and the *Times* rather than in a dispatch from his consul in Le Havre. He had no more information than the average British reader.

To make matters worse, on 18 May, the *Times* published a letter condemning the murders in the longboat and, by implication, British policy. "However the United States and British Consuls at Havre may attempt to palliate the transaction relative to the passengers of the *William Brown*," it began, "I for one shall never be persuaded that any circumstances whatever can possibly justify so gross an outrage on every generous, and human, and just feeling." The author identified himself as "Homo," short for *Homo sapiens,* a polite, nineteenth-century way of saying, "just a man who comments from the perspective of humanity."

"One might perhaps have expected to hear that such an act had been perpetrated among the savage and heathen inhabitants of the North Seas, though I should doubt whether savages themselves would not possess a greater nobleness of nature," Homo editorialized. "But [that] a ship's company sailing under the flag of a Christian nation, a nation sufficiently boastful of its advancement in civilisation, should have been guilty of one of the most revolting deeds of inhumanity and meanness is almost beyond credibility."

That was it, exactly. There was a *meanness* to the reported events. Where, Homo asked, was the "noble example of self-devotion, or even [of the sailors] subjecting themselves to an equal lot with the rest?" Absent nobility, there were, at least, he implied, the proprieties of fair play. One might not expect the average seaman or mate to sacrifice himself for a passenger, but, failing the ideal of self-sacrifice, every Englishman knew that an equal sharing of dangers was only fair.

"At the least," Homo's letter argued, "it will be allowed that the carrying out of the measure, if really necessary, should have been decided by lot, and that the mate and crew themselves should have participated." This was the crux of the matter. "For an individual to sacrifice the life of his companions in danger in order to make his own secure, would be an atrocious outrage on humanity," Homo fumed. "Yet here the heinousness of the deed was peculiarly aggravated by the circumstance of the parties sacrificed being persons who had implicitly committed themselves to the protection and safe conduct of the officers and crew of the vessel."

The centerpiece of Homo's argument was an attack on British law and policy. At that time, no law or statute regulated the responsibilities of a ship's officers and crew to the passengers they carried. In no maritime country had the issue ever been dealt with. Therefore, there was no precedent by which the murders could be judged, no standard in law that could be applied. The subtext of Homo's letter was an argument *for* a precedent, for a legal judgment, to ensure that in future ship officers and crew could not drown passengers with impunity.

Legal historian A.W. Brian Simpson dismisses Homo as a crank and the letter as inconsequential. Certainly, it was a minor if politically disturbing departure from the stories that more or less supported the Rhodes/Ball version of events, and thus the consuls' argument of necessity. But it would be a mistake to underestimate its significance. The importance of the letter rested upon the identity of its author. The *Times* was not in the habit of publishing anonymous letters from just any citizen. For Homo's critique to be published, he had to be known to the newspaper—and if only readers knew his *real* name, to them as well—as a man of standing. The likelihood was that Homo was a member of the opposition and that the letter was a political barb aimed at Lord Melbourne's government. By implication, it criticized the Foreign Office, and thus Lord Palmerston himself, as the minister in charge of foreign affairs.

Like the *Morning Post* story, Homo's letter drew attention to a glaring omission in the law that the government had not addressed. Because seamen and their officers sailing in international waters were a law unto themselves, there was nothing to prevent them from dispatching cargo or passengers when it seemed expedient to do so. When would the government act? At the least, Homo's letter implied, the *William Brown* was a case that should be severely dealt with by a government that so far had failed to protect British subjects at sea.

As if to add weight to Homo's letter, the day before the *Times* had run a story culled from a Canadian newspaper, the *Quebec Mercury:* "It again becomes our duty to record a calamity involving destruction of human life to an awful extent. Four of the crew and four of the passengers of the brig Minstrel, Captain Outerbridge, arrived here yesterday, bringing the disastrous intelligence." Like the *William Brown*, this was an emigrant ship, albeit a larger one, sailing from Limerick to Quebec with 141 settlers. On 21 April it struck a reef in Canadian waters. "Upwards of 100 passengers embarked in the boats, but their doom was quickly sealed." The *Minstrel* sank so quickly that the "painters of the boats could not be cast off, and the people who had embarked in the boats perished."

Here was the normal course of a shipwreck. There had not been sufficient lifeboats, of course. There never were. But in this wreck, sailors and passengers shared the danger and died together. And, most damning when compared with the *William Brown*, the captain chose to go down with his ship: "Captain Outerbridge, of the unfortunate Minstrel, behaved most gallantly during the awful scene, until he perished with the rest. He declared that he would not leave the vessel until his passengers were saved, and he was the last person seen by those who were in the gig."

HAD GILBERT GORDON BEEN AWARE of what British newspapers were saying, he might have written a different report. As it was, however, after sending his letter to London, he thought his work was done, except for some minor matters. On 18 May, for example, the day Homo's letter appeared in the *Times,* Beasley and Gordon together deposed Captain George Ball of the *Crescent.* His statement was relatively short. On the morning of 21 April, Captain Ball "was at the mast head of his ship con-ing [conducting] her through the ice under close reefed fore and main top sails when he perceived a boat about a point and a half on the weather bow." He came down from aloft, mustered all hands, and "every exertion was made to get them on board immediately." Ball then described care-fully sailing through the ice, the contrary weather he experienced and, modestly, his every kindness to the survivors.

Ball's deposition also summarized his ship's 2 May encounter with the *Ville de Lyon.* He mentioned that, needing fuel for the cooking fire, he had burned his own longboat rather than the damaged boat from the *William Brown,* "as it was thought it might be necessary hereafter, to pro-duce that of the William Brown as evidence of its condition."

The next day, the 22nd, the two consuls had three ship masters exam-ine the longboat and certify its state of disrepair. With that done, Gordon wrote to London to ask permission to pay Captain Ball "fr. 642.60 (about £25.9) for the subsistence of British subjects during 21 days they were on board this vessel." Gordon also asked for, and later received, an additional "fr. 500 (about 19.16) for the longboat that he [Ball] was obliged to break up for firewood, not having sufficient on board for so great a number of persons." The Foreign Office note of 28 May authorizing payment is reproduced here.

An order from the British Foreign Office to pay Captain Ball for expenses incurred in the rescue of the survivors of the wreck of the *William Brown*, 28 May 1841.

On 20 May, the *Times* ran a brief follow-up story titled "The Loss of the William Brown." Datelined Havre on 16 May, it reported "the surviving passengers of the William Brown, brought to this port by the Crescent, request that their names may be inserted for the satisfaction of their friends at home." It then listed the names of all "those saved, many of them being witnesses to the awful, heart-rending scene of their brothers, sisters, cousins and other relatives being launched into a watery grave." As if the verb "launched" were not enough to remind readers of the murders, the *Times* writer piously added, "It is not correct that the hands were cut off from those who clung to the sides of the boat."

This was the first that *Times* readers learned of the rumour that the hands of some survivors had been cut off as they clung to the side of the longboat. Denying a rumour to give it credence was and remains a fine rhetorical device, a way of at once inserting the unproven fact while simultaneously disclaiming responsibility for it. Palmerston was not amused. Nor was he pleased to read that in Le Havre "Subscriptions are in progress here for the purpose of getting them all [survivors] sent out to New York with the next packet."

The story was becoming ever more charged, more ruinous to the government's image. To have British subjects helped by a public subscription in France—its ancient enemy—was insupportable. They might be shipwrecked, but to have them displayed as paupers was humiliating to the government, and, therefore, to the nation. The man whom Lord Palmerston blamed was the consul who was supposed to make sure the Foreign Office would not be caught unaware.

On 25 May, Lord Palmerston's secretary, John Bidwell, penned a stinging letter to Gilbert Gordon, informing the consul that his superiors found his handling of the *William Brown* incident a marvel of incompetence. "You give no account of your proceedings, nor of the steps you took in this business to investigate a transaction in which so many British subjects were violently put to death by foreigners." The trade in emigrants, Bidwell implied, had been endangered by Gordon's incompetence. He made absolutely clear that, for London, the real issue was the murder of British subjects by foreign sailors on board an American ship, acknowledging, "It may have been necessary for the American crew to sacrifice a certain number of the passengers to save the lives of the rest of the public in the boat." But, the letter continued, "however horrible such an expedient may have been, yet if the necessity were fully established, a veil might be drawn over the murders of those so committed."

Gordon's superiors did not accept his argument of necessity any more than did Homo, or the *Morning Post*'s editors. Nor, Bidwell informed him, was it Gordon's job to independently investigate the affair. "It was your duty as British Consul, specially charged with the protection of His Majesty's subjects, to have taken steps for bringing this matter to strict investigation before a judicial tribunal. If there be yet time, I am directed by Lord Palmerston to desire that you will do so forthwith."

A judicial tribunal meant a London courtroom in which defendants would be tried under British law. It did not matter that international jurisdiction was at best unclear or that the United States would certainly protest if its citizens were hauled before a British court for actions that had occurred on an American ship at sea. Britain in the mid-nineteenth century was at the height of its power and wanted to make the point that British subjects, even Irish emigrants, were protected wherever they might be. Britain also wanted to prove its maritime primacy, and, therefore, its right to set precedents irrespective of where the British subjects might be in the world. Today, it may seem unbelievable—a British tribunal judging Americans (or the citizens of other nations) for actions that took place in international waters—but in those days, it seemed reasonable and appropriate to Lord Palmerston. In what was almost an afterthought, Bidwell then demanded an explanation of "how so many females happened to be onboard the *William Brown* without any of them bearing the same surnames." Why, in short, were single women travelling from Great Britain to America? It offended Palmerston that so many apparently single women were travelling without gentlemanly escort.

That Bidwell rather than Palmerston signed the letter was itself a calculated rebuke. Usually, correspondence from the Foreign Office to the consul in Le Havre carried the foreign secretary's signature, as if Palmerston had penned the letter himself.

It was unfortunate for Gilbert Gordon that Lord Palmerston was a thorough-going professional politician of the Irish noble classes. Born Henry John Temple, he succeeded to the Irish peerage, and his title, after his father's death in 1802. He entered Parliament in 1807 at the age of twenty-two. Palmerston was so valuable as a minister that, during his career, he served in both Tory and Whig governments. He first became Secretary of State for Foreign Affairs in 1830 in the government of Earl Grey and held the position under three regimes. Queen Victoria roundly disliked him, in part because of his libertine behaviour, particularly when he was found one morning in the rooms of one of her ladies-in-waiting, Lady Dacre. What truly separated Palmerston and his sovereign, however, were their distinct political priorities. The queen believed Britain should do what it could to help preserve Europe's royal families against republicanism, whereas Palmerston believed "the main objective of the government's foreign policy should be to increase Britain's power in the world." In the 1840s, this meant keeping control of the seas.

A portrait of Lord Palmerston some years after the sinking of the *William Brown.*

ON 30 MAY, Gilbert Gordon hastened to begin to repair the damage. "I cannot lose a post without expressing my regret that I have in the opinion of Lord Palmerston failed in my duty respecting the unfortunate and melancholy affair the William Brown," he wrote to John Bidwell. In the next paragraph, Gordon identified the source of his miscalculation. "In what I did I was certainly inclined to be guided by the long experience of Mr. Beasley, the United States Consul, a Gentleman of the highest Honour and Character here, and who has acted in that capacity for upwards of 30 years—and as a man of honour, I can assure you, that the greatest impartiality has been shown in this business."

Poor Gordon. Reading this, Lord Palmerston's secretary understood what the consul still did not: he had been snookered. The American consul must have been delighted and relieved when the people of Le Havre took up a subscription to pay the fares of the surviving emigrants to the United States. Not only would they travel to American jurisdiction but at no cost to his nation. That their publicly subscribed passage carried as well an implication of British miserliness was something he doubtlessly appreciated.

For the next month, Gordon was involved in damage control. On 3 June he sent, at London's request, a copy of the letter he and Beasley had written to the editor of the *Journal de Havre* about the *William Brown.* Palmerston had criticized what he perceived as the letter's (and thus the consuls') attempt to justify "the drownings at sea." The motive, Gordon pleaded, "was not to justify the dreadful loss of life but to contradict the false and exaggerated reports that were in circulation." On the same day, under separate cover, he dispatched copies of "the depositions of the crew and passengers saved from the *William Brown,* taken by the U.S. Consul and myself."

Regarding Lord Palmerston's most important demand, however, Gordon could not comply: "I regret that it is not in my power to have the crew examined before a judicial tribunal in compliance with Your Lordship's command. Of the passengers, James Patrick, wife, and child returned to Ireland by the Dublin steamer on the ninth, and James Black and wife are now in London. The rest left on the twenty-sixth on board the Richmond bound to Baltimore from whence they will be forwarded to Philadelphia."

Gordon was, however, able to satisfy his superior on another matter: "The reason why there were so many females on board the William Brown without any men bearing the same names arises from the fact that they were going out to join their relations already established in the United States."

A news brief describing the rescue of the *William Brown*'s Captain George Harris went unnoticed, or at least unremarked, in this flurry of activity. On 16 June the *Times* reprinted a short paragraph from a Cape Breton newspaper reporting Harris's arrival there "with Eliza Rafferty, second mate Walter Parker and six crewmen. After having been in the jolly boat six days, they were picked up by a French lugger on the fishing ground and carried into St. Pierre. They were in a dreadful state of exhaustion, and were sent to the hospital, where several of them remained at the date of the last advice."

After the departure of the *Richmond,* Britain's part in the events came to a close. Stuck in the Foreign Office files, buried amid the depositions, is a brief note dated 23 July in Lord Palmerston's own hand: "This was a calamitous event, and nothing more need be said about it." Had Rubin Beasley been

Lord Palmerston's final note about the *William Brown* in the Foreign Office files, 23 July 1841.

less adept, or Gilbert Gordon more astute, the trial and its resulting precedent might have given to Britain the next chapter of this story.

HAVING CUT BRITAIN out of the picture, Beasley now had to find someone to make an example of, a sailor for American officials to charge. He might have recommended Francis Rhodes, who was clearly in command of the longboat. But Rhodes's power came from his captain, and to impugn the first mate was to implicate the master. That, in turn, might open the question of ship safety generally, and the Americans were no more eager than the British to do that. Moreover, Rhodes was a native-born American citizen. There would be sympathy for him that a foreign member of the crew would not garner. Indeed, it would be best if the person chosen was neither American nor British. The United States did not want a diplomatic battle with its principal trading partner.

Ruling out both British and American subjects considerably narrowed the field. And, of course, irrespective of nationality, the man charged had to be Caucasian. Blacks were still considered property in the southern United States, so the cook and steward were also disqualified. And if that were not reason enough, they weren't *sailors*. That left the foreign crewmen, and among them, "Alexander Williams," actually Alexander William Holmes, was the obvious choice. He had participated in the drownings of passengers. That was a fact. But Holmes also had returned to the ship to save the life of Isabella Edgar. And it was Holmes who had taken command when Rhodes was unmanned the morning after the killings. Finally, Holmes had not relished the work, ending his participation part way through the task.

Charging Holmes would put the best possible light on the whole sordid affair. His punishment, if any, would not be onerous—he was, after all, a hero—and thus any potential criticism arising from the conviction of a sailor for following a superior's orders would be diminished.

As soon as Beasley learned that the emigrants would be sailing to the United States on the *Richmond*, he wrote to his superiors in Washington before the ship sailed on 26 May. In his letter, he reported on all of the events surrounding the *William Brown* and arranged to have American officials meet the ship when she arrived in Philadelphia.

THE CHARGE

OR A TIME, the story of the *William Brown* almost disappeared from public view as the principals travelled by sailing ship from the Old World to the New. The summer of 1841 was like a theatre performance at intermission, the time when the faint sound of stagehands can almost be heard as one set is struck and another erected, readying for the final act.

In late June and early July, most of the survivors from the *William Brown* arrived in Philadelphia and Boston, carrying the story wherever they went. The first to arrive was sailor John Messer, who had been released early by consul Rubin Beasley. Messer had shipped on the *Angelo*, arriving in New England at the end of June. He told his story to the *Boston Post;* it was picked up and run by other papers in North America, the *Philadelphia Public Ledger and Daily Transcript,* for example, and in Great Britain by the *Glasgow Times* and, later, the *Times* in London. "Still in a very weak state of health, from his sufferings in the boat," the story said, Messer "called on the editor of the Boston Post and furnished him with a statement relating to the loss of the ship and the circumstances connected with the heartrending affair in the longboat."

In spite of the *Boston Post*'s claim that Messer walked into its office with a statement prepared, the story reflects the polish of a professional journalist behind the text, prompting and searching for the most horrifying details. At every turn, however, Messer refused to talk about what he had not personally seen or heard, refused to judge or condemn what he himself had not witnessed. All this makes his statement more interesting and more believable. Unlike Francis Rhodes, who insisted that under his command the *William Brown*'s sailors were instantly active after the collision, Messer remembered a long wait between the striking of the iceberg and the call mustering all hands on deck. "We felt the collision below, but did not think of hurrying on deck, especially as we were not called. Nearly 20 minutes, I think, elapsed before we were called, and then the not unusual cry of 'All hands shorten sail!' roused us on deck." He added, "The captain . . . then went down into the forecastle in order to ascertain what damage had been done, and, upon ascertaining, he exclaimed, 'My God, we can't save the ship, it's no use; clear away the longboat.'"

Messer then described the jolly boat and longboat being cleared from the deck, but again, unlike the others, he was frank about the undisciplined panic. When the longboat was in the water, he said, "The passengers made a rush, and I believe that several of them perished in their haste to get on board. In the meantime the stern-boat [the jolly boat] was lowered down, but, as I did not see what transpired I will not state anything upon hearsay."

Praising Captain Harris as "an able, experienced commander" and a "generous, noble-hearted man" (Messer was, after all, a sailor who would be seeking another berth), he briefly described the discussion between Harris and Rhodes, saying there were "some communications, which I did not distinctly hear that passed between the captain and mate, to which the Captain replied, 'I will not hear such talk.' The mate then distinctly said, 'We must cast lots—we all cannot live—some of us must die, the boat is so leaky.' The captain again remonstrated with the mate."

After the day alone at sea, said Messer, "towards nightfall the mate consulted, in a low voice, with several of the crew about lightening the boat. I was at the time with my back against the stern. At last he said to me and another man who was near me, 'Well, I suppose you have no objection to lending us a hand to lighten the boat?'

"I inquired how he intended to do so, and while I was speaking I heard a splash alongside, and the whole boat was in an uproar—the work of death had commenced. The other man and myself had both remonstrated against such cold-blooded proceedings." Messer also said he told Rhodes that to be fair, they should cast lots.

Messer was at some pains to deny the worst rumours that swirled around the case. "There were no hands cut off, nor any blood spilt," he said firmly. And he downplayed the sensational rumours of the physical resistance on the part of the passengers thrown overboard. "The unfortunate passengers offered no resistance; prayers and entreaties were all they used. 'Oh! Spare me! Spare me!' several of them cried, even while they were half overboard. I will not attempt a description of this awful story it would melt a heart of stone. I believe there were sixteen thrown overboard."

In conclusion, Messer turned to the survivors' salvation by the *Crescent*, and his ongoing anger at his own treatment. "The following morning I discovered a sail, and communicated the fact to the mate, who said, 'By God, Jack, you're a lucky fellow; you have saved your life.' The ship that picked us up, as is already known, was the Crescent. So strong was my indignation against the Negro, that upon reaching the Crescent's deck I seized a heaver and threw it at his head."

This was surely the story that Beasley heard from Messer and immediately dismissed, not because he did not believe it but because he did. Messer had assumed that the other passengers, and perhaps his crewmates, would tell the same story. By the time he understood his error, there was no other place to tell it but to a newspaper. The official story had been announced and journalists were the only people who would listen.

Had Messer's story been published in the *Journal de Havre* when first the *Ville de Lyon* and then the *Crescent* arrived in Le Havre, it might have made a difference. Even had it not sparked some of the others to speak openly and critically, it would have been fuel for those who, like Homo, regarded the drownings as unacceptable. Gilbert Gordon would have known, upon hearing Messer's story, that he needed to seek his superior's instructions. But by the summer of 1841 the *William Brown* was old news, worth but a few paragraphs in the back pages of a newspaper. Messer's story was of only passing interest.

Sixteen-year-old seaman William Miller's version, printed 1 July in the *Philadelphia Public Ledger and Daily Transcript*, attracted even less attention and added nothing to the stories already written. Mostly, Miller blamed the passengers, who, "in order to avoid the severity of the storm created some commotion and in their fruitless attempts to seek shelter unfortunately forced the plug out of its place." Worse, as the water rushed in—"It was a trying moment," Miller said—the passengers panicked. "After using every exertion himself to replace the plug without effect, in consequence of the obstinacy of the passengers, he [Rhodes] exclaimed, 'My God! It must be so—lighten the boat, men.' "

Miller insisted that the murder of the passengers was necessary if the bailing plug was to be replaced. After all, he stated, only "those passengers nearest the plug-hole were passed overboard, and the plug was replaced," not later but almost immediately. That the plug was not checked until after the murders were committed was a fact he confidently omitted. Indeed, Miller insisted, the concern over the drowning of the passengers was overblown. "The whole affair did not occupy three minutes," he said. Nobody, not even Rhodes, had so minimized the deaths. In the United States, Miller's story was not taken seriously, and, later, no official requested that he testify at the trial.

In Britain, meanwhile, Lord Melbourne's government, which had been tottering for months, finally fell. But the new government did not change any policy regarding sailing ships and their owners or masters. Neither the new prime minister nor his cabinet saw the need for legislative action. As for Lord Palmerston, he was too valuable a bureaucrat to lose to something as ephemeral as an election. A few years later, he was returned to his post as Secretary of State for Foreign Affairs.

Bridget McGee and most of the other surviving passengers and crew arrived in Philadelphia, the *William Brown*'s home port, on 13 July. By that time, stories from British newspapers had already made the rounds. The *Philadelphia Public Ledger* was indignant, demanding that "the mate and sailors of the William Brown who threw the passengers overboard to save themselves, should be put upon trial for murder." Editorials in other papers were no less vehement.

McGee took lodgings on Decatur Street, and though officials made sure they knew where to find her, she was not formally questioned until a grand jury was convened in October. That did not mean she was silent, however. In the summer and into the fall, she told her story in the Irish community. Something had to be done about the *William Brown* and its longboat, McGee insisted, and about the drowning of the emigrants. The Irish in America had to protect those who would follow in other ships. In their turn, the Irish community's leaders pushed for a trial. They complained to the Philadelphia district attorney, demanding justice. Officialdom acquiesced. Alexander Holmes was arrested in July and detained in gaol and held pending a grand jury hearing on multiple charges of murder. He would be there for a while. It would be more than a hundred years before the *Miranda* decision ensured that men like him would be advised of their rights. Nor did nineteenth-century courts guarantee a speedy trial for the accused.

Bureaucrats in Washington and jurists in Philadelphia had to decide on the precise charges, and it took them until October to devise a plan. On 11 October the *New York Herald* announced with enthusiasm: "Next week, a very important trial is expected to come off in the District Court of the United States, for murder." Alexander Holmes, and he alone, would stand trial for the murders in the "small boat of which several human beings were hurled into the sea." Someone had decided to treat the case as a simple murder under Pennsylvania statute and not as a federal crime to be tried by a federal prosecutor.

This case, the *Herald*'s Philadelphia correspondent promised, would make for fascinating entertainment. The trial was not really about the guilt (or innocence) of a single Swedish seaman. Rather, at issue was human nature and moral philosophy. "There will many nice questions arise for settlement," announced the newspaper. "Among others to be considered, the determination of the extent of the law of self-preservation." In addition to its moral significance, the trial would be even more interesting because of practical concerns, the newspaper enthused. At issue was "Whether public carriers of passengers have a right to sacrifice the lives of those very passengers, which they have impliedly pledged themselves to land at a designated point—whether they have a right to throw them into the sea to save the lives of themselves or of any others."

Did self-preservation take precedence over a man's duty to others, especially those who had paid for the privilege of international maritime travel? Should selfish human nature be an excuse in law for acts of self-preservation? The answer would dictate maritime policy and affect all who sailed in international waters. What better way for men of leisure to entertain themselves than to attend the trial and hear these questions argued by worthy members of the legal profession?

The trial was set up so that nobody would ask *why* the *William Brown* was under full sail without a special watch in waters that were known to be ice filled. Nobody would ask why there were only two auxiliary craft and who was responsible for their condition. All that was needed to make the official approach work was for the grand jury to indict one sailor from the *William Brown* for the death of at least one passenger.

As a boon, the concerns of the Irish would be assuaged in the bargain. Only the man accused, an otherwise insignificant Swedish sailor, would suffer.

The Philadelphia district attorney's office lined up its witnesses, including Bridget McGee. Prosecutor George M. Dallas and his colleague, Oliver Hopkinson, were so confident of an indictment that they scheduled the trial to begin in Judge Archibald Randall's courtroom even before they presented their case to the grand jury. All they had to ask the witnesses was: "Did that man,

A sinking "coffin ship," one of many ill-repaired and overloaded ships in which emigrants on their way from Britain to America died in the mid nineteenth century. From *Harper's Weekly*

Mr. Holmes, throw overboard the passengers whose deaths are named in the murder indictment out of the longboat?" Since the answer was bound to be yes, the jurors would indict Holmes for the longboat murders.

In those days, when hearings and trials were a public spectacle and a forum for general entertainment, Judge Randall was a popular choice. The first week of that October, for example, he presided over the widely reported trial of "Caldwell, *alias* Edwards, the great forger and swindler." Caldwell's lawyer had sought a writ of *habeas corpus* for his client, who was fighting extradition to New York state. Nobody doubted his guilt (or identity), but his bonhomie and his audacity had won him many fans. "Mr. Dallas [the prosecutor] spoke about two hours yesterday and one and a half today. That he was plausible and eloquent it is unnecessary to say—he never speaks otherwise," a local newspaper enthused. But while the defence "fought over every inch of ground," it was Judge Randall who carried the day. His response to the lawyer's speech "was about an hour's length" and "had all the zeal and eloquence" that characterized his first detailed ruling on the case.

Judge Randall was what Mark Twain called a "speech-a-fier," an orator who could hold his own with the most long-winded of attorneys. A case before his court would be well argued and peppered with pretty speeches. Who better to hear a trial on the tragedy of human nature, on selfish survival versus heroic self-sacrifice?

In the end, Randall did not get the chance. On 15 October, the grand jury refused to return murder indictments against Alexander William Holmes.

Then as now, grand juries are in most cases a formality, a check-less balance to the power of the state, a useless guarantee under law. It is not their task to decide the guilt or innocence of the accused, only whether or not there is sufficient evidence to bring a person to trial for the specified offence. Usually, that requires so little effort, so minimal a burden of proof, that prosecutors assume a grand jury's true bill as a matter of course, and some bragged they could have a hitching post indicted. The jury's refusal to indict Holmes was, therefore, a serious embarrassment.

There was no doubt that Holmes was one of the seamen who had thrown passengers out of the longboat. Bridget McGee said so. So did the other emigrants whom prosecutor George Dallas paraded before the grand jury. Hell, Holmes himself admitted it. The sticking point was not the facts of the case, but its nature. Whatever Holmes had done, the jurors' judgment said, was not a murder like the ones they read about each day and understood as a capital offence under the laws of Pennsylvania. Holmes should not be tried, they decided, in the same way, and with the same capital penalties, as a miscreant who had shot, knifed or bludgeoned a shop owner in an attempted robbery, or a neighbour in a local dispute.

It did not take long for officials to rethink the case. Within weeks, a new set of charges was presented to a new grand jury. This time, Holmes was charged under not state but federal law "for the punishment of certain crimes against the United States." These included "manslaughter on the high seas," in this case the death of Francis Askin.

The 1790 law under which Holmes now was charged was a catchall for extraterritorial crimes against American citizens in cases where legal jurisdiction might otherwise be in doubt. The new indictments alleged that Holmes, "first and with force, etc. unlawfully and feloniously did make an assault, and cast and threw Askin from a vessel into the high seas by means of which Askin, in and with the waters thereof, then and there was suffocated and drowned." The maximum punishment Holmes faced under the federal charge was three years' imprisonment, however, not the death sentence given to those convicted of murder under Pennsylvania state law.

Prosecutor George Dallas and his colleagues argued at least four counts of manslaughter (and several lesser charges) before the federal grand jury. These were, in effect, two identical counts put forward together to solve a legal problem. Holmes was charged, first, with manslaughter on board the ship *William Brown*, belonging to Stephen Baldwin, a U.S. citizen, and again under identical charges on board the ship *William Brown*, belonging to Joseph P. Vogel, also a U.S. citizen. To make the federal case, the prosecution had to show that the deaths occurred on an American vessel whose pedigree was clear. However, the ownership of the *William Brown*—and thus her longboat—was a matter of some confusion.

The owner of record, Baldwin, had sold the ship to Philadelphia businessman Joseph P. Vogel on 30 December 1840, with the sale to take effect on delivery of the ship to Philadelphia. The prosecutors worried that the defence might argue that an indictment naming the ship as Baldwin's might be challenged as inaccurate, since he had sold the ship to Vogel. Similarly, if the prosecutors insisted the ship was Vogel's, then defence attorneys might argue that the ship in fact still belonged to Baldwin, since it had never been delivered. Either way, it was the type of legal knot that might tie up the case for years on appeal. That was an outcome nobody wanted.

The solution was to bring separate counts of manslaughter reflecting each possibility and to let the grand jury sort it out. It did not matter which set of indictments was returned as long as one of them was accepted. Out of pique rather than legal technicalities—Dallas was still smarting from the first grand jury's refusal—the grand jury was asked as well to indict Holmes on a charge of theft. "In the impotency of disappointed revenge," as Holmes's defence attorney later put it, the prosecutors accused Holmes of "larceny in having stolen a quilt of the alleged value of three dollars." The quilt in question was the one used to make a sail for the longboat in the hours before the *Crescent*'s rescue.

The grand jury refused to indict Holmes for theft or on the indictments assuming Baldwin's ownership of the ship. In the legal Latin of the day, the charges were "ignoramused" (rejected). But people *had* died in the longboat, and manslaughter seemed to fit the facts of the case. And so the grand jury approved the prosecutor's request for a charge under federal law of manslaughter on the high seas against Alexander William Holmes.

Nobody really wanted Holmes to be hanged except, perhaps, Bridget McGee. She had never forgiven him for trying to order her out of the longboat, or for her uncle's murder. For their part, the prosecutors were well content to try Holmes on the federal manslaughter charge. The "many nice questions" that the case promised to address—and that the prosecutors were eager to argue—could be more easily judged with a maximum sentence of three years rather than a death penalty. A jury reluctant to convict Holmes of a capital crime might be more than willing to send him to prison to make a political or philosophical point. As a bonus, that the charge was under federal law meant the federal government itself would be involved, giving Washington an opportunity to impress the new emigrant interests with its concern.

Federal charges required a federal judge, one sitting in the Third Circuit covering eastern Pennsylvania. And though Judge Randall was commissioned to that court early in 1842, he was not to hear the case of the *United States v. Holmes*. The court's chief justice, Henry Baldwin, reserved that pleasure for himself. A prestigious senior jurist first appointed to the District Court in 1830, he was seasoned, politically connected and generally admired as a legalist. In his younger years, he had proudly published the text of a patriotic (and politically partisan) 4 July speech he had given to a group of Republicans celebrating Independence Day in the 1820s. Later in his career, he authored several volumes of circuit court cases, as well as a tome on the Constitution.

Baldwin was just the man for the job. He was ready to use the court to deal with the issues raised, of which the fate of an insignificant Swedish seaman was the least important.

The winter of 1841–42 was a hard one, with heavy ice again reported in the North Atlantic. In early spring, the shipping news was filled with sightings of icebergs. En route from Le Havre to New York, for example, the packet ship *Albany* "Spoke bark Frederick Warren, of and for Boston, from Bangor, Wales, 41 days out, 2d [sighting] in Lat. 41°44' and from Long. 48°30' to 49°11'. The ship paused between icebergs—the weather being clear they were as far north and south as we could see."

The conditions that had given rise to the nightmare of the *William Brown* had not changed and would not go away.

As important, shipping was then in the doldrums, so it would not do if the charges against Holmes were transformed into an investigation of the industry and its many failings. Hundreds of ships sat idle in port, many of them for sale and without the likely prospect of immediate buyers. The situation was grievous, according to the *New York Herald:* "It cannot be denied but that this country was never in a more healthy condition internally than now, with large and increasing crops every year. Yet, here we see hundreds of vessels lying idle and rotting, at our docks, for the want of some business to send them to sea."

The problem, the paper editorialized, was the lamentable state of Washington politics and its deleterious effect on business in general. In 1842 candidates already were jostling for position in the next presidential election; all assumed that Henry Clay would run against President John Tyler—and with the outcome of that struggle lay the potential salvation of businessmen. Judge Baldwin understood politics and was sure to prevent contentious issues that might affect the industry—the rights of ship owners and their captains, for example—to be raised in his courtroom. The only matters to be considered would be the guilt or innocence of a sailor and the more general issue of a crewman's responsibility to the passengers aboard his employer's vessels.

District Attorney George Dallas was delighted with the court assignment. The outcome of the trial, he believed, was an almost foregone conclusion. Arguing with him and his Philadelphia colleague, Oliver Hopkinson, would be William M. Meredith, counsel for the United States. This was, after all, a federal case.

The prosecution's joy was the defence team's despair. The defence lawyers were in trouble from the start. They did not even have copies of the depositions made in Le Havre. We do not know who paid David Paul Brown, Isaac Hazlehurst and Edward Armstrong to defend Holmes. No matter how popular a defendant's case might be, public subscriptions were not often constituted to pay for the defence of the accused in the nineteenth century. The Seamen's Friend Society, which supported Holmes's cause and his eventual appeal, may have helped to secure Brown, one of Philadelphia's best-known trial lawyers, to defend Holmes and may have contributed to his defence costs. Or, perhaps, the defence team served *pro bono* in the hope that a highly publicized, well-argued case would raise their professional profiles. Maybe they even believed that Holmes deserved a good defence because he had been made a scapegoat.

However they were paid, the defence lawyers knew that the manslaughter charge was virtually unassailable. Holmes *was* one of the sailors who had drowned the lifeboat's passengers. Survivors would swear to it, and Holmes himself did not deny it. The only real defence would be to blame someone else, making Holmes the tool of another's culpable action. The defence could argue that Holmes was only following orders, as the crewmen had promised Captain Harris they would; or, were John Messer to be believed, that Holmes acted out of necessity, out of fear that Francis Rhodes would order Holmes's own life taken if he failed to follow orders. Since Rhodes had ordered the killings, he was the most obvious one to blame.

But to make these arguments, the defence would need Rhodes, Messer and Captain Harris on the witness stand. In fact, it might be useful to have all the sailors who had been in the longboat—certainly all those who had made depositions in Le Havre—available for the defence. After the indictments were handed down, the defence team, therefore, almost surely began to argue for the subpoenas that would enable them to keep at hand the men they wanted to parade before the jury.

The prosecutors would have opposed the blizzard of legal requests the defence put forward, on the grounds that it would be unreasonable to restrain a ship's captain on land for months so that his opinion of a subordinate's actions could be heard. In the same vein, they would have argued that to restrain sailors would be a hardship on them as they made their living upon the sea. Of course, Alexander William Holmes had been detained since July and would be held in custody at least until the trial was finished and a verdict reached. But that was different. He was the defendant and how long he was held did not matter.

Judge Baldwin gave both sides some of what they requested. Clearly, Captain Harris's testimony was important. So, too, was the testimony of Holmes's watch commander, Walter Parker. But these were seamen and their livelihoods depended on being free to ply their trade. Holmes's lawyers would have time to depose Captain Harris and Parker, Judge

Baldwin decided, and those depositions could be read as testimony at the trial, but neither man would be subpoenaed and required to stay ashore until the trial was held.

That meant the defence would have no real witnesses. All of them would be at sea: Captain George Harris, Francis Rhodes and Walter Parker. Indeed, all the sailors who had returned to North America had left again, scattered to a score of sailing ships. They could not be asked about Holmes's heroism, about Rhodes's inability to command, or about the possibility the first mate might have turned on Holmes and them—as he did on Messer—had they refused his order.

David Paul Brown could have Holmes take the stand, but to have the accused testify in his own defence is always a risky strategy. Even so, Holmes might have been called, but for the fact that, alas for the defence, he was honest to a fault. Strongly built but pale from his months on land, he sat quietly as his lawyers tried to find a better defence for their client than the God-given selfishness of base human nature.

The problem was that while a better than competent sailor, Holmes was wholly lost in the world of law. If he saw danger, he faced it. When given an order, he carried it out. He did not understand why he was charged or how anyone could believe he had done something wrong. It was not his place to question a superior's command, to stand with knife drawn against the order of his first mate. Had Messer been charged with refusing Rhodes's order, Holmes would have served ably as a strong prosecution witness.

HOLMES SPENT HIS FIRST American Thanksgiving in a Philadelphia jail. On 9 December, prosecution and defence lawyers deposed Walter Parker, Holmes's immediate superior, and Captain George Harris. At the least the defence needed an unimpeachable witness who had seen Holmes's rescue of Isabella Edgar.

After Parker was sworn in, he told defence lawyer Isaac Hazlehurst: "I was on board the ship William Brown on her last voyage . . . I was Second Mate. I was on deck and Captain Harris was on deck. It was my watch—Holmes was in my watch when the accident occurred." The weather was thick, he said, when "she struck very heavy, which drove me from my feet, and stopped the headway of the ship."

Parker then described his own part in lowering the jolly boat—his assigned role—and in taking aboard his captain. He argued the small boat was so loaded that it was unable to accept more passengers and still be safe. He did testify to Holmes's rescue of Isabella Edgar, however. "I saw Holmes myself take a sick woman down by the tackle falls and put her in the [long]boat. This was as she was coming along by the ship's side. There was great danger in this, both of him and the female: he was a strong man, no man of moderate strength could have done it. He brought in the last passenger, who was this woman. He was the last man that went into the longboat from the ship."

As to the events of the following morning, Parker testified: "I recollect Captain Harris giving his advice to the men to obey Mr. Rhodes the same as if he, Captain Harris, was in the boat." Did he have the men promise to this, Brown asked? Did Holmes promise to this? "Holmes made his answer, as the rest of them, that he would obey," said Parker. After that, Parker and Captain Harris departed in the jolly boat. "All I heard Holmes say when we were parting was good-by. He was in his shirtsleeves—he gave his coat to the women; all the men were in their shirtsleeves." He testified that Holmes was a good, obedient sailor who caused no trouble within the crew and always did his job. Parker had liked having him in his watch.

Prosecutors George Dallas and William Meredith then cross-examined Parker, seeking to limit his usefulness to the defence. Parker was not really a threat, as he had not been in the longboat when the passengers were drowned and so could speak only to the time that Holmes had served on the *William Brown*, and especially the night of its sinking.

After the ship was struck, Dallas suggested, there must have been great confusion on board. "The passengers all ran on deck that could run, at the first strike. I believe that all, every one, ran on deck at first shock," said Parker. When asked about the jolly boat, he said, "After the others got in our boat was as much crowded in comparison as the other boat. I was much alarmed." Parker was concerned about the passengers, but his greatest concern was the longboat itself: without a serviceable rudder, it was unmanageable. "I mean to say he [Rhodes] could not put the boat to any point for safety; they could not put her head around from one point to another. She was going around like a tub, she was like her own mistress; they could not keep her head one way or another even for a minute."

It was bad enough, the prosecution reasoned, that Holmes had returned to the ship to effect a rescue. That he was in his shirtsleeves, implying that he had given the clothes off his own back to others, was a sharp point to be blunted. Did Parker *see* Holmes give his clothes to any of the passengers? Meredith asked. No, Parker replied. But his last memory of Holmes, as the jolly boat pulled away, was that the man was without the heavy peacoat he had worn on watch the night before. When Dallas asked if other sailors had given clothes to the passengers, Parker said that yes, many had.

After the lawyers paused for refreshment, Captain George Harris was sworn in. He had his story ready for David Paul Brown. "I was Captain of the William Brown on her last voyage from Liverpool to Philadelphia," he stated, then gave the names of all the crew members and a list of her 559½ tons of cargo: salt, coal, crockery, hardware and passengers, "of which I have a list of those who were saved."

He had been on the weather deck, Harris said, when they struck the iceberg. He then told the same story that Francis Rhodes had told Captain Ball, though in his version it was he, not Rhodes, who called the hands to shorten sail, who investigated the damage to the hull, who did everything a master could do before ordering his men to abandon ship.

The defence lawyers then walked him through the launching of the jolly boat and longboat, and those who were left to drown. "I left thirty-one on board the ship, there were nine on board the jolly boat and forty-two on board the longboat," he said. "They were all allowed to get onboard as they could, with the exception of a sickly woman who was carried on Holmes's back." And you saw this, Brown asked. No, Harris replied, he was told about it later.

The defence team closely questioned the captain about the longboat. Was she seaworthy? Absolutely, he replied. "If the boat had been a leaky boat she would have gone down with them, she could not have supported one half she had in her had there been a moderate blow, even with a leak." When asked why he had sailed away in the jolly boat, leaving the longboat behind, Harris paused a moment, as if in thought, and replied: "I could render the longboat no more service—I had done all for them I could. I found she was unmanageable and that it was useless for me to waste longer time there and I made for land, which was two hundred and fifty miles."

Brown next asked Captain Harris about Holmes and his character. "Holmes was kind, obliging in every respect to the passengers and his shipmates, and to everybody," Harris replied. "He was a first rate man. I heard speak of his kindness on board the vessel, in the longboat, and everywhere—I never heard anyone speak against him." That was good. But one important issue for the defence was the crew's swearing obedience to Rhodes. And that was a question that Harris could best answer.

According to Captain Harris, "The mate, Rhodes, observed, as near as I can recollect, that his boat was unmanageable and that there were so many in it he would be obliged to draw lots and throw some overboard." Harris made no mention of the damaged rudder. He then carefully conflated the suggestion that "something must be done" and the equality of drawing lots. "I remarked to him [Rhodes] to let that be the last resort, that I did not wish him to say anything about it then." Rhodes's worries that morning were premature, Harris suggested, especially when stated in the presence of dispirited passengers and crew.

Finally, the defence lawyers asked Captain Harris if, when he left the longboat, he believed its passengers might be saved. "At the time I left the longboat I knew there was no chance of being saved except by their being picked up, and there was slim chance of being picked up among the ice and fog; there was poor chance of a ship in such ice."

The prosecution's cross-examination was brief and focussed mostly on the condition of the longboat. Captain Harris testified it was a well-found boat in good condition. Before leaving, he made sure the longboat was well provisioned with water and sea rations. She was overloaded, but so was the jolly boat. As to the events in the longboat after his departure, he knew nothing first hand, of course, so could not speak.

When had Captain Harris last seen the first mate, William Meredith asked. "I saw Francis Rhodes in July last, either July or June; he was then in Philadelphia, both in the street—at the corner of Front—and in the house of Stephen Baldwin, former owner of the *William Brown*." Rhodes had met with his former captain at the ship owner's house, presumably to report on the sinking and on what had happened in the longboat. Neither prosecution nor defence followed up on this conversation. It would have been hearsay and thus inadmissible in court.

Just to be clear, Captain Harris was asked, did the *William Brown*'s course deviate from the normal path of transatlantic vessels? If so, the question implied, Harris might have been reckless in sailing along a dangerous route. If not, well, then it was fate that had wrecked the vessel. "The generality of vessels pass in the track, or about the track that I took the William Brown. It is the thoroughfare between Europe and America, and particularly the North of Europe and the United States." Didn't this mean there was a good chance that the jolly boat and the longboat would have been rescued if they had stayed together? Certainly, there was a chance, Captain Harris replied. But he added that the sea is broad and ships are small. To be seen in the ice was possible but by no means a certainty. That the longboat had been rescued so quickly was, in fact, enormous good fortune.

The final question put to Captain Harris by the prosecution concerned those with whom he had discussed the case. "The persons with whom I have conversed, and from whose conversations I have formed my opinions, were the sailors Holmes, Smith, Miller, and Rhodes, and the Edgars." All those conversations had taken place after Holmes was arrested but before he was charged.

Harris's deposition had something for everyone. The defence had his assertion that their client Holmes was an upstanding fellow and a first-rate sailor who answered to every order. The prosecution had the image of a competent captain giving clear orders to his men. George Harris believed that his deposition would ensure that his honour and reputation would not be impeached.

On 13 April the jury was empanelled. Two potential jurors were excused from serving: John Hopkins "entertained conscientious scruples against sitting upon a jury in a case of homicide" and George Weevil "admitted to have formed an opinion in the case." The other jurors—all male, and, of course, all white—were duly selected. Lawyers for the defence and the prosecution were ready and so, too, was Judge Baldwin. John Wallace, the court reporter, was ready to take down the testimony: beside him at his table were reams of paper and a collection of pens with sharpened nibs. The courtroom was packed. Many of the city's leading citizens were present for the show. There was, as well, a small group of Holmes's supporters from the Seamen's Friend Society and spectators from the local Irish community. Also present were Philadelphia reporters and correspondents writing for more distant newspapers, including the *New York Herald*.

The court clerk called the case in the time-honoured fashion: "Oyez! Oyez! All those with business before the Third District Court of the United States, Judge Henry Baldwin presiding, come forward and be heard." All rose as Judge Baldwin entered, sitting down again after he settled into his chair. The newsmen held their quills poised expectantly over their travelling writing desks, ready to record the events. First, however, Judge Baldwin had a surprise for them.

Like other conservative justices, Baldwin was troubled by a higher court ruling that prevented judges like him from finding journalists in contempt for reporting a trial in progress. It was part of what was wrong with the country, he believed, part of a popular permissiveness that would not serve. People should wait until a verdict was rendered before reviewing the myriad details presented by district attorneys, defence counsel and, perhaps most importantly, a presiding judge. This trial, he had decided, would not be the subject of daily comment by slackers and layabouts.

"Although this court is deprived, by the act of March 2, 1831, of the power to punish, as for a contempt of court, the publication during trial, of testimony in a case," Judge Baldwin announced, "yet, having power to regulate the admission of persons, and the character of proceedings within its own bar, the court can exclude from within the bar any person coming there to report testimony during the trial." In effect, anyone with the temerity to write about the trial while it was underway would be barred from attending the next day. Not only would their access to the trial be lost but the judge might bar them from future trials, too. Thus, even before the trial began, it set a legal precedent permitting the restraint of public reporting while assuring the judge control of the timing, if not the content, of courtroom reports. It was a sufficiently noteworthy action that Judge Baldwin's restraint of the press was included as the first formal headnote, the summary of a case's important legal findings, in the official legal record of *United States v. Holmes*.

AFTER JUDGE BALDWIN had put the press in its place, the prosecution opened the proceedings. It fell to one of the local prosecutors, Oliver Hopkinson, to offer, in his opening remarks, "some of the circumstances

Case No. 15,383.

UNITED STATES v. HOLMES.

[1 Wall. Jr. 1.] [1]

Circuit Court, E. D. Pennsylvania. April 22, 1842.

CONDUCT OF TRIAL—ADMISSION OF PERSONS WITHIN BAR—HOMICIDE BY SEAMEN—SHIPWRECK —ABANDONMENT OF PASSENGERS.

1. Although this court is deprived, by the act of March 2, 1831, of the power to punish, as for a contempt of court, the publication during trial, of testimony in a case, yet. having power to regulate the admission of persons, and the character of proceedings within its own bar. the court can exclude from within the bar any person coming there to report testimony during the trial.

[Cited in U. S. v. Anon., 21 Fed. 768.]

2. Seamen have no right, even in cases of extreme peril to their own lives. to sacrifice the lives of passengers. for the sake of preserving their own. On the contrary, being common carriers, and so paid to protect and carry the passengers, the seamen, beyond the number necessary to navigate the boat, in no circumstances can claim exemption from the common lot of the passengers.

3. In the case here reported. the relative obligations of seamen and passengers, in the event of shipwreck or maritime disaster, are examined and stated.

4. The indictment charged that the prisoner did commit manslaughter on the high seas (1) by casting F. A. from a vessel belonging. etc., whose name was unknown; (2) by casting him from the long-boat of the ship W. B.. belonging. etc. The indictment is sufficiently certain.

The American ship William Brown, left Liverpool on the 13th of March, 1841, bound for Philadelphia, in the United States. She had on board (besides a heavy cargo) 17 of a crew, and 65 passengers, Scotch and Irish emigrants. About 10 o'clock on the night of the 19th of April, when distant 250 miles southeast of Cape Race, Newfoundland, the vessel struck an iceberg, and began to fill so rapidly that it was evident she must soon go down. The long-boat and jolly-boat were cleared away and lowered. The captain, the second mate, 7 of the crew, and 1 passenger got into the jolly-boat. The first mate. 8 seamen. of whom the prisoner was one

---

1 [Reported by John William Wallace, Esq.]

The headnotes defining the precedents in the case of *United States v. Holmes,* 22 April 1842.

attending to the loss of the ship William Brown, and the throwing overboard from the longboat of several of the passengers, among whom was Francis Askin."

His speech, like those of others who participated in the trial, is summarized in *United States v. Holmes* and in the *Trial of Alexander William Holmes,* a pamphlet published later that year by an anonymous author, probably the court reporter John Wallace. In addition, newspaper reports on the trial were published in the *Philadelphia North American,* the *New York Herald* and several other papers. These are all summaries, however. Like the depositions, they are a secretarial, or at best journalistic, abridgement of hours of question and answer boiled down to a few paragraphs. If a verbatim record was kept, it has been lost. What we know about the trial is found only in these summaries. Still, it is possible, especially after reviewing the depositions, to reconstruct both the lawyers' questions and the witnesses' answers, sometimes terse, sometimes verbose.

The official record is at its best when reporting a lawyer's speech, because these were rehearsed orations with copies made for admirers and often for the court reporter. Thus, we do have a near complete text of the opening and closing statements of both the prosecution and the defence. Here, for example, is the overture, Oliver Hopkinson's opening statement.

"Learned colleagues, Mr. Justice Baldwin, members of the jury and citizens of this fine city, we are here to attend to the lamentable events which occurred last year on an American ship returning from Great Britain. On April 19, 1841, the sailing ship William Brown, registered in this city, struck an iceberg in the icy waters of the North Atlantic, carrying with her thirty-two persons and all her cargo to the deeps. This was a tragic event although it is one we know of too frequently. You are not here to lament the passing of those poor souls or to praise the salvation of fully more than half the ship's complement. Over forty souls were saved to a large overcrowded longboat, and more in a small, heroic jolly boat. The latter was under the command of the William Brown's Captain Harris, from whom you will hear. He delegated command of the larger vessel to his first mate, Francis Rhodes.

"The two small vessels separated the day after the William Brown's sinking and on that first night of solitude the crew of the longboat drowned sixteen of their passengers. Testimony to be given at this trial will make it clear that one who did these deeds was the accused, Alexander William Holmes. Members of the jury, you are here to consider the charge of 'unlawful homicide,' only, and not of a felonious or malicious homicide. In other words, the prisoner is charged with the commission of a homicide without premeditation or malice, on the one hand, and without justification or excuse upon the other."

After pausing for effect, Hopkinson carried on to state the essence of the matter: "The trial of such a case has never before occurred in any nation, nor have the writers of law, with perhaps one exception, ever considered the particulars of the case before you. The learned Judge Baldwin will instruct you in the law. But for our purposes I may say this: If you believe the defendant was justified in killing others in the base hope of his own survival, you will acquit him. Should you decide, upon hearing all the evidence, that there was a duty to the passengers above and beyond the sailor's own salvation, you must find him guilty."

Hopkinson then tackled the sticky legal point of the ownership of the *William Brown*. "The indictment of the prisoner has been framed in such a manner as to meet any technical objections which might be urged from the fact that the homicide occurred from on board a boat without a specific name," he said, with a glance at the defence counsel. That the longboat itself was unnamed might, he worried, make it seem a legally stateless vessel and thus raise jurisdictional issues. To forestall this, he stated the obvious: "It can only be described as the 'longboat of the ship William Brown' whose owners, men of this city, will testify to you as to that fact." The problem of which Philadelphian owned the ship when it sank was one he would tackle when questioning the witnesses.

"In your deliberations," Hopkinson concluded, "please keep before you the only issue you are asked to judge: Did the prisoner, on the night in question, attack and drown the passenger Francis Askin, a passenger in that longboat, or not?"

THE TRIAL

THE COURTROOM WAS PACKED on the first day of testimony, Thursday, 14 April. Journalists sat quietly in the rows reserved for them by Judge Baldwin, a press box their reward for not publishing stories during the trial. The air of excitement made it feel like an important event. "The courtroom was crowded for near a week with much of the beauty, fashion, and intelligence of the city," according to defence lawyer David Paul Brown. The newspapers had promised a show, and Oliver Hopkinson's opening remarks for the prosecution the day before had been, all agreed, a better than acceptable prologue to the drama that was about to unfold.

Bridget McGee, the most vocal survivor of the *William Brown,* was the prosecution's lead witness. Dressed in a decent but inexpensive dress, she was the Irish colleen all had heard about, attractive and demure and outspoken at once.

Oliver Hopkinson understood his audience, and his judge. It was his place to open for the prosecution, to prepare both judge and jury for his senior colleague, George Dallas. Hopkinson's plan was to start his questioning slowly, to give both judge and jury time to warm to Bridget McGee and her testimony. He knew that her version of the events in the longboat would serve the prosecution well.

"Please tell us, Miss McGee, your relation to the William Brown and the events that occurred on its voyage," Hopkinson began. "I was a passenger on board the William Brown," she replied. "We left Liverpool on the 13th of March, 1841. But it was on the 19th of April when we struck on the iceberg."

"And where were you when that happened?" Hopkinson asked kindly.

"We were all in our beds," Bridget said primly. "When a man said we were sinking, we all rushed on deck where the sailors were getting out the longboat and the jolly boat. I waited until the longboat was got out and then I got in...some of the other passengers were before me."

"And when you entered the longboat, seeking your place, did anyone try to dislodge you?" Hopkinson continued. "Yes," she replied, looking directly at Holmes. "He called to me after I got in and said we must get out of the boat and go aboard the ship again."

"You mean the defendant," Hopkinson asked, "Alexander William Holmes?" "Yes, sir," she said, pointing, "that man over there." McGee then added, "I was in the stern of the boat when he ordered me out. But I told him I would not leave the boat and go back to the sinking ship. He turned from me and said no more."

"And were you the only one so addressed?" "No," the witness replied. "He ordered Bridget Nugent to leave the boat, too. But when she refused, he said no more, and never gave a reason for his order."

In pretrial strategy discussions, the prosecution lawyers had decided to introduce Holmes's rescue of Isabella Edgar at the beginning of the trial in order to defuse its power. Hopkinson, therefore, next asked McGee if she had seen anyone leave the longboat. Nodding again toward the defence table, she said, "I saw Holmes leave, climb back aboard and then bring one more passenger into the longboat. Her name was Isabella Edgar." The whole was told matter of factly, as if it were not an important point. But it was, of course. Holmes's rescue was the defence's strongest argument for his character.

"When your complement was complete, how many passengers were you?" Hopkinson next asked. "When the boat pushed away from the ship we were thirty-two passengers aboard," McGee replied. "The ship went down a little afterward."

"Then Captain Harris departed, didn't he?" "No," McGee answered. "The captain's boat—the jolly boat—and the longboat stayed together until morning, when the captain gave Francis Rhodes, the mate, a compass and chart and told him he was 250 miles from land. In the morning the captain took down the names of the crew and the passengers in our boat and then he left. During that day, Tuesday, the sailors and passengers bailed and rowed constantly."

"Now we come to that painful night, the night of Tuesday, April 20," Hopkinson prompted. "Please describe the events as you experienced them."

The courtroom grew still as Bridget McGee paused, remembering. The only sound was the scratching of pen quills across paper as reporters scrambled to catch up. "About 10 o'clock they commenced throwing the passengers out of the longboat. The first I heard was Owen Riley. I heard him cry to the Scotch woman, Mrs. Edgar, to speak to the sailors to spare his life. I don't know who was the next man, but they caught hold then of Francis Askin. He, too, first called on the Scotch woman to speak to the sailors to spare his life, but she said nothing at either time. When they came to throw him over, Frank said that all he had was five sovereigns but he would give them if they would spare his life until morning. Nobody cared. Mr. Askin had two sisters in the boat. One named Mary said that if they threw her brother over, they might as well throw her after him. After they did as she said, they looked for and threw over the other sister, Ellen, too."

McGee's deposition, made in Le Havre, however, stated that she had not seen anyone dispatched, that she only heard the cries of some of those thrown overboard. It also said she believed that she had been kindly treated by the crew. The defence could not question her about these inconsistencies, however, because the Le Havre depositions were never made available to them.

Hopkinson slowly turned from Bridget McGee to the jury, and from them to the audience at large, as she calmly recited the names of the persons who had been drowned. Now he turned back to her and asked in a low, almost inaudible voice, if that had been the end of the carnage. She shook her head as if to dislodge his interruption, a distraction to her memories. "The next I know of, Holmes there was catching hold of James Black. He was a passenger. Holmes caught a hold of him and said, 'Who is this?' Black answered, 'Why, it's James Black.' When the mate heard this, he said to Holmes, 'Don't part man and wife,' and they did not throw him over. Then Holmes came to Charles Conlin, who was sitting next to me. When he saw Holmes coming, Mr. Conlin said, 'Holmes, dear, you will not put me out, will you?' 'Yes, Charlie, you'll go, too,' Holmes answered. And he did."

There were two ways to interpret this. The defence might argue it was evidence that Francis Rhodes was indeed in command, ordering the killings as a captain directing men sworn to obey. To the prosecution, however, this was evidence that Holmes was an active and willing independent murderer.

Here Bridget McGee paused, and Hopkinson asked if that was the end of her tale. She indicated it was not, and continued: "Mr. Conlin was the last person they threw out of the boat that night, but there were two others that remained in the boat they did not see. In the morning, the sailors saw these other two men; one of them was under a seat, and the other under the stern of the boat. They had hid themselves there, John Nugent and another man whose name I don't remember. At daylight these two commenced bailing the boat and when they had done, the sailors threw them out, too. About an hour and a half after that, we were picked up by the Crescent."

Hopkinson asked whom it was that Bridget McGee meant when she talked about "the sailors." "I mean that Charles Smith, Alexander William Holmes, Jack Stetson and a coloured man, the cook, Henry Murray, did so."

And the mate, Hopkinson asked, did he participate? No, McGee said. She didn't see him drown any of the longboat's passengers.

There was a sigh of satisfaction in the courtroom. This was what they had come to hear: the tragic tale of people saved from the sinking of a sailing vessel only to be drowned in the longboat by its crew. The prosecution had made its point, and, with the recitation of persons killed, had stated the essential facts of its case.

Now Hopkinson went on to focus on the details. Was the longboat filled with water during the journey or during that horrible night? No, Bridget McGee replied. "There was not much water in the boat the second night; there was more on the first."

And, prompted Hopkinson, the passengers helped by bailing? Yes, she answered, they would stop and start, as each saw fit, or as directed by the sailors. But, the lawyer continued, wasn't there water in the longboat on that second night? Yes, she said, but the water was from the eternal rain and not from a leak.

Hopkinson suggested that perhaps the boat was so crowded there was no room to bail or work the oars. What he really wanted—to reinforce the prosecution's strategy of casting doubt on the defence of necessity—was the answer that Bridget McGee was pleased to give, the insistence that such was not, in fact, the case. "There was plenty of room to work the boat," she claimed, "and for bailing and rowing it, too. There was enough room for this before the passengers were thrown out."

"Thank you, Miss McGee," Hopkinson politely concluded.

As Hopkinson sat down, defence lawyer David Paul Brown gathered his notes before standing up. He knew it would be a mistake to attack Bridget McGee too fiercely. The last thing he wanted was for her to gain more sympathy. All he could do on Holmes's behalf was to blunt the edge of the essential fact to which she testified and which he could not dispute: Bridget McGee had seen Alexander William Holmes throw Francis Askin and others from the longboat into the sea.

"Prior to today," Brown began, "who has questioned you about this case?" She thought a moment and then replied, "I have not been examined in regard to this matter before. I had my statement taken in writing in France, but not since I came to America." Brown seemed puzzled by this and asked, "But didn't you testify on this matter last autumn?" She explained that testifying and being examined were, to her, different matters. "I was examined before the grand jury, and have been examined by Mr. Dallas," she said with a nod to the prosecution's benches, "but by no one else."

"And when you left Ireland, Miss McGee, did you travel alone?" Brown asked. No, she said. "My uncle, George Duffy, shipped with me at Liverpool. He was one of those thrown out." Before Brown could ask another question, she added, "I was not related to any other person on board the vessel nor had I seen any of the passengers before I went on board at Liverpool. I didn't know where they came from, but I was on friendly terms with them on the voyage."

"And the crew, Miss McGee, were you friendly with them, and perhaps Mr. Holmes, on the voyage?" Brown asked. "I never spoke to Holmes on the voyage but once, I think," she replied. "But you had an animus toward him?" When she looked at him blankly, Brown hastened to choose another word: "That is to say, perhaps, a disregard." No, she said. Holmes had never shown her or Bridget Nugent or any of the others any unkindness during the voyage until that night.

Changing gears, Brown asked her to remember the night the ship sank. When did she first learn the ship was in trouble? "It was a quarter of an hour after the shock when James Black called down that the ship was sinking. I heard them pumping as soon as the ship struck, but there was no water in the steerage when I left it," she began. "I saw Holmes as soon as I got on deck. He was throwing wood and things from the longboat over the side, before they launched the boat. The cook and Jack Stetson were helping him. The jolly boat was hanging out of the bow, and the sailors were getting her ready to put into the water. The longboat was then launched by Holmes and other sailors."

"So you were first into the boat, Miss McGee?" No, she replied. "I can't say who got into her first. Bridget was in when I got in. The boat was nearly full. There were men and women in her when I got in, but James Black and his wife came after me."

"And this," Brown asked carefully, "is when you say the defendant asked you to leave?" Yes, she nodded, looking at Holmes in the dock. "It was before James Black and his wife came in that Holmes ordered Bridget Nugent and me to go on board the ship again. Holmes addressed himself to me even though there were others in the boat who were afterwards thrown out." And so, Brown persisted, he ordered the others out as well? "I heard him tell no one else but Bridget and me to leave the boat. He gave no reason but took hold of Bridget by the shoulders when he told her to go onboard the ship. I heard her saying he might pull her about as much as he pleased but she would not get out."

"But the defendant did not force you or Bridget Nugent away, did he?" Brown pressed. "No," McGee admitted, "he did not." There was no need for Brown to suggest that McGee had not forgiven Holmes for trying to remove her from the longboat. That was clear to all and to emphasize it would have been overkill.

Brown then asked, "And of all the sailors and passengers in the longboat or the jolly boat, was he the only man who returned to the William Brown to attempt a rescue, let alone the only man among passenger or crew to effect one?" She nodded agreement but said nothing, her silent refusal to credit Holmes implying a great deal, until the lawyer asked her to again describe the moment. "I heard this girl's sisters cry out for her from the boat. Her mother was on board. He climbed up and went on board to carry the girl on his back. It was about an hour after Holmes came on with the girl that the ship went down but by then we were half a mile from the ship."

Brown now turned to the condition of the longboat, to the fact that the drownings took place in extreme conditions when the sailors and passengers alike feared for their lives. "You told Mr. Hopkinson that the passengers bailed as they saw fit, or as the sailors ordered. I take it the longboat was leaky, and water-filled?" McGee responded, "Some hours after Holmes tried to put us out that first night, I discovered water in the boat. No part of me was wet but my feet, sir. And the next morning Mr. Rhodes did not complain to the captain that she was leaky and that day they could bail with the passengers sitting up. There was room for it."

Damn woman, Brown must have thought. Others would insist the boat was overcrowded with people and filling with water. But to hear Bridget McGee tell it, there was plenty of room and no more than a few inches of water lapping at her shoes. "And so there was no time when the boat seemed on the verge of being overwhelmed by the sea?" he asked incredulously. "You didn't hear the sailors cry for God's help because of the water?" No, she replied, never. "The water came into our boat once from her canting," she stated, "but I never heard them say in the boat, 'God help us, we are all sinking.'"

Did she at least see Holmes give his warm peacoat to one of the passengers? No, McGee said, she saw the first mate give his coat to one of the Edgars, but not Holmes, because, "I was in a different part of the boat."

Brown then turned to the drownings, to the other sailors who were involved. But again Bridget McGee remembered mostly Holmes. "I don't know who threw Riley or Duffy over, but it was one of the four sailors I mentioned. I know Holmes threw Conlin over, and that Mary Carr got hold of him and said he should spare Conlin as he was the father of a family of fifteen. And I know," she hurried on, "that he assisted in throwing out the rest. I knew it was he from his voice and the calling to him. I know Askin's sister was thrown over, too, but not who by. And she had nothing but her nightclothes on, and when they were about to throw her over she begged them to give her a cloak."

There was another collective sigh from the audience, involuntary and heartfelt. The testimony was grand, graphic, horrifying. They had been promised a show and a philosophy lecture. The latter was to come, but the drama of it all certainly matched and perhaps exceeded their expectations.

Brown next asked about the morning of 21 April, when the last two passengers were drowned. Bridget said she did not see their murders but insisted that the men were obviously not comatose, since they'd been bailing until they were shoved overboard by Smith and Joseph Stetson. That would have been devastating testimony had they been on trial, but they were not. Holmes was. And because Holmes was charged only with the death of Francis Askin, the details of the others were tangential, though perhaps damaging to the minds of the jury. Brown realized that the prosecution wanted all the deaths to be described and discussed not because they were relevant to Holmes's guilt but to encourage the jury to convict someone in the case. Against this there was no defence but to excuse the witness as soon as possible.

"I am finished, Your Honour," Brown said, then returned to his seat. It had been as bad as he had expected and perhaps a little worse.

Next, Oliver Hopkinson called Joseph P. Vogel, who testified simply that he owned the *William Brown* when she was lost. "I purchased her from Stephen Baldwin on the 30th of December, 1840, without reference to that final voyage. She was to have been delivered to me in this city but never did arrive."

On cross-examination, David Paul Brown asked Vogel how he could own a ship that was never delivered. Since he had paid for her, Vogel shrugged, he owned her. Because the deal had not involved the profits of the last voyage, they were not his concern. He was out his money and out his ship and that was enough proof of ownership, he said. From this, we finally learn the answer to Rhodes's question of Captain Harris: the ship was not insured for loss.

The last witness of the day was Mary Corr. When Brown questioned her, she said that on that first night, "After the ship went down one of the women discovered that the plug in the bottom of the boat was out. It was Sarah Carr who put her hand over the hole and gave a piece of her dress to stop it." "And so," asked Brown, "the sea was stopped by a bit of female clothing?" Yes, Mary Corr agreed, "at least until the sailors cut another plug with an axe."

"Before the drownings, did you hear folks crying that the boat might be filling, or sinking, or words like that?" asked Brown. Yes, she replied, and Brown could have kissed her for that memory. "There were

TRIAL

OF

ALEXANDER WILLIAM HOLMES,

ONE OF THE CREW OF THE SHIP

WILLIAM BROWN,

FOR

MANSLAUGHTER ON THE HIGH SEAS,

BEFORE THE CHIEF JUSTICE OF THE UNITED STATES CIRCUIT COURT
FOR THE EASTERN DISTRICT OF PENNSYLVANIA.

———

PHILADELPHIA, 1842.

The title page of the pamphlet *Trial of Alexander William Holmes,* published in Philadelphia in 1842.

exclamations of 'the boat is sinking' before and at the time the passengers were thrown overboard." She added, "As I swore before the grand jury and swear now, I heard the mate say, after the men had been bailing some time, 'This work won't do, the boat must be lightened.'"

And with that the trial ended for the day.

ON THE THIRD DAY OF THE TRIAL, Friday, 15 April, Judge Baldwin took a moment to compliment the journalists who sat in his courtroom. None had published a word the day before, and he was "gratified to observe the editors of your newspapers have acquiesced in regards my request not to publish these proceedings while the trial is in progress."

Oliver Hopkinson then called young Owen Carr to the witness box. He had been asleep when the ship struck the ice and "threw me from my bunk by the impact. When James Black hallooed his wife to come and fetch a blanket with her for the ship was sinking, I went on deck where they were cutting the boats from the side of the ship. I went down again to get some clothes—I was nearly naked—and when I came up the longboat was going over the side of the ship. I tried to get in but fell out, when Julia McCadden pushed me in again."

In the longboat the first night, Carr saw Joseph Stetson put the bailing plug back into its hole, the plug Mary Corr said had been dislodged. Some others said it was Holmes who first fixed the plug, but the inconsistency went unremarked. The next morning, Carr continued, the captain left, and all that day they rowed until nighttime, when "they began to throw the men overboard." "Who did this?" asked Hopkinson. "The cook, Stetson and Holmes threw them over—laying hold of and forcing them over," Carr replied. That was exactly what the prosecution wanted, another witness naming Holmes.

Now it was time for George Dallas to stand and finish the questioning for the prosecution. How big was this plug, he asked, the one that had been dislodged and the sailor Stetson had replaced. "It was not as big as my fist," Carr said. "It was, say, the size of a chair post." At this, Dallas raised his hand and brought thumb and forefinger together to make an oval perhaps an inch in circumference. "And was the boat wet?" he asked. "There was a little water there," the boy replied. "Some came in at the plug and some was the rain. I couldn't know what was from where." Some of the sailors said the makeshift plug was too small, he remembered hearing, but that was all.

"When the sailors threw over the passengers, where were you sitting?" Dallas asked. "I was back of Mary Carr when they commenced," he said, "back toward the stern. I heard Holmes say nothing except when Charles Conlin stood up and said, 'Holmes, you won't throw me over,' and Mr. Holmes said, 'Charlie, you must go.' And then he did. I know this 'cause Conlin was beside me."

David Paul Brown then rose to try and mitigate the damage. It was time to focus on the captain, and on Francis Rhodes, to see if they could be presented as the real culprits in the affair. And so Brown asked Owen Carr about the meeting between the captain and Rhodes the morning after the sinking. Carr said, "The captain said he believed he would be going away. The mate said he might stay the day but the captain, he made no reply. The mate then asked the captain to take some of the passengers into the jolly boat as ours was deeply loaded, but the captain, he said he had enough."

When pressed, Carr insisted, "I didn't hear nothing about them casting lots. I don't recollect anything said by the mate, or Holmes, or anybody, for I fell over asleep after the captain left us." "But," Brown protested, "you told the grand jury the sailors said the boat was sinking before they threw the passengers over." "I don't recollect that," Carr said, "and I don't know that they said it so." Almost piteously, Carr restated that he was cold and tired and that he had lost his family the night before when the *William Brown* sank. There was nothing for him to do on the longboat, so he slept through most of its voyage, hearing only a little, and what he heard he had testified to. Of the rest, well, he had sworn God's oath to tell the truth and that was what he was trying to do.

A woodblock print featuring a banner with the motto "Don't Give Up the Ship."

The witness was excused and Brown sat down, trying hard to hide his satisfaction. Owen Carr's testimony had been blunted. He had said one thing to the grand jury and another to the court. And since he admitted to having slept through most of the events on the longboat, his testimony had to be at least discounted if not wholly disregarded by the jurors.

The rest of the day's witnesses corroborated and filled out Bridget McGee's testimony, each offering a little bit more detail. Next to be sworn was Ann Bradley, who told the court she "saw Frank Askin thrown over by Holmes, and three or four others. Frank was sitting between his two sisters, and when they came up to him, one of his sisters said they ought not to separate him from them. Holmes laid hold and called for the others to help him or Askin would have him over, he struggled so. Frank begged for his life, saying he would work like a man if they would spare him for that night." Where was she sitting through these events? As the passengers were being thrown overboard, Ann Bradley said, she quietly moved from her place in the centre of the longboat toward the stern, "because I was afraid they would throw me over, too."

Bradley remembered sailors fixing the bailing plug the first night and that most of the water she saw in the boat was from rain that fell after the passengers were thrown out. "I heard one of Mrs. Edgar's daughters say the boat would sink," she testified, but because of where she sat she did not see the passengers being drowned. All she knew was what she had heard.

The next witness, Julie McCadden, told George Dallas that she had refused Holmes's command to give up her seat in the longboat. She, too, saw Holmes bring Isabella Edgar on his back into the boat. And, like the others, she saw "Holmes and the coloured man—the cook—throw Owen Riley out of the boat. They first told him to stand up. I thought they were going to make him bail, but when he stood, they took hold of him and they threw him out, and he cried three times to Isabella Edgar and to her mother but received no answer from them." "Why," Dallas asked, "did they call to the Scotch woman and her daughter?" McCadden shrugged. "I thought it strange to hear the man's cry."

"And who was next drowned?" Dallas asked. "They laid hold of Duffy, who told them he had a wife and three children on land and asked for the honour of God they save him for his family's sake. But they told him it was no use and put him over. Then Frank Askin asked them to spare his life till morning and offered them five sovereigns. He told them if they would spare him till then and God sent no relief that he would go over himself." "Did they listen?" Dallas queried. "No," McCadden replied. "They put him out."

And were anyone's pleas for salvation answered by the crew? Yes, she said. "I sat alongside of the Scotch family on Tuesday night. Mrs. Edgar called Holmes and asked him if they would throw her or any of her family out. Charlie Smith answered no, and Holmes did the same, saying they should not be thrown out, that they—the sailors—would themselves go first." The implication was clear. The murders were not random, but considered. The sailors had chosen their victims.

"Was the boat wet?" Dallas asked. "Well," Julie McCadden replied, "on Monday night I felt some water coming into the boat very fast and I called Holmes and put his hand down to the place and told him the boat was beginning to leak. And then I pulled some rags out of me pocket, rolled them up and put them to the place. Holmes, he looked for the cork or something, but when he could not find it the sailors took an axe and made a new plug to put it in. Afterwards that night I heard some say the plug was coming out again. And that's really all I know."

Despite a gruelling cross-examination, she offered little for the defence. When David Paul Brown asked about Isabella Edgar's rescue, she said she had seen it and that the girl had cried, "I am coming, Mother, I am coming," as Holmes carried her on his back from the deck of the sinking ship. And, like some of the others, she had heard Rhodes say to the captain, before the boats separated, "that his boat was so overcrowded they would have to cast lots. The captain replied, 'Say no more about it. I know what you will have to do.'"

The defence lawyer circled this point again and again, focussing on Rhodes's pleas and his later failure to consider a lottery. Did the mate ever ask the passengers to draw lots? Did they ever draw lots among themselves? What did she think the captain meant when he said, "I know what you will have to do"? "Oh yes," Brown added, changing gears, "did you see anyone rise from the longboat to offer a rescue for any passenger, excepting Holmes rescue of the Edgar girl?" And did she think Holmes had a reason to favour the Edgars, at least any more than the captain did? McCadden patiently, almost doggedly answered each question. No, she saw nobody else rise from the longboat to attempt a rescue. No, she did not think Holmes was especially nice to the Edgars excepting, of course, that he rescued the daughter. Otherwise, "I don't know what else the captain might have meant and never heard anyone in the longboat say they were casting lots."

It is hard to tell who was the more frustrated by what the *Trial of Alexander William Holmes* calls "a very rigorous cross-examination." The defence wanted both an acknowledgement of Holmes's heroism and of the culpability of others but, somehow, they could not get Julie McCadden to admit those. When Mr. Brown told her she might leave the stand, the witness nodded very significantly and said, "Well, good-bye to ye!"

The next witness was Sarah Corr, who told Hopkinson that first mate Francis Rhodes had tried to give up command of the longboat. "I heard the mate ask one of the men if he knew navigation. The man replied yes. Then, Rhodes said, 'I give up all charge of the boat.'" And while she thought it might have been Rhodes's voice, she couldn't swear that it was he who said, just before the killing began, "God help me, this won't do. Men, fall to work."

Corr was still somewhat scandalized that, when the sailors grabbed James MacAvoy, most of them wanted to refuse his request for five minutes of prayer before his death. "Fortunately for his immortal soul," she added, "Murray, the coloured man, said he should have the time. McAvoy then said a prayer and they threw him out. Frank Askin told them if they would spare him till morning and then cast lots, he would go out himself if it came his turn. But they threw him out then anyway, and after that his sister Mary. Then they said they might as well throw Ellen out, too."

She added, "After they had thrown most of the men out, the sailors looked for more, and told the women not to hide them as they would not leave a damned soul of them in the boat. And then the next day they found Keegan [Hugh Keigham], who Jack Stetson pushed over head first after getting him to stand up and bail."

"Was this shocking?" Hopkinson asked. "Indeed it was," she replied. "Even the mate on seeing this cried 'Lord! Cruel, cruel.'"

Sarah Corr would have been a fine witness for the prosecution if Jack Stetson were on trial, or even Francis Rhodes. At this trial, however, all she did was spread the blame to those who, free of any legal charge, were safely at sea.

It was mid-afternoon when, for a change of pace, the prosecution called Stephen Baldwin to testify that he had owned the *William Brown* and had sold it to Joseph T. Vogel, who was the owner when the vessel was lost. Baldwin had transferred ownership of the ship to Vogel before 19 April. If there was any legal question about ownership, and thus the wording of Holmes's indictment, this testimony was designed to quash it.

On cross-examination, David Paul Brown asked Baldwin to comment on Captain Harris's character, hoping to hear, perhaps, that the man was a cowardly drunken lout. Maybe he wanted exactly what he got, however, the prosecution's strenuous objection to the question of character. "I had only hoped to avoid calling the captain later in the trial, Your Honour," Brown said. "But as my learned colleague objects, I will not here press the issue." It was pure theatre, of course. Captain Harris was at sea and unavailable to the defence.

The last hour of the afternoon was spent with Bridget Nugent, whose testimony was almost identical to that of the other women, her friends. A year had passed since the affair of the longboat, and the young women had been together, first in Le Havre, then on the *Richmond* and since then in Philadelphia's Irish community. No wonder their testimony was so alike and so consistent. They had been retelling it to each other for all that time.

ON SATURDAY, 16 APRIL, William Meredith, the federal attorney, informed the court that the prosecution's case was complete. He had been central neither to its planning nor its presentation, but because Holmes was charged under federal statute, it was Meredith's job to announce that the prosecution would rest.

Now it was the turn of the defence team. David Paul Brown, Isaac Hazlehurst and Edward Armstrong had no secret witnesses, no brilliant legal strategy. All they could do was attempt to prove necessity and introduce witnesses who might help them do so. And, of course, they could argue eloquently on their client's behalf. A natural experiment in philosophy and ethics had been promised. That is what the audience would get.

THE DEFENCE OF NECESSITY

Isaac Hazlehurst rose on Saturday, 16 April, to open for the
defence. "Is this a case for the application of the federal law, the act of
Congress that prescribes the punishment for manslaughter on the
high seas?" he asked the jury. "Does this case body forth those exhibitions
of violence, heat, and passion," he asked rhetorically, relishing each word,
"which are indispensable to consummate the crime? Let not the excitement of friends, or the melancholy and distressing recital of details, draw
you from the truth, the great truth, to which your attention is directed.
Though friend after friend may have perished on that awful night—
though scenes of the most heart-rending character have been presented
by surviving friends and relatives—let us press onward in the inquiry to
find in the terrible reality of the case a legal refuge for the prisoner."

In doing so, Hazlehurst insisted, the law itself would be vindicated
and the nation's reputation for justice satisfied. And so, having equated
Holmes's salvation with the well-being of a just nation, he reviewed once
more the details of the *William Brown*'s sinking and the salvation of the
surviving passengers in the longboat. It took him at least a half an hour of
heavy oratory to describe the danger of the longboat—overloaded and
filling with water—and of the sense of doom that sailors and passengers
had shared as they watched the *William Brown* sink.

"Toward the end of the first day, the sea, which had been calm now
became rough and night closed upon them under circumstances of the
most appalling character. The longboat which during the day was scarcely

able to float now required the aid of all who could work her to keep her from sinking. The sailors were unable to secure the plug in the boat, the boat was half full, her gunwales on a level with the water, and was so crowded from stem to stern that the oars could not be used. The sea and the ice washed over them, those in the boat could distinctly hear the ice grating against the vessel as it rushed past.

"What would you do in such a situation? What course was to be pursued in an emergency so awful, so sudden, and which had fallen upon them under the signal dispensation of the Almighty? The danger was instantaneous—the emergency demanded an instant effort of power. What is the active principle at such an hour of hopeless despair?" he asked the jury. "Self-preservation," he answered, as if the word were itself a token of power. "What will justify it, you ask? The law of nature, that great principle which is paramount to all obligations, common to all men, that is constant, immutable, eternal. Self-preservation is a principle that the rudeness of ignorance cannot stifle, the inanition of refinement cannot extinguish."

That's the ticket, the audience thought. This is what we came to hear: duty versus self-preservation, man for others or each man for himself.

Hazlehurst continued. "It was thus, by the natural principle of self-preservation, that the prisoner was impelled. There was no malice under pretence of necessity; there could have been none in the bosom of the mariner as he gazed upon the helpless crowd clinging to him on that awful night. There was no passion to swell the horrors of the dread necessity—for the arm of the prisoner was extended even then to protect the weak and the timid.

"On the deck of the William Brown the prisoner had served the passengers to the utmost of his power—his arm had been extended to save as long as safety was possible. Wasn't he the last to escape from the sinking ship, young Miss Edgar on his back?"

And Hazlehurst then offered necessity as a defence in law, a shield of rectitude for the man charged with manslaughter who was, in fact, a hero. "If the evidence will present that case of necessity which I have described, the course of the defendant was justified by a principle which can only be appreciated under the terrible circumstances detailed here. The law of nature herself permits it not upon the principle of simply impunity but upon a higher obligation traced to the absolute approbation of The

Author of all laws. The prisoner had a right to preserve himself. He was justified in lightening the vessel. The preservation of his life was lawful in itself, and the means were made lawful by being unavoidable."

Holmes must have hated this. To save him, his own lawyer was impugning his actions, his very self-respect. He was innocent, the defence claimed, because he was a natural coward acting for himself, albeit understandably, at the expense of others. Never mind that his captain had told him to follow Rhodes's orders and that those orders, given at least three times, had been followed by others as well as by Holmes.

Then Hazlehurst quoted a range of writers, including Francis Bacon, Blackstone's legal commentaries and William Shakespeare, on the nature of man. He reminded the jury that the friendless Swedish prisoner had been nine months detained while awaiting trial. Nine months, he reminded them, was an eternity to a sailor used to the open world of the sea. "A stranger here, no heart beats for his return, no voice of recognition reaches him; no arm is extended in friendship to renew the assurances of gratitude for what he did do for the survivors of this terrible tragedy. The perils of the sea have given place to the perils of this trial."

Hazlehurst took more than an hour to finish his argument, insisting that Holmes was first a victim of the longboat—he, too, had suffered—and secondly of the law under which he was charged. He entered into evidence the depositions of Walter Parker, the second mate, and of Captain George Harris. The court reporter slowly read to the jury the statements and cross-examinations of the two witnesses who were happily at sea. By the time the reading was finished and the depositions formally entered as evidence, it was time for lunch.

That afternoon, it was David Paul Brown's turn. He began by calling Jane Johnston Edgar to the stand. Unlike Bridget McGee, she had found the longboat crowded and wet. "The boat was so crowded that my head was pressed almost off against a seat and an oar. I put my hand on the edge of the boat to lift myself up and my hand was then in the water outside the boat." "And were you afraid?" Brown asked kindly. Yes, she replied, "I said to Isabel we should all be lost. She said we must trust to the Almighty."

"The night of the drownings, did you hear the mate tell his men to lighten the boat?" Brown asked. "I heard the mate say this work would not do and tell the men to go to work or they would all be lost. I felt the boat move backward and forwards as the men got up on their feet. They sat down again afterward and the boat was still."

"And then it was over?" Brown prompted. No, Jane Edgar said, "That was only the first attempt, the one before the drownings truly began. The mate again called them up and said they must fall to work or all would perish. I heard them lay hold of a man near me and I lifted the cover I had on my head against the rain and saw it was Owen Riley. I heard him call on Mrs. Edgar and Isabel three times, and on Julie McCadden, too. Because my head was covered, I did not see but I heard him and the others going over. I heard Frank Askin call on Mrs. Edgar, and while she answered something, I did not hear her words. I heard his sister, Mary, say she would die the death of her brother. I heard when they took hold of Black the mate said they should not part man and wife."

"And the next morning, after the drownings, what did you see?" Brown questioned. "I saw Holmes with a quilt belonging to James Patrick," Edgar replied. "He tried to raise a sail but the wind was too strong. Then he stood up and saw the masts of a vessel. We were all going to rise with him but he told us to sit down as the ship would not take us aboard if they saw so many of us. Then he walked forward with an oar to loosen us from the ice at the front of the boat."

"And so Holmes was in charge at this time?" Brown pressed. "It was the prisoner who ordered your efforts for rescue?" Yes, she answered. "Before this the mate had asked the men what to do. Holmes said we ought not to steer for Newfoundland as we could never reach it, but to go south, as it would be warmer and we might meet a vessel. The mate said he would do as he, Holmes, wanted. And so he did and we were saved."

Brown paused to let this information sink in before asking if Holmes had seemed to her a violent, wanton man, or one concerned for the welfare of all. "I saw nothing unbehaving of him in all the time we were aboard," she replied. "After Askin was thrown over, someone asked if the sailors were going to throw any more, and Holmes said, 'No, no more should be thrown over. If any others were to be lost we would all be lost together.'"

George Dallas's cross-examination of Jane Johnston Edgar was mercifully brief, as the case against Holmes for the manslaughter of Francis Askin was made. Others might be more culpable than the prisoner, but it was the Swede who was on trial. More for form's sake than out of real interest, Dallas wanted to know if there had been a great deal of water in the longboat. "Indeed there was. It was on Tuesday night that the water was nearly up to my knees. When they bailed, the water went down, but it was always there around my feet at least."

Jane Johnston Edgar was the last witness that Saturday, and the trial recessed until Monday.

On Monday, Susannah Edgar was the first defence witness to be called to the stand. She was eloquent on both the state of the longboat and Holmes's kindness. "Was the boat crowded, Miss Edgar?" David Paul Brown asked. It was, she replied. "In bailing, one man filled the bucket and another passed it over the side, as it was impossible for the man that filled the bucket to get up to empty it on account of the crowded state of the boat." And yes, she said, the boat rode dangerously low in the water. "The gunwale of the boat was so near the water's edge just before the passengers were thrown out that my fingers touched the water when I grasped the side of the boat to raise myself up. When they raised the longboat aboard the Crescent, I saw a hole in her bottom and thought to myself, there's the one that caused this all," she testified.

"What was Holmes's demeanour?" asked Brown. "The passengers looked very distressed on Wednesday morning before he spied the Crescent," she answered, "but Holmes said we should keep our hearts up, and hope."

Next called was Eliza Lafferty, the one emigrant in Captain Harris's jolly boat. Of all the survivors, she was perhaps best qualified to speak to the conversation between Harris and Rhodes who, she testified, had not wanted command of the longboat and would have preferred to be in the jolly boat with the captain. In fact, she said, Rhodes first sat there, but the captain told him his place was elsewhere. "Rhodes was put into the longboat because he knew navigation. He objected to going at first because the longboat was very full, the gunwale near the water."

Had she heard Rhodes speak to the captain the next morning before the jolly boat sailed for Newfoundland? She replied that she had heard some of what was said. "The mate told the captain that the longboat could not live, and the captain said he understood but should say no more."

Eliza Lafferty then opened her purse and offered a letter she had recently received from James Patrick, who had returned to Ireland, refusing to chance the ocean again. Brown seemed surprised, but thought Patrick's comments on the case—and the lamentable events of the longboat—might be of interest. He told Judge Baldwin, "I have not read this letter myself, but it is pertinent to ask that—contents unseen—it be offered into evidence." George Dallas objected, of course. He wanted no surprises to affect the otherwise smooth path toward Holmes's conviction. "It's nothing I have seen or read or known about and it should not be entered at this time," he protested. Judge Baldwin agreed and the letter was not read in court.

Next, Mrs. Margaret Edgar was called to the stand. For all the testimony about her by others, she had little to say for herself. Yes, Holmes gave her his jacket as a cover, and yes, he had gone back to the ship to rescue her daughter. No, she had known nothing of the happenings in the longboat. Her head was covered against the rain, and she saw little throughout her ordeal. All she knew was that there was an eternal fight against the water, men bailing all the time, and that they were rescued by the grace of God in the person of the *Crescent* on Wednesday morning.

The penultimate defence witness was Isabella Edgar. "I had been sick from the time we left Liverpool until the day we struck," she said, "and had not been on deck before that final night." After putting on a dress, she went "on deck where I helped my mother to the side of the ship where someone helped her into the longboat."

She was a dutiful daughter, and a modest one. After dressing, her first thought was her mother's safety. The jury was in love. "The cook then pulled me back from the side of the boat and said I should go to the stern, where they would swing the longboat and where I might get in. But I fell on deck in going there," she said, "and missed my chance. Then the cook came and picked me up, lifting me on Holmes's shoulders, and he carried me down by the rope into the longboat. I held on by one hand to his neck and he swung down by the rope, holding it with one arm."

"Did others ask that he rescue them instead?" Brown asked. "Mrs. Anderson said Holmes should carry her down and that she would give him as much money as he could earn in a twelve-month if he would." "But he refused this offer?" the lawyer asked, in an incredulous tone. "Yes," she replied. "He said money was no object to him—all he wanted was to save lives."

Brown paused for a moment to make sure the jury took in this point. He then asked if Isabella was reunited immediately with her mother in the longboat. "No," she replied. "It was some time before I found her, the boat was so crowded, and even then I could not sit down but had to lay across Jane Johnston's and my sister Susannah's shoulders."

"Where was Holmes at this time?" queried Brown. "When the ship was going down, he struck and twice missed the rope that attached the longboat to the ship," she said. "The waves made the boat rock, and it was only on the third blow that he could cut the rope and let us swing away from the William Brown."

The defence's point, made late but firmly, was clear. Not just Isabella Edgar but all the survivors in the longboat owed their lives to Holmes. He cut the rope that had held them to the sinking ship; he took charge after the murders when Rhodes was unmanned; he spied the Crescent and raised the signal that brought it to their side. This was the hero, the defence implied, whom the courts had charged with murder.

"On the night of Tuesday," Brown then asked, "did you see the sailors throw any of the passengers overboard?" "The only man I saw at the work was Holmes," Edgar replied. "But I heard two go over and one say, 'God's blood and wounds, let me go myself.'"

At this point, Judge Baldwin decided to adjourn the trial until the next morning, 19 April, the anniversary of the sinking of the William Brown.

THE NEXT DAY, Isabella Edgar returned to the witness box and the prosecution's cross examination. Like a football team with a substantial lead at the end of the fourth quarter, the prosecution needed to do little but defend, stall and wait for time to run out. Her cross-examination was, therefore, perfunctory and after a few questions, she was released.

The last witness, Isabella Edgar's sister, Margaret, was sworn in. She had little to add, so the defence's case ended almost lamely. Yes, the boat was crowded. Yes, it was wet. No, she did not see the passengers being drowned. No, her family had no friendship or enmity with the prisoner who had indeed saved her sister from certain death.

With that, the defence rested its case and, as a prelude to the final act, the indictments against Holmes were read again to refresh the jury's memory. Judge Baldwin paused to consult his pocket watch. Since there was only an hour or so left in the day, the prosecution should begin its summation the next day, he decided.

And so on the 20th, George Dallas rose to speak. "Gentlemen of the jury," he said, "you must be satisfied from the testimony that an offence against the laws of the United States was committed in the melancholy sacrifice of many of the passengers of the ship William Brown. In this case the vengeance of the law was not invoked merely to punish the prisoner at the bar. There are, as you have heard, many circumstances in his favour, and it is gratifying to know that no verdict that can be rendered against him will reach to his life. He is charged not with murder but with manslaughter and that is not a capital crime. In his favour we can say he is a young, a robust, a brave and an adventuring seaman. But the justice and dignity of this country require the crime which was perpetrated under the extraordinary circumstances which form the basis of his charge must be punished.

"The defendant has pleaded 'not guilty' to the charge. It is not that he denies having taken the life of Francis Askin but that he had no ill will toward him. He did it not from malice, he argues, but from 'absolute necessity,' and if he has proven this I admit in all candour that he could not have made a better defence."

Consul Rubin Beasley's inspired invention of necessity, crafted to explain the deaths to newsmen, was the defence's only hope. For necessity to serve as a defence, however, Dallas argued, the danger must be "real, present, impending, and an inevitable necessity." But, he insisted, the evidence showed that inevitable necessity did *not* serve. After all, the survivors of the longboat were rescued the morning after the drownings, less than a day after Francis Askin met his death. Although the boat had filled with water, it had also been bailed. And although heavily loaded, the longboat *was* seaworthy, the proof being the simple fact that Holmes and the others had survived. Had not the captain of the *Crescent* kept the longboat and burned his own? Would he have done that if the *William Brown*'s longboat was too damaged to serve?

Yes, Dallas continued, the plug in the bottom of the boat had come unfixed, twice. But it had been replaced twice, too. And the passengers who were drowned had themselves served the longboat by bailing the water the rain and waves shipped in. Indeed, "the whole current of the testimony proves that not one of them was ever insensible or helpless. The ability they showed to go up the side of the ship Crescent on the Wednesday morning shows that the passengers retained their senses and their strength however much they might have suffered from cold, exposure, and want of nourishment or rest."

None of this was to argue that the other sailors and officers of the *William Brown* were blameless, Dallas admitted, not even the captain—especially not the captain. "By the testimony of the witnesses, and Captain Harris himself, they had two hours after the ship struck to attempt to save the crowd of helpless human beings on board his vessel. And nobody has suggested that during this time he ordered his men to fashion a raft or otherwise attempt a provision for them.

"Unlike the heroic captains of other such wrecks he did not stay with his men, cast his fate with that of the longboat's passengers, but made off on his own for Newfoundland, made off to save himself." But to say the captain's actions were less than heroic did not speak to the case at hand. It was not Captain Harris but the seaman Alexander William Holmes who was on trial for drowning the passenger Francis Askin. And it was to *this* charge that the jury's efforts must be directed. This neatly evaded the question of why Holmes and not Harris, Rhodes, Smith or Stetson had been charged.

Dallas then pointed out there was an important principle at stake: "It will not do for the crew of a ship to unite together for their own protection by the sacrifice of others. They must submit to an equal risk with their fellows in necessity, and endure the fate that falls to their lot unless they be exempted by common consent." That, Dallas insisted, was what the jurors were to decide: should sailors be exempted from at least equal danger? Did they have a duty to those who paid for passage upon the ships they worked? If they did, then the sailor Holmes was guilty. If they did not, if the jurors wished to permit sailors always to look to their own lives before those of their passengers, then Holmes should go free.

This was the point of the exercise, the principle that the government and the prosecutor, and earlier, Beasley, wanted inscribed in law. The jury could convict Holmes and protect the emigrants who were coming to America or release him and put current and future generations of sea travellers at risk.

Next, it was Edward Armstrong's turn to speak for the defence. His job was to warm up the jury so that David Paul Brown could pull out all the stops in a final plea on behalf of Holmes. It took the rest of Wednesday and much of Thursday before the defence's closing arguments were complete.

"The theories of philosophy," Armstrong began, "are here reduced at once to frightening reality." Who among the audience or the jury could say what they would have done had they been in the defendant's place? Would *they* have returned to the *William Brown* to rescue the young Isabella Edgar? Would they have refused Mrs. Armstrong's offer of a year's wage? Would they have cowered in the longboat with the other passengers?

Armstrong depicted Holmes as a friendless stranger who had come to the United States believing he had done no wrong, only to be arrested on charges he did not comprehend. There was the implication but never the statement of machinations against a simple, honest man. Here he was, the sole hero of the *William Brown*, charged with murder. "He scrutinizes each face but finds no welcome features, until at last he is reminded—the terrible reality rushes upon senses—that he is arraigned."

"Why look to the sailor when Captain Harris is so close at hand?" Armstrong asked. Even the prosecution had questioned the captain's judgment. "Yes, Captain Harris," Armstrong thundered as if the man were in the courtroom, "you had the atrocious coolness to procure the names of those you had every reason to believe would perish." Did the captain take even one extra person into his boat? Did he choose to link the fates of the jolly boat and longboat as had more heroic captains in the past? "Where," Armstrong asked, "was the noble pity evidenced by the heroic Holmes, this friendless seaman, who heard the cry of another and risked his own on her behalf?"

Then Armstrong spent an hour talking about "necessity" and the frailties of human nature. Here, he noted, they were all at a disadvantage. "Understand," he told the jurors, "the courtroom is a poor venue for so weighty a subject as the one you must consider." It is one thing, he pointed out, to make an argument in the comfort of a courtroom or a classroom. It is quite another to apply it to a situation of extreme peril.

David Paul Brown would speak next day for the defence. A brief note promoting Brown's oratory had earlier been sent to the *New York Herald*

SPEECH

OF

Dabid Paul Brown,

IN DEFENCE OF

ALEXANDER WILLIAM HOLMES,

ONE OF THE CREW OF THE SHIP WILLIAM BROWN,

INDICTED FOR MANSLAUGHTER UPON THE HIGH SEAS,

APRIL 21, 1842,

BEFORE THE CIRCUIT COURT OF THE UNITED STATES, FOR
THE EASTERN DISTRICT OF PENNSYLVANIA.

PHILADELPHIA:
ROBB, PILE & M'ELROY, PRINTERS,
LODGE STREET, NEAR THE EXCHANGE.
1858.

The title page of *Speech of David Paul Brown in Defence of Alexander William Holmes*, published in Philadelphia, 1858.

by its correspondent but was printed two days later, after the jury reached its verdict. "The verdict is involved in much doubt," the news brief said. "The prosecution has been most vigorously enforced and the accused no less ably and zealously defended."

Brown's closing argument on 21 April—all twenty-six typeset pages—was published several years later in a volume of eloquent legal arguments. His oration—there is no other word for it—did not disappoint. In it, he picked up and then hammered home his colleague's central theme: to judge Holmes, the jurors needed to put themselves in the situation where he had found himself.

"This case," Brown told the jury, "ought to be decided in a longboat, hundreds of leagues from the shore, loaded to the very gunwale with forty-two half-naked victims, with provisions only sufficient to prolong the agonies of famine and of thirst, with all the elements combined against her, leaking from below, filling also from above, surrounded by ice, unmanageable, from her condition, and subject to destruction from the least change of the wind and the waves. Decided at such a tribunal, nature, intuition, would at once pronounce a verdict not only of acquittal but of commendation."

Brown went on to imply that the jury had no jurisdiction because they were landsmen who could not know the choices Holmes had faced. And even if they despised Holmes's actions, Brown suggested, the Swedish seaman had suffered enough. Since arriving in the United States, an innocent sailor seeking a berth on a sailing ship, the prisoner had already spent "nine months of suffering and of obloquy" in detainment. Acquittal would not recompense Holmes for the indignities he had endured, but "he would at least enjoy the satisfaction always to be derived from a consciousness of rectitude."

At heart, Brown continued, the case was about the dignity and justice of the nation that had charged Holmes under its laws. "You can form some idea of the dignity of the United States in this case by observing how it has been cheapened. An indictment brought against the defendant, one 'ignoramused' by the Grand Jury, was for the theft of a quilt. And this very quilt is that which was converted by Holmes into a sail for the boat in a moment of the extremest peril in order that he might save the lives of those very beings who gratefully appeared here in order to convict their benefactor of these imputed crimes. Is this justice? Is this the nation's majesty?"

For reasons he could not fathom, Brown insisted, the United States had charged a hero, the man who had returned to the *William Brown* to save a young woman. "On that dreadful night, the crew and half the passengers having taken to the boats—the agonizing voice of a mother is heard even beyond the tumult and the clamour, calling for the preservation of her daughter who in the consternation of the moment had been forgotten and remained onboard the fated ship. In an instant, you may see a gallant, athletic, and powerful sailor passing hand over hand, by dint of a slender rope, until he regains the vessel.

"And you may further behold him upon the quarterdeck, one arm entwined around a sickly and half naked girl, surrounded by the wind and wasteful ocean, while with the other he bravely swings himself and his almost lifeless burden by means of the boat tackle falls from the stern of the sinking ship into the boat below. Yet today, I say it to the disgrace of the law, after months of solitary imprisonment you here see that selfsame, heroic sailor arraigned upon the odious charge of having voluntarily and wantonly deprived a fellow creature of his life. That, gentlemen of the jury, is the charge that I am to argue and you are to determine."

Brown took several hours more to review the testimony of the witnesses, including the depositions of Captain Harris and his second mate, Walter Parker. From each, Brown pulled testimony that supported his client, dismissing whatever seemed to indict him. He closed with a bow to the prosecution, saying, I am "perfectly sensible of the power of the learned counsel opposed to me," and then offered "the destiny, the worldly destiny of the prisoner" to the jury's hands. "Do with him as you would be done by," Brown pleaded, offering a bit of the Bible to take into their deliberations. "With what judgment ye judge, ye shall be judged, and with what measure ye mete, it should be meted unto you again."

Even Judge Baldwin appeared to be impressed.

Next, it was William Meredith's turn for the prosecution. As the United States attorney, it was his right to close the federal case. Although not eloquent, he was workmanlike and thorough. He, too, censored Captain Harris for the questionable decision to abandon the longboat to the sea. It did not hurt to shift a portion of the blame as long as it did not affect the charge at hand.

Meredith's job was to secure a conviction of manslaughter under federal law. From the government's perspective, a charge of murder under Pennsylvania statute might have served, but this way was better. Officials wanted the precedent that Dallas had stated, and to have it argued in a federal court gave it added power. At first, they had wanted to try the case simply because Beasley feared that England wanted it, too. And later, perhaps, they pursued it because the case had become a cause that needed to be defused. Finally, they sought it because of the points in law and philosophy it raised.

To all these ends, Meredith reminded the jury that the suggestion made by some that those drowned were almost dead, comatose, was wrong. They were active, vigorous, protesting people who were killed by the sailors, including Holmes. And while the longboat did leak, or at least take on water, that did not justify the crew's murder of passengers, he said, in hopes of saving themselves. As to necessity, they were rescued the next day. As a problem in moral philosophy, the answer, he suggested, was simple. Holmes was guilty and "necessity" was not an issue. Humans might indeed be self-centred and selfish but that was no excuse to kill.

On Friday, 22 April, it was Judge Baldwin's turn to gather his notes and present his charge to the jury. He knew his presentation would be a legal marker, one cited in future cases, and so he had put considerable effort into crafting it. He began by stating it would have afforded "much relief, if these terrible events occurred by means which could not be averted by human power, leaving no ground for imputing to any survivor any wrongful act of commission or omission." But the grand jury had returned an "official accusation against the prisoner at the bar, charging him with the unlawful taking of the life of Francis Askin, and on the truth of that we are called to decide."

The jury was instructed to consider "the whole conduct of the person, the accused" in their deliberations. They were directed to "look into his mind, his heart, the governing motives, the ruling passion that was in the ascendant at the time." That said, Baldwin warned the jurors against the "indulgence of misapplied humanity. It is one thing to give a favourable interpretation to evidence in order to mitigate an offence. It is a different thing when we are asked not to extenuate but to justify the act." Judge Baldwin was instructing the jury in a manner that demanded a conviction.

As to necessity, the judge continued, "It is not a case of necessity if any other means of preservation remain. All must be exhausted, the peril must be imminent, present, and apparently avoidable only by the destruction of another." In effect, he argued, the only defence would have been absolute proof that drowning Francis Askin was the *only* way the sailors could have saved their lives and those of the surviving passengers.

Baldwin then ruled that the failure of the sailors to draw lots should not be a factor in the jury's deliberations. Although there were precedents for a lottery, sailors were not required to make common cause with their passengers, to offer their lives as equals. Indeed, Baldwin reasoned, there was good reason to think a lottery would not have been the best course. The sailors were more important than the passengers because it was they who had the skills to keep the boat afloat. And so if they decided against a lottery that included them, the judge argued, it might be because they understood their value in the situation and not because of cowardliness or any other less than salutary sentiment.

Nor, the judge said, should the jury consider Francis Rhodes's order to "get to work" as one that the sailors were required to obey. "An unlawful order would be no justification to the seamen, for that even seamen are not justified, in law, by obedience to commands which are unlawful," Judge Baldwin told the jury. In this he conveniently ignored the fact that, at sea, a sailor who refused orders lawful or not—might be keelhauled, whipped or hanged from the yardarm.

However much the jurors might wish to find Holmes innocent, Judge Baldwin's interpretation of the law made it impossible. Holmes's promises to Captain Harris mattered no more than the orders Francis Rhodes gave his sailors. Holmes and Holmes alone was responsible for his actions, the judge instructed the jury. That they took more than a day to agree on the verdict spoke eloquently if impotently to the general sympathy many felt for the sailor.

"The learned Judge concluded his charge with but a few other observations in reference to the case," the *New York Herald* later reported, "and submitted the whole to the jury." During the sixteen hours of deliberation, the jurors returned once to inform Judge Baldwin they could not reach a verdict. For a moment, there was a spark of hope at the defence table. It was dashed when Judge Baldwin urged the jurors to try again. He sympathized with their difficulties but insisted they had the information needed to return a verdict and a duty to render it in court. Word finally came late Saturday morning that the jury was ready to pronounce.

The courtroom filled rapidly. "What say ye?" the jury was asked. The foreman rose to say that they unanimously agreed the prisoner, Alexander William Holmes, was guilty of manslaughter on the high seas. "The prisoner is, however, recommended to the mercy of the court." The message was clear: under the law, at least as Judge Baldwin had interpreted it, the jurors had no choice but to find the defendant guilty. But they sympathized with Holmes and wished his penalty to be mild, his incarceration brief, if indeed he were to be jailed at all.

David Paul Brown immediately moved that the verdict be set aside and that the judge issue an order of acquittal, an action that, while rare, is permitted by law. Sentencing was deferred until the appeal could be heard.

With the jury's decision, Baldwin's ban on publication was lifted. Reporters from the *Philadelphia Public Ledger and Daily Transcript* had been summarizing the testimony of each witness day by day, both their direct statements and their answers under cross-examination. The type had been set and pressmen waited throughout Saturday morning. As soon as the verdict was announced, a reporter raced to the office and the presses began to roll. By late afternoon, the newspaper was on the streets, beating by better than a day other Philadelphia and New York newspapers. The story took up two full broadsheet pages.

Almost everyone applauded the verdict. It gave the government the legal precedent it wanted, without restrictions on the maritime industry, a relief to ship owners and their captains. The Irish seemed satisfied, at least in Philadelphia, and congratulated themselves on avenging the deaths of their own. Members of the Seamen's Friend Society were disheartened. They had supported Holmes throughout the case. But the verdict was not unexpected.

A reporter from the *Ledger* (which incorrectly identified Holmes as Finnish) was close enough to the accused in the courtroom to report his reaction. "Holmes seemed at first indifferent to the verdict, but further

THE TRIAL OF HOLMES.—This important case was concluded yesterday. A full report of the testimony for the United States will be found on the first page of this paper, and will be read with much interest. The details of the melancholy loss of the ship William Brown, and of the awful fate of many of those who betook themselves to the boats when she sunk, cannot fail to excite the commiseration of the reader, while they engross his attention. Like the trial itself, the circumstances upon which it is founded are without parallel. Marine disasters are at all times fearful and full of peril, but this must have been terrible beyond conception. Here were between sixty and seventy human beings in a gallant ship, plunged in a moment from hope and safety into danger and despair, by an accident as unexpected as it was fatal in its consequences. Thirty-one of the passengers went down with the ill-fated vessel. The rest embarked with the crew in the boats. Sixteen of those who took refuge in the long boat were subsequently thrown overboard by the crew, in the panic of a cry that the boat was sinking. The remnant of the survivors were afterwards picked up by the ship Crescent, after enduring cold, exposure and privation, which must soon have terminated in death.

Holmes, the defendant in the case referred to, was one of the crew of the unfortunate ship, and one of those who assisted in throwing the passengers from the boat. He is a young man, a native of Finland, of excellent character, and of a bold and vigorous constitution. He does not deny his participation in the awful tragedy, but justifies the sacrifice on the ground of impending and unavoidable necessity. The testimony produced by him on the trial, and the speeches of his eloquent legal advocate, were all directed towards the establishment of this defence. How far it has succeeded remains to be seen by the judgment of the jury and of the world. The charge of Judge Baldwin was generally understood to be unfavorable to the prisoner, so far as the law of necessity was concerned.

conversing with a few friends who were near him he became much affected and wept. He remarked to those about him that, 'it was hard to be convicted in the manner he had been by the testimony of the very persons whose lives he had saved at peril of his own.'"

SENTENCING WAS DEFERRED until the appeal could be heard. It was not that anyone believed Judge Baldwin would reverse the judgment but rather that he needed the time to consider the sentence. To do that, he had to gauge both public and official sentiment. Should he let Holmes go with nothing but time served, or should he make an example of the man by imposing the law's maximum penalty?

The *Philadelphia North American* argued it was time to show some Christian mercy to the man who had saved lives as well as taken them. The newspaper pointed out that the Swedish sailor was simply a convenient pawn in the legal game of precedent and principle: "The court and jury thought they could not save Holmes without acknowledging a principle in maritime law liable to a fearful abuse." Holmes was convicted, in other words, to make the point that sailors could not "destroy a portion of their number without the equal chance of life to each which is secured in men that desperate expedient of casting lots." It was not that Judge Baldwin said lotteries were not important; it was that they were not important in this case.

"It was deemed wiser and better to convict the accused, and leave the question of the penalty to Executive clemency. That the convicted in this case will be pardoned, and that he ought to be pardoned, we entertain without a doubt." The call for clemency underscored a concern on the part of some that too harsh a sentence would not be good for the maritime industry. The newspaper worried that if sailors always had to give up their seats to passengers, "Who but a madman, or a fool, would take that berth?"

The *North American* argued for what it called a "fate principle," one that gave passengers an equal but not greater chance of survival. The goal was to share risks, not to load them all on to another, weaker group. Were sailors to carry all the risk themselves, however; if passengers were all necessarily privileged, the result would be to encourage sailors "to escape this last necessity in the longboat by leaving the passengers on board [a sinking vessel]."

Finally, the *North American* castigated the survivors who had testified against "a poor sailor to whose energy they were mainly indebted for the salvation of their lives. Gratitude and a sense of their own peril should prompt a different course. We should be the last to put the hand in irons that has been stretched to save us from a watery grave." That those same hands also had helped the survivors' friends and relatives into a watery grave introduced a level of ethical complexity the editorialists conveniently ignored.

The trial of Alexander Holmes was also front-page news at the *New York Herald*, which incorrectly identified him as the *William Brown*'s first mate. It made a better story, removing the thorny subject of levels of

To Certain Subscribers—Those who Paid Curns the New Orleans Defaulter.

We have been requested by a subscriber of New Orleans to send him the Herald post paid, because he had paid Curns in advance the subscripton and the postage. We do not, and never will, hold ourself responsible for any such subscription. Every person who pays for the Herald in advance to an agent, does so on his own responsibility. All those subscribers who paid Curns in advance, will no longer receive the Herald—we have lost enough without anything additional. Also, our new agents at New Orleans will please to attend to our instructions, otherwise we shall change them at once. We never shall put faith in any man's honesty hereafter. Amen.

Interesting Trial of a Shipwrecked Sailor for Throwing Passengers Overboard

We give in this day's paper the report of a trial which took place last week in Philadelphia, of Holmes, the mate of the William Brown, accused of manslaughter, in throwing overboard several passengers to save his own life.

The Jury on Saturday came into Court with a verdict of guilty, but his counsel has moved for a new trial. The punishment is five years' imprisonment in the State Prison.

This trial is probably one of the most unique and singular that ever took place. It is full of thrilling interest—discloses the weakness of human nature in her most awful moments—and surpasses in pathos anything that we ever read in poetry or prose. Talk no more of morals and fiction—read fact such as this, and be astonished.

responsibility, of Captain Harris's refusal to discuss a lottery and of Rhodes's uneasy command of the longboat. The fiction of the *William Brown* that began on the *Crescent* and was formed in Le Havre thus was given another simplifying twist.

Good tragedies should not be too complex. Good law should be unambiguous. Soon everyone would forget about the captain and the mate. The *Herald* told the fable of a sailor in charge of a longboat who drowned the passengers in an effort to save his own life. The complex story was now a simple tale of how justice was served in the United States courts, which understood that selfish human nature must be constrained by the law of the land. To raise the stakes, the *Herald* unilaterally increased the potential maximum sentence for manslaughter on the high seas from three years to five.

The *Herald*'s editors were not themselves believers in the common man, however, or in the decency of human nature. Above the short piece on the *William Brown,* the newspaper announced its owners would not be responsible to New Orleans subscribers who had paid for "Curns the New Orleans defaulter" for their paper. Curns had not paid the New York office, so his subscribers would not receive their papers. "We have lost enough without anything additional," the paper groused. The problem here, as in the trial reported in the next paragraph, was venal human nature. "We never shall put faith in any man's honesty hereafter. Amen," the *Herald* promised.

SEVERAL WEEKS LATER, David Paul Brown argued Holmes's appeal before Judge Henry Baldwin. It was a quixotic gesture. In essence, he was asking the judge to admit he had been wrong in his charge to the jury: "Because the Court, instead of telling the jury that in a state of imminent and deadly peril, all men are reduced to a state of nature, and that there is, then, no distinction between the rights of a sailor and passenger, adopted a contrary doctrine."

The federal and state prosecutors thought so little of Brown's chances they did not even show up. Judge Baldwin formally rejected Brown's request on the grounds that "During the trial they [the jury] had given to the subject studious and deliberate consideration, and they had paid like regard to what was now urged."

The only question that remained was how long Holmes would have to spend in prison. The official trial record summarizes Baldwin's judgment: "When the prisoner was brought up for sentence, the learned judge said to him that many circumstances in the affair were of a character to commend him to regard, yet, that the case was one in which some punishment was demanded." The maximum sentence was three years' imprisonment and a fine of $1,000 (a huge sum in those days). But "in view of all the circumstances, and especially as the prisoner has been already confined in gaol several months," Holmes was sentenced to a fine of twenty dollars and six months' "imprisonment in the Eastern Penitentiary of Pennsylvania (solitary confinement) at hard labor."

Taking the *Herald's* suggestion, the Seamen's Friend Society sought an order of executive clemency from President John Tyler, who was disinclined to leniency "in consequence of the court's not uniting in the application." That meant unless there was a joint application by prosecution and defence, one accompanied by the blessings of the judge, President Tyler would not consider weakening the legal precedent that officials and diplomats had worked so hard to create. Neither the federal nor local prosecutors had any intention of joining in an appeal whose merits Judge Baldwin had already rejected.

From our perspective, the sentence does not sound very long. But in those days, six months in prison was hard indeed. Charles Dickens, who visited Eastern Penitentiary in 1842, called its "rigid, strict, and hopeless solitary confinement... in its effects, to be cruel and wrong." It was not the mindless, meaningless repetitive labour prisoners were required to carry out in their cells that shocked him. In itself, that was no more onerous than the mindless, repetitive labour that thousands of factory workers endured. What he described as Eastern Penitentiary's "torture and agony" was that prisoners were forbidden any human contact at all. The prisoner "sees the prison officers, but with that exception he never looks upon a human countenance, or hears a human voice. He is a man buried alive; to be dug out in the slow round of years."

In *The Old Curiosity Shop*, Dickens described prison this way: "Every prisoner who comes into jail comes at night, is put into a bath and dressed in the prison garb, and then a black hood is drawn over his face and head, and he is led to the cell from which he never stirs again until his whole period of confinement has expired."

PRESUMABLY, ALEXANDER HOLMES survived his prison sentence. At least there are no newspaper stories describing his dying in prison. Nor, however, did any document his release. There is no record anywhere of his later years. He had served his purpose for the lawyers, politicians and reporters who used and then disposed of him. Afterward, he was as relevant as last month's newspaper.

THE LEGACY

I N THE END, nothing changed as a result of the trial of Alexander
William Holmes. The Great Migration continued as millions of
British, Irish and Scottish citizens left Great Britain for North
America. As the century passed, steam came to replace sail, shortening
the time it took to cross the North Atlantic. Later, Italians, Poles, Germans
and Russian emigrants travelled in the crowded steerage holds of cargo
ships that ever more speedily, and profitably, made the North American run
their own. Progress, everyone said. It was grand. Shipping interests thrived.

Into the twentieth century, traditional sailing vessels and new steamships alike continued to use the same dangerous route that the *William
Brown* had taken. Why not? It was the shortest route, and that meant less
time and, therefore, more profit. Every year icebergs were sighted. Every
year a few ships were lost and more were damaged. It was the cost of
business, the occasional loss offset by the higher expense of a safer but
slower passage. As a *McClure's Magazine* story explained in the 1880s: "A
day lost to one of these ocean ferries means in coal, and food, and wages,
and so on, a matter of one thousand pounds or so out of the pockets of
her owners, and this is a little sum they do not care to forfeit without
strong reason . . . They expect their captains to drive the boats along as
usual, and make up for the added risk [from icebergs] by increased watch-
fulness and precaution, and a keen noting of the thermometer for any
sudden fall which should foretell the neighborhood of ice."

Occasionally, an exceptional disaster was used to argue for more fun-
damental changes. When the ss *Arctic* sank in 1852, for example, newspaper

editorials were filled with questions for a few days, perhaps a week. Why were there insufficient lifeboats for all on board the ship? Who could be blamed? The same thing happened two years later when the *City of Glasgow*, with its 480 passengers and crew, disappeared at the end of February in the same icy waters that had wrecked the *William Brown*. What, editorialists asked, should we do? Later, in 1870, the *City of Boston* left Halifax at the end of January and vanished, presumed lost to the icebergs that flowed early that year. Newspapers again demanded to know what could be done to stop the deaths on the North Atlantic run.

Into the twentieth century, ever more ships steamed through the North Atlantic in the winter and spring. The sheer volume of traffic ensured that the number of incidents would increase. The frequency of these disasters gave rise to a spate of short stories and critical novels. In 1898, for example, *McClure's Magazine* published *The Wreck of the Titan*, a novel

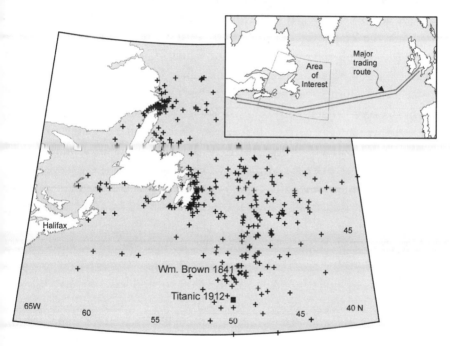

A map of approximately three hundred known locations of ship collisions with icebergs off Newfoundland, 1700–1920. The *Titanic* location is marked by a square. Data courtesy Brian Hill

about "The largest craft afloat and the greatest of the works of men … a glorious luxury liner carrying two brass bands, two orchestras, and a theatrical company, the *Titan* was wrecked upon an iceberg in the North Atlantic in the spring." Most of its crew and many of its passengers died in the scramble for the few lifeboats that the supposedly invincible ship carried. The author, Morgan Robertson, was a ship's captain who knew the business and the pressures of steamship owners to increase speed and to increase their profit margins. The subtitle of the book was "Futility."

In April 1912, a real luxury liner, a true engineering wonder, sailed from Great Britain for America. Some later claimed that the *Titanic*'s name was inspired by the story of the *Titan*, reality overtaking literature in a singular act of hubris. On its maiden voyage, the *Titanic* was sailing at full speed when the night turned cold and foggy. The sailors on watch remarked upon it, as had, seventy-one years before, the sailors on the *William Brown*. In spite of the warning that this weather change gave, and in spite of six telegrams alerting the ship's officers to the presence of icebergs, the *Titanic* did not slow down until it struck an iceberg.

More people might have been saved had the eighteen lifeboats that were launched, some of which were only half-full with mostly first-class passengers, returned to the site after the *Titanic* went down. Just one lifeboat chose to pick up those who survived the ship's sinking only to struggle weakly, for a time, before drowning in the freezing Atlantic waters. Like Captain George Harris in his jolly boat, most of the survivors would not risk their own safety to save others.

"The Titanic crime," the *New York Evening Journal* editorialized, was that "the lifeboats will hold only a few more than a quarter of the number of men, women, and children who have committed themselves to the care of this steamship company." Shocking. "The company simply took the risk," the newspaper concluded. "They staked the lives of passengers and crew on the chance that kind of accident would not happen." How, the paper asked, could this have happened, and how might it be prevented in the future?

There were inquiries, of course. Both the United States Congress and the British Parliament held extensive hearings. What the newspapers called a disaster, the officials called a tragedy, blaming no one for the deaths. Studies were commissioned and bureaucracies were formed. In 1913 the British Board of Trade held a thirty-six-day hearing into the loss

The iceberg struck by the *Titanic* on 12 April 1913. Courtesy United States Coast Guard

of the *Titanic* and the first International Conference on the Safety of Life at Sea was convened in London. As a result, the next year the ss *Scotia* was sent to map and study the airs and currents of the North Atlantic, and the icebergs they carried.

An international ice patrol was established to chart the location of icebergs and warn mariners. Every spring, warnings were issued by telegram, and, later, by more modern communication methods, to inform ship masters of dangerous obstacles. After the *Titanic*, ship captains even took heed. More importantly, perhaps, ship owners and maritime officials alike agreed to shift the normal sailing route across the North Atlantic slightly to the south, so that, in April, ships could avoid the icebergs that congregate in those waters. It even became standard practice for ships to carry sufficient lifeboats to save the entire complement of passengers and crew in the event of a wreck.

It has been a long time since a luxury liner sank after striking an iceberg in the North Atlantic in April. The International Ice Patrol does its job well, as do modern radar and telecommunications. Still, every year, there are one or two "incidents" involving cargo ships, but damage rather than destruction is the typical result. Today's ships are more strongly built, and if one is in danger of sinking, rapid rescue service is usually available.

There still are storms, and sailors desperate for a faster route are sometimes caught in them. But for most who sail the North Atlantic, the fears of nineteenth- and early twentieth-century mariners and their passengers are just history, and the *William Brown* is no more than a historical footnote.

HONED AND SIMPLIFIED first by Francis Rhodes with the help of Captain George Ball, and then by the United States consul in Le Havre, the complex story of the *William Brown* was transformed over the years into a simple morality tale. A sanitized version of the story first debuted in 1845 in the *Highwaymen and Pirates' Own Book*. Its author, Henry K. Brooke, made a nice living summarizing popular tales of death and disaster, year by year. The story now went like this: A seaworthy and well-captained ship tragically sank after striking an iceberg in April 1841. Half the passengers went down with the ship and half were saved to the ship's doughty longboat. The next night, fearing the boat might sink from the weight of its passengers, crewmen drowned sixteen of those saved the day before. This aroused the "sympathy of all classes for the unfortunate victims of the catastrophe, and aroused a feeling of detestation toward the individuals of the crew who had been so active in consigning their fellow creatures to a watery grave." Justice was served when the sailor responsible, Alexander Holmes, was brought to trial in the United States.

The story glossed over the ship's sinking and the demise of the passengers who were left on board; it was the longboat murders that Brooke emphasized. And even here, the murders were less important than the questions they raised. "The case assumes a still greater importance from the fact that it is without precedent or parallel in the legal history of any nation. The result of the trial is the settlement of a principle of considerable importance of the wayfaring part of the world."

As Brooke told it, justice was served both through Holmes's conviction (evil was punished) and through the establishment of a principle of law that would, in the future, prevent sailors from trying to save themselves at the expense of their passengers. The rules of what today we call "lifeboat ethics" were born: in dire circumstances, some *must* die that others may live. But when driven to this necessity, a fair procedure—the lottery being the best known—must be followed.

Through the rest of the nineteenth and across the twentieth century, the simplified story of the *William Brown* has been cited from time to time, its complexities obscured. When in 1884 the British courts tried the sailors from the *Mignonette,* a private sailing ship, for resorting to cannibalism after their ship was sunk in the Indian Ocean, lawyers cited *United States v. Holmes* as an example. The *New York Times* resurrected the story in an 1884 review of both the *Mignonette* and the shipwrecked Greeley expedition.

In the first case, the judge ruled the U.S. precedent did not apply because it dealt with lotteries that were inappropriate in this case. Obviously, he had not read Judge Baldwin's charge to the jury. In the second case, Lt. Adolphus Greeley, the leader of a shipwrecked military party, shot a private who was stealing food from the meagre stores that remained for all the crew. In the *Times* story, the analogy was clear. The murdered private was like Holmes, who drowned passengers on his boat to assure space for himself. The private took food just as Holmes took lives to assure his own survival.

Over the years, *United States v. Holmes* has become a general rather than a maritime precedent. In the late 1990s, for example, its defence of necessity—and of human nature—was used after a Canadian farmer, Robert Latimer, was convicted of killing his young daughter. He did it, he said, because his daughter was severely disabled and he could not stand to see her suffer. During Latimer's appeal to the Supreme Court of Canada, his lawyer argued that the farmer had killed his daughter out of love. It was human nature—impervious and demanding—that necessitated and thus justified the act. The defence failed, again. Latimer's appeal was rejected.

The story of the *William Brown* took on new life and new meaning, when, in 1991, Louis Lasagna, a dean at the Tufts University School of Medicine, invoked it as a metaphor for modern medical rationing. He used the simple form of the tale put forward in Brooke's book and made it even more concise. A good ship struck an iceberg and half the passengers were saved to the lifeboat. Overloaded, it was about to capsize when the crew threw sixteen passengers overboard. One of the sailors involved in this desperate act was later tried and convicted for manslaughter.

We can think about the costs of medical care and its contemporary scarcities, Lasagna said, in terms of the longboat, where there was not room enough for all. The cost of modern medical services like organ transplantation is great enough to swamp the financial boat of the entire health care system, just as the full complement of the longboat's passengers presumably threatened to swamp that vessel. More generally, Lasagna said, the question becomes who will be granted a seat in the medical lifeboat and who will be jettisoned for want of resources. Thus, the story of the *William Brown* has in our time become a metaphor both for health care rationing and for the protocols of choice in the face of necessity. Where scarcity reigns, the ethics of the lifeboat must rule.

David Thomasma, a doyen of modern bioethics who was perhaps unaware of the *William Brown* story, chose the *Titanic* as a similarly simple metaphor for "the problems associated with the lifeboat ethic."

Nor is the lifeboat metaphor limited to health care. It applies in *every* area (education, housing, welfare, etc.) and at every scale where the supply is insufficient for everyone. In 2002, for example, the *Joplin Globe* in Missouri retold a simplified version of the story of the *William Brown* to ask if lifeboat ethics "could conceivably have other applications such as, say, in a worldwide hunger crisis. Which starving nations should be fed?"

THE PROBLEM with the simplified story of the *William Brown* and the metaphor of "lifeboat ethics" it has bequeathed us is that it ignores the causes of scarcity, the generative conditions of disaster. It prohibits important questions from being asked (why was there only one longboat on board?) under the guise of considering real and important concerns (who will be thrown overboard?). The metaphor assures we will consider preventable tragedy as a theological judgment, that we will blame God for the heat wave that cooks us, the winter cold spell that freezes the homeless, the dam that breaks and drowns townspeople who could not afford to live away from the riverbanks. That none of these events is necessary—and none necessarily the act of a capricious deity—is a fact hidden by the stories we tell ourselves about the inevitability of it all.

The accepted metaphor of lifeboat ethics that began with the *William Brown* and later grew with the *Titanic* looks only at the disaster and never questions its contributing elements. Whether the subject is health care, housing, or the "hunger crisis," the metaphor assures that, like Holmes's legal accusers, we, too, will accept the necessity of sacrificing a portion of our passengers (the medical longboat, the food longboat, the education longboat, etc.). The only question the metaphor permits is how those to be sacrificed will be chosen.

The real lesson of the *William Brown* is that we do not have to be in this quandary of scarcity and necessity; we do not have to be in the lifeboat at all. The simplified story of the longboat was a lie perpetrated by those who wanted to deflect public attention from the problem of rapacious ship owners who sent ill-equipped ships on dangerous courses with a demand for excessive speed.

The moral of the *William Brown*, and the *Titanic*, should be that we can make sure there are enough lifeboats for all, and perhaps, that we can avoid the necessity of their use. In this way, the metaphor of the lifeboat stands not as an excuse but as an indictment of the constructions that assure the scarcity that appears to pervade our world.

WHY NOT USE THE STORY of the *William Brown* as a cautionary tale saying that this is what happens when the demand for maximum profit and industry protection is given precedence over minimal care standards for the public? As it is, because we take the simple story rather than the complex history as our standard, we always indict an Alexander William Holmes, rarely a Rhodes, a Harris or a ship owner. We are still more than willing to make a scapegoat of this sailor, or that nurse, doctor, parent or social worker whose desperate action results from the scarcity society imposes.

For almost 170 years we have relied upon a telling that assumed a necessity that need not have a risen, a culpability that was incorrectly assigned. Alexander Holmes did help drown the longboat victims on the evening of 20 April 1841. He did not act alone, nor was he solely or even primarily responsible. In the end, however, he was as much a victim of Captain Harris's sloppy seamanship, Francis Rhodes's failed leadership, and the owner's greed as were the Irish emigrants whom he helped to throw overboard. This is the final great lesson the history of the *William Brown* teaches: when we insist upon the simple tale and accept the parameters of the world it offers, the best we can hope to be is an Alexander William Holmes. Even when we try to do our best in the longboat, we will fail.

ENDNOTES

The Second Strike

The reconstruction of the last hours of the *William Brown* is drawn from several sources. Two were especially critical. The first was *Trial of Alexander William Holmes*, a pamphlet published the year after the trial, and *United States v. Holmes*, the official legal summary of court testimony. Another source was the formal, third-personal depositions given by survivors in Le Havre weeks after the ship's sinking. In addition, several newspaper accounts were used to add to knowledge of the nature and position of the icebergs in those North Atlantic waters in April. With contemporary news accounts, these formal records give the sense but not the exact words, which are re-created here in the first-person for the sense of moment.

7 *The sounds and smells* B. Greenhill and A. Giffard, *Traveling by Sea*, 14. A New Bedford whaler's description also serves: "The whole was in equal parts composed of foul air, tobacco smoke, sea chests, soap kegs, greasy pans, tainted meant, foreign ruffians and seasick Americans." From P. Harris and D. Lyon, "In New Bedford, a Return to the Days of 'Moby-Dick,'" *Boston Sunday Globe*, 6 July 2001.

8 *"Thunder is no more"* W. Gliddon of Barnstaple wrote the description in 1855 for the *Western Standard*, a British newspaper. The article is quoted in Greenhill and Giffard, *Traveling by Sea*, 19.

10 *"a sort of rumbling"* W.A. Lord, *A Night to Remember*, 5.

15 *From the seventeenth* For more on the use of the thermometer in navigation, see T.F. Gaskell, *The Gulf Stream*, 5–7.

15 *This practice* For more on Benjamin Franklin's map, see Gaskell, *The Gulf Stream*, 5–7, and H.M. Wallis and A.H. Robinson, *Cartographical Innovations*, 152–53.

16 *After the first strike* Quartermaster George Thomas Rowe of the *Titanic* later

commented on what he and his mates called "Whiskers 'round the light," tiny splinters of ice in the air that reflected bright colours from the deck lights. Lord, *A Night to Remember,* 3.

THE LAST WATCH

See the headnote for the previous chapter "The Second Strike."

20 *The first purpose-built* I am obliged to *Great Britain* archivist and librarian Jean C. Young for data on the ship's lifeboat complement. See http://www. ss-great-britain.com.

26 *In January 1873* For more on the *Northfleet,* see A.W.B. Simpson, *Leading Cases in the Common Law,* 243–45.

27 *The longboat, rigged only* Page 360 of *United States v. Holmes* states: "The long-boat was 22½ feet long, 6 feet in the beam, and from 2½ to 3 feet deep." Modern methods of calculating capacity for small boats (length × breadth × beam divided by 15) indicate that the longboat should have carried a maximum of twenty-two or twenty-three people, when it actually held more than forty.

28 *The smaller yawl-rigged jolly boat* Although many people later commented on the jolly boat's being smaller than the longboat, the jolly boat's dimensions are nowhere given in the trial testimony or in other period reports on the wreck of the *William Brown.* On page 164 of *Cannibalism and the Common Law,* A.W.B. Simpson writes: "There were two boats, a jolly boat rigged as a sailing cutter and a shallower longboat propelled by oars. The jolly boat was between 19 and 20 feet long and the longboat 22½ feet and some six feet in beam." Neither beam nor draft for the jolly boat is given. Using the modern method of calculating capacity, were the jolly boat 19 feet long with a beam of 3 feet and a draft of 3 feet, it could have held eleven people, when it actually carried only ten survivors. With a beam of 4 feet and a draft of 3 feet, it could comfortably have held fifteen people. It's possible that the length of the jolly boat given by Simpson is incorrect.

28 *The story was much* Lord, *A Night to Remember,* 121.

29 *"Both in the revolutionary Navy"* A. McKee, *The Wreck of the Medusa,* 184.

34 *Survivors of the* Lord, *A Night to Remember,* 100.

ALONE IN THE NORTH ATLANTIC

36 *In April 1805* The story of and quotations about the *Jupiter* are from S.H. Tappan, *Memoir of Mrs. Sarah Tappan,* L. Tappan, *The Life of Arthur Tappan* and D.L. Tappan, *Ancestors and Descendants of Abraham Tappan of Newbury, Massachusetts, 1606–1672.*

38 *By 1841 everyone knew* The *Essex* is, perhaps, the most studied of all nineteenth-

century maritime disasters. From O. Chase, *The Wreck of the Whaleship Essex*; Chase et al., *Narrative of the Wreck of the Whale-ship Essex*; N. Philbrick, *In the Heart of the Sea*; T. Nickerson, O. Chase et al., *The Loss of the Ship Essex*.

38 *That the survivors* N. Hanson, *The Custom of the Sea.*

39 *Everyone also knew* See McKee, *The Wreck of the* Medusa.

39 *A popular book* For a detailed account of the publication, see M. Ryan, "Liberal Ironies, Colonial Narratives, and the Rhetoric of Art" in *Théodore Géricault.*

40 *"experienced a gale of wind"* "Maritime Herald," *New York Herald*, 11 October 1841.

41 *"lat. 42° lon. 47°"* "Maritime Herald," *New York Herald*, 15 April 1842.

41 *In a seven-year period* J. Fowles, *Shipwreck*, 48.

41 *Brian Hill of the Institute* See B. Hill, Ice Charts, http://www.nrc.ca/imd/ice/.

43 *A top-class sailing packet* P.J. Hugill, *World Trade Since 1431*, 127.

44 *The first steamship* P.K. Kemp, ed., *The Oxford Companion to Ships and the Sea*, 353.

44 *On its maiden voyage* Hugill, *World Trade Since 1431*, 126–28.

45 *As historian M.L. Hansen* See M.L. Hansen, *The Atlantic Migration*, 173.

47 *Only after the* Titanic *sank* See G.K. Batchelor, *The Life and Legacy of G.I. Taylor*, 1.

47 *In 1841 the extent* For Brian Hill's calculations of the extent of ice flows from 1810 through the 1950s, see his website www.nrc.ca/icc/nic4.txt.

49 *The* William Brown's *survivors* Facts in this section are from *Trial of Alexander William Holmes* and depositions given in Le Havre, British Foreign Office 227/634.

AT SEA

Sources used in reconstructing the events that took place on the longboat are similar to those for the reconstruction of the *William Brown*'s last hours: *Trial of Alexander William Holmes, United States v. Alexander William Holmes* and depositions made at Le Havre. These formal records give the sense but not the exact words, which are re-created here in the first-person for the sense of moment. In addition, I used newspaper stories about the longboat murders that were published in both European and British newspapers. Most of these newspaper stories cite the versions reprinted in the *Times* (London), whose records today are the most complete and the easiest to research. A.W.B. Simpson's re-creation of the longboat murders in *Cannibalism and the Common Law*, long the only detailed study of these events, is a model whose organization I generally followed.

60 *Sea biscuits were a staple* Hanson, *The Custom of the Sea*, 59.

60 *Later, Rhodes claimed* In his Le Havre deposition, Francis Rhodes insisted that passengers had heard him talk to his men.

61 *"This won't do"* Several survivors later testified in both depositions at Le Havre and at the eventual trial that these were Rhodes's words. He, however, remembered them slightly differently in his deposition and insisted that he never ordered his men to "get to work." He remembered telling them if they did not drown some passengers that all would die.

63 *Owen Riley, a married man* Different authors have given different reports on the order of those who were drowned, and their names. The progression of murders given here is the best guess based on the survivors' depositions, the trial records and the work of later scholars.

63 *"Good God"* From Simpson, *Cannibalism and the Common Law*, 168.

65 *"Blood-an-ouns"* A curse that usually is interpreted as "Christ's Blood on you."

65 *"I heard a splash"* John Messer's story was originally published in the *Boston Post* and reprinted in other papers in North America and in Great Britain; reprinted as "The Ship William Brown," *Times* (London), 24 July 1841.

69 *Everyone knew the story* Hanson, *The Custom of the Sea*, 126–27. For an analysis of this and similar cases, see Simpson, *Cannibalism and the Common Law*.

69 *The wonder is* E.E. Leslie, *Desperate Journeys, Abandoned Souls*, 176.

71 *"Everyone noticed"* Lord, *A Night to Remember*, 139 and 159.

72 *"So strong was"* Originally published in the *Boston Post*; reprinted as "The Ship William Brown," *Times* (London), 24 July 1841.

THE CRESCENT

No documents survive to describe the attitude of the passengers and crew who were rescued by the *Crescent*. What they may have been thinking is speculation based on later depositions and statements. An understanding of the Irish emigrants' perspective is based upon research of the prejudice against the Irish during the mid-nineteenth century and general work on the North Atlantic migration by authors like E.C. Guillet *(The Great Migration)* and M.L. Hansen *(The Atlantic Migration)*.

75 *But at sea* According to S. Junger, *The Perfect Storm*, 277: English Common Law "saw death at sea as an act of God that ship owners couldn't possible be held liable for. Where would it end? How could they possibly do business?"

75 *Even today* Junger, *The Perfect Storm*, 277. In the 1990s the *Death on the High Seas Act* was used to limit liability for air carriers whose planes crashed more than three miles from the coast of the United States. In 2000, the Federal Aviation Administration reauthorization legislation (H.R. 1000) amended the act to distinguish between maritime disasters and most categories of

aviation disaster occurring over the sea. See www.avweb.com/news/avlaw/181903-1.html.

75 "removed from commerce" Hansen, *The Atlantic Migration*, 177.

75 "twenty souls" Quoted in Guillet, *The Great Migration*, 17.

76 In the mid-nineteenth century Hansen, *The Atlantic Migration*, 120.

76 The science of the day For more on the Irish at this time, see C.E. Mewburn, *Imaging the Body Politic*.

82 "In consequence of this" British Foreign Office 27/634.

82 The previous August The James Dixon case is mentioned several times in British Foreign Office files 27/634.

84 If an example In 1874 the British used the case of the *Francine (Regina v. Keyne)* to declare its right to try a foreigner for an offence committed within British territorial waters, a matter of three miles from sovereign land. Simpson, *Leading Cases in the Common Law*, 231–43.

84 Without informing Gordon "The Ship William Brown," *Times* (London), 24 July 1841.

85 "the American consul" "The Ship William Brown," *Times* (London), 24 July 1841.

86 Dreadful Shipwreck "Dreadful Shipwreck," *Times* (London), 15 May 1841. Originally published in *Journal de Havre*, 11 May 1841.

89 "There is a suspicious" Simpson, *Cannibalism and the Common Law*, 171.

89 The depositions began British Foreign Office 27/634.

THE STORY

Newspaper reports and the deposition summaries in the British Foreign Office 27/634 are the primary sources used in this chapter. Many of the stories originated with small newspapers like *Galignani's Messenger*, but the originals do not survive. Most were reprinted in the *Times* (London), however, and for the sake of consistency—and convenience—these were the versions used. The attempt to re-create the attitudes of the British and United States consuls are just that, re-creations based on the data. No letters have survived supporting these, other than those in the British Foreign Office.

94 In this decade For an engaging, nontechnical treatment of the penny black stamp, see B. Maitland *The Chalon Heads*. For a more detailed understanding, see J.B. Seymour, *The Penny Black of Great Britain* and *Stanley Gibbon's All World Stamps*, http://www.allworldstamps.com/.

95 Then as now This was the birth of the modern fourth estate whose principal function was (and remains) to broadcast the affairs of the first three estates. For more on the estates, and the role of the news domain, see T. Koch, *The News as Myth*.

96 *In the first ten months* "London Post Office," *Philadelphia North-American,* 16 October 1841.

96 *A Paris-based* I am obliged to Michael and Jane Phillips of the Maritime History website for their help on this point. www.cronab.demon.co.uk.

96 *"Dreadful Shipwreck"* From *Galignani's Messenger,* 12 May 1841; reprinted "Dreadful Shipwreck," *Times* (London) 15 May 1841.

99 *On Thursday, 13 May* The quotations in this section are reconstructed from the summarized depositions in the British Foreign Office 27/634.

102 *The American consul had* We can reconstruct what John Messer told Rubin Beasley from "The Ship William Brown," originally published in the *Boston Post* and reprinted in other papers in North America and in Great Britain; reprinted *Times* (London), 24 July 1841.

102 *"when the longboat"* The quotations in this section are reconstructed from the summarized depositions in the British Foreign Office 27/634.

105 *A Letter to the Editor* Published in the *Journal de Havre* and the *London Morning Post* and other newspapers; reprinted as "Letter from English and U.S. Consuls," *Times* (London), 18 May 1841.

105 *The next day* The quotations in this section are taken from the summarized depositions in the British Foreign Office 27/634.

A MELANCHOLY AFFAIR

Documents in the British Foreign Office archives and the changing tenor of news stories permitted the reconstruction of the attitudes and attentions of officials to the wreck of the *William Brown.* Perhaps more than any chapter, an understanding of the events required surmises based upon that data.

110 *"My Lord,"* Letter from Gilbert Gordon to Lord Palmerston, 15 May 1841, British Foreign Office 27/634.

111 *To criticize the* Lord Melbourne's government would fall within the year.

114 *The William Brown—Havre* "The William Brown," *London Morning Post,* 13 May 1841; reprinted *Times* (London), 17 May 1841.

117 *"I for one shall never"* Homo, letter to the editor, "The Loss of the William Brown," *Times* (London), 18 May 1841.

118 *Legal historian* Simpson, *Cannibalism and the Common Law,* 171–72.

118 *"It again becomes our duty"* "Melancholy Shipwreck—One Hundred and forty-eight lives lost," *Quebec Mercury,* 22 May 1841; reprinted *Times* (London), 16 June 1841.

119 *"was at the mast head"* British Foreign Office 27/634.

119 *"fr. 642.60"* Gilbert Gordon to the British Foreign Office 27/634.

120 *The Foreign Office note* British Foreign Office 27/634.

121 *"You give no account"* John Bidwell to Gilbert Gordon, British Foreign Office 27/634.

122 *Born Henry John Temple* For a brief but comprehensive biography of Lord Palmerston, see the British Schoolnet website http://www.spartacus.schoonet.co.uk/Prpalmerston.htm.

123 *"the main objective"* Biography of Lord Palmerston at http://www.spartacus.schoolnet.co.uk/Prpalmerston.htm.

123 *"I cannot lose"* Letter from Gilbert Gordon to John Bidwell, 30 May 1841, British Foreign Office 27/634.

124 *"was not to justify"* Gilbert Gordon to Lord Palmerston, 3 June 1841, British Foreign Office 27/634.

124 *"After having been"* No headline, *Times* (London), 16 June 1841.

124 *"This was a calamitous"* Note by Lord Palmerston, British Foreign Office 27/634.

THE CHARGE

This chapter is based on news stories, primarily from Philadelphia sources, and the *Trial of the Alexander William Holmes*. Where sources seem to be in conflict about details, the latter, based on the fullest possible trial materials, was used.

126 *"Still in a very weak"* Messer's story was originally published in the *Boston Post* and reprinted in other papers in North America and in Great Britain; reprinted as "The Ship William Brown," *Times* (London), 24 July 1841.

128 *"in order to avoid"* "Another Statement," *Philadelphia Public Ledger and Daily Transcript*, 1 July 1841.

129 *"the mate and sailors"* From *Philadelphia Public Ledger and Daily Transcript*, n.d., quoted in http://people.brandeis.edu/~teuber/lawspelunk.html.

130 *"Next week"* "Postscript: Philadelphia," *New York Herald*, 11 October 1841.

131 *"Caldwell, alias Edwards,"* "Postscript: Philadelphia," *New York Herald*, 11 October 1841.

132 *"for the punishment"* Story's Laws 83 Stat. 115, quoted in *United States v. Holmes*, 383.

132 *"first and with force"* *United States v. Holmes*, 383.

133 *"In the impotency"* D.P. Brown, *Speech of David Paul Brown in Defence of Alexander William Holmes*, 1858, 10–11.

134 *And though Judge Randall* and *The court's chief justice* J.T. Scharf and T. Westcott, *History of Philadelphia*, 1844.

134 *In his younger years* H. Baldwin, *An Oration Delivered by Hon. Henry Baldwin, at the Request of the Jackson Democratic Republicans of This City July 4ᵗʰ, 1827*.

134 *Later in his career* H. Baldwin, *Reports of Cases Determined in the Circuit Court*

of the United States, in and for the Third Circuit and *A General View of the Origin and Nature of the Constitution and Government of the United States.*

134 *"Spoke bark Frederick Warren"* "Maritime Herald," *New York Herald,* 14 April 1842.

135 *"It cannot be denied"* Port—Stagnation in Business," *New York Herald,* 15 April 1842.

135 *In 1842 candidates* "Movements for Mr. Clay," *New York Herald,* 24 April 1842. John Tyler was the first U.S. vice-president to assume the presidency upon the death of his superior.

137 *Holmes spent his* This section is based on the pretrial depositions of Walter Parker and George Harris, summarized in *Trial of Alexander William Holmes,* 9-11.

141 *"entertained conscientious"* and *"admitted to have"* From summaries of statements by John Hopkins and George Weevil in *Trial of Alexander William Holmes,* 1.

142 *"Although this court"* and *It was a sufficiently* J. Wallace, *Cases in the Circuit Court of the United States for the Third Circuit,* 28.

142 *"some of the circumstances"* From the summary of Oliver Hopkinson's speech in *Trial of Alexander William Holmes,* 1.

THE TRIAL

The reconstruction of the trial is drawn from several sources: *Trial of Alexander William Holmes* is the most complete and is the principal reference, *United States v. Holmes* is the authoritative legal summary and *Speech of David Paul Brown in Defence of Alexander William Holmes* offers another perspective. Newspaper reports—especially those in the *New York Herald* and the *Philadelphia North American*—were also used. These records provide summaries that give the sense but not the exact words, which are re-created here in the first-person for a sense of immediacy.

THE DEFENCE OF NECESSITY

See the headnote for the previous chapter, "The Trial."

172 *"The verdict is involved"* "Philadelphia," *New York Herald,* 23 April 1842.

172 *"This case"* D.P. Brown, *Speech of David Paul Brown in Defence of Alexander William Holmes.*

175 *"The learned Judge"* "Interesting Trial of a Shipwrecked Sailor for Throwing Passengers Overboard," *New York Herald,* 25 April 1842.

176 *Reporters from the* "United States Court: Before Judge Baldwin and Randall," *Philadelphia Public Ledger and Daily Transcript,* 23 April 1842.

176 *"Holmes seemed at first"* "Local Affairs: Conviction of Holmes," *Philadelphia*

Public Ledger and Daily Transcript, 23 April 1842.

178 *"The court and jury"* "The Holmes Case," *Philadelphia North American and Daily Advertiser*, 25 April 1842.

178 *The trial of* "Interesting Trial of a Shipwrecked Sailor for Throwing Passengers Overboard," *New York Herald*, 25 April 1842.

180 *"Because the Court"* and *"During the trial"* Wallace, *Cases in the Circuit Court.*

181 *"in consequence of the"* See *United States v. Holmes*, 369.

181 *"rigid, strict, and hopeless"* C. Dickens, *A Tale of Two Cities: American Notes/Pictures from Italy.*

181 *"Every prisoner"* C. Dickens, *The Old Curiosity Shop*, quoted in Hanson, *The Custom of the Sea*, 272.

THE LEGACY

182 *"A day lost"* C. Hyne, "The Liner and the Iceberg," *McClure's Magazine*, August 1898, 333.

182 *When the ss* Arctic *sank* D.W. Shaw, *The Sea Shall Embrace Them.*

183 *The same thing happened* B.T. Hill, "Ship Collisions with Icebergs," 7.

183 *Later, in 1870* Shaw, *The Sea Shall Embrace Them*, Chapter 19. See also Hill, "Ship Collisions with Icebergs," 7. The death of 480 passengers aboard the *City of Glasgow*, which sank after striking an iceberg in 1854, was the largest number of passengers drowned in a single incident until the sinking of the *Titanic* in 1912.

184 *"The largest craft afloat"* M. Robertson, *The Wreck of the Titan: Or, Futility*, 1.

184 *On its maiden voyage* Lord, *A Night to Remember*, 2.

184 *"The Titanic crime"* "The Titanic Crime," *New York Evening Journal*, 15 April 1912.

185 *As a result* Batchelor, *The Life and Legacy of G.I. Taylor*, 1. Also see D.J. Matthews, *Ice Observation, Meteorology, and Oceanography in the North Atlantic Ocean.*

186 *A sanitized version* H.K. Brooke, "The Loss of the Ship *William Brown*, and the Trial of Alexander William Holmes for Manslaughter" in *Highwaymen and Pirates' Own Book.*

187 *When in 1884* See *Regina v. Dudley and Stephens* and M.G. Mallin, "In Warm Blood," *University of Chicago Law Review.*

187 *The New York Times resurrected* See "The Right of Self-Preservation," *New York Times* 28 September 1884.

187 *In the late 1990s* See *Regina v. Latimer.*

187 *The story of the* William Brown *took* L. Lasagna, "Mortal Decisions" in *The Sciences.*

188 *"the problems associated"* D. Thomasma, S. Hellig and T. Kushner, "From the

Editors," *Cambridge Quarterly of Healthcare Ethics* 8:2 (1999): 263.

188 *"could conceivably"* G. Plagenz, "Lifeboat Ethics," *Joplin Globe,* 22 February 2002.

188 *The metaphor assures* For a modern example of how pervasive this thinking is, see the review of E. Klinenberg's book *Heat Wave* (on the Chicago heat wave of 1995) by M. Gladwell, "Political Heat," *New Yorker,* 12 August 2002.

BIBLIOGRAPHY

Baldwin, H. *A General View of the Origin and Nature of the Constitution and Government of the United States*. Philadelphia: J.C. Clark, 1837. New York: Da Capo Press, 1970.

——. *An Oration Delivered by Hon. Henry Baldwin, at the Request of the Jackson Democratic Republicans of This City July 4th, 1827*. Pittsburgh: Cramer and Speer, 1827.

——. *Reports of Cases Determined in the Circuit Court of the United States, in and for the Third Circuit*. Vol. 1. Philadelphia: J. Kay, Junior and Brother, 1837.

Batchelor, G.K. *The Life and Legacy of G.I. Taylor*. Cambridge: Cambridge University Press, 1960.

——. *The Scientific Papers of Sir Geoffrey Ingram Taylor*. Vol. II. Cambridge: Cambridge University Press, 1960.

Brooke, H.K. "The Loss of the Ship *William Brown*, and the Trial of Alexander William Holmes for Manslaughter." In *Highwaymen and Pirates' Own Book*. Philadelphia: John B. Perry, 1845.

Brown, D.P. *Speech of David Paul Brown in Defence of Alexander William Holmes*. Philadelphia: Robb, Pile, & M'Elroy, 1858.

Butler, H. *Abandon Ship*. Lincolnwood, IL: NTC/Contemporary Publishing, 1974.

Chase, O. *The Wreck of the Whaleship* Essex. Ed. by Haversack and B. Shepard. New York: Harcourt, Brace, 1993.

Chase, O., et al. *Narratives of the Wreck of the Whale-ship* Essex. 1935. New York: Dover, 1989.

Curtis, P.L., Jr. *Anglo-Saxons and Celts: A Study of Anti-Irish Prejudice in Victorian England*. Bridgeport, CT: University of Bridgeport Press, 1968.

Dickens, C. *The Old Curiosity Shop*. Oxford: Oxford University Press, 1951.

——. *A Tale of Two Cities: American Notes/Pictures from Italy* London: Educational Book, 1910.

Foster, R.F. *Paddy and Mr. Punch: Connections in Irish and English History.* London: Allen Lane, Penguin Press, 1993.

Fowles, J. *Shipwreck.* London: Jonathan Cape, 1974.

Gaskell, T.F. *The Gulf Stream.* London: Cassell, 1972.

Gibbons, S. *Stanley Gibbon's All World Stamps.* Accessed 20 November 2001. www.allworldstamps.com/.

Greenhill, B., and A. Giffard. *Traveling by Sea in the Nineteenth Century.* New York: Hastings House Publishing, 1974.

———. *Women Under Sail.* Newton Abbot: David and Charles, 1970.

Guilbaut, S., M. Ryan and S. Watson, eds. *Théodore Géricault: The Alien Body: Tradition in Chaos.* Vancouver: Morris and Helen Belkin Art Gallery, 1997.

Guillet, E.C. *The Great Migration: The Atlantic Crossing by Sailing-Ship Since 1770.* 2d. ed. Toronto: University of Toronto Press, 1963.

Hansen, M.L. *The Atlantic Migration: 1607–1860.* 2d ed. New York: Harper Torchbooks, 1961.

Hanson, N. *The Custom of the Sea.* New York: John Wiley & Sons, 2000.

Hertzman, O. "Oceans and the Coastal Zone." In *The Surface Climates of Canada,* by W.G. Bailey, T.R. Oke and W.R. Rouse. Kingston, Ont.: McGill-Queen's University Press, 1998.

Hill, B.T. "Ice Charts and Ship/Iceberg Database." Institute of Marine Dynamics in St. John's, NF. *Icebergs.* Accessed 20 November 2001. www.nrc.ca/imd/ice/.

———. "Ship Collisions with Icebergs: An Historical Record of Collisions in the Seas around North America and Greenland." *Proceedings of the 16th International Conference on Port and Ocean Engineering under Arctic Conditions.* 2 vols. Ottawa: 2001. 2:997-1002.

Hugill, P.J. *World Trade Since 1431: Geography, Technology, and Capitalism.* Baltimore: Johns Hopkins University Press, 1995.

Junger, S. *The Perfect Storm.* New York: W.W. Norton & Co., 1997.

Kemp, P.K., ed. *The Oxford Companion to Ships and the Sea.* London: Oxford University Press, 1976.

Kinsella, J. "Irish Immigrants in America during the 19th Century." Accessed 20 May 2001. www.kinsella.org/history/histira.htm.

Klinenberg, E. *Heat Wave: A Social Autopsy of Disaster in Chicago.* Chicago: University of Chicago Press, 2001.

Koch, Tom. *Scarce Goods: Justice, Fairness, and Organ Transplantation.* Westport and London: Praeger, 2001.

———. *The Limits of Principle: Deciding Who Lives and What Dies.* Westport and London: Praeger, 1998.

——. *The News as Myth: Fact and Context in Journalism*. Westport and London: Greenwood Press, 1990.

Kurlansky, M. *Cod*. New York: Penguin, 1997.

Leslie, E.E. *Desperate Journeys, Abandoned Souls: True Stories of Castaways and Other Survivors*. New York: Houghton Mifflin, 1988.

Lord, W.A. *A Night to Remember*. New York: Bantam Books, 1956.

"Lord Palmerston." Schoolnet. *Prime Ministers*. Accessed 6 January 2002. www.spartacus.schoolnet.co.uk/PRpalmerston.htm.

McKee, A. *The Wreck of the* Medusa: *The Tragic Story of the Death Raft* 1975. New York: Signet, 2000.

Maitland, B. *The Chalon Heads*. New York: Orion, 1999.

Matthews, D.J. *Ice Observation, Meteorology, and Oceanography in the North Atlantic Ocean: Report of the Work Carried Out by the* S.S. Scotia, *1913*. London: H.M. Stationery Office, 1915.

Mewburn, C.E. "Imaging the Body Politic: The Social and Symbolic Spaces of Citizenship in Maxwell's History of the Irish Rebellion." Vancouver: University of British Columbia Department of Fine Arts Master's Thesis, 1996. Chapter 1.

Nickerson, T., O. Chase *et al. The Loss of the Ship* Essex, *Sunk by a Whale: First-person Accounts*. Eds. N. and T. Philbrick. New York: Penguin Books, 2000.

Philbrick, N. *In the Heart of the Sea: The Tragedy of the Whaleship* Essex. New York: Viking, 2000.

Philips, M. "The Dreadful Shipwreck of the *William Brown*, 1841." Accessed 29 September 1999. www.cronab.demon.co.uk/brown.htm.

Regina v. Dudley and Stephens. 1884. 14 Q.B.D. 273.

Regina v. Keyne. 1976. 2 Ex. D. 63, Cox Crim. Case 403, 47 LIMC 17. See Simpson, *Leading Cases*.

Regina v. Latimer. 2001 SCC 1. File No. 26980. 2000: June 14; 2001.

Robertson, M. *The Wreck of the Titan: Or, Futility*. New York: *McClure's Magazine* and *Metropolitan Magazine*, 1898.

Ryan, M. "Liberal Ironies, Colonial Narratives, and the Rhetoric of Art: Reconsidering Géricault's *Radeau de la Méduse* and the *Traite des Nègres*." In *Théodore Géricault*, ed. by S. Guilbaut, M. Ryan and S. Watson. Vancouver: Belkin Art Gallery, 1997. 18–51.

Scharf, J.T., and T. Westcott. *History of Philadelphia 1609–1884*. Vol. II. Philadelphia: L.H. Everts, 1884.

Seymour, J.B. *The Penny Black of Great Britain: An Adaptation from 'The Stamps of Great Britain.'* London: Royal Philatelic Society, 1934.

Shaw, D.W. *The Sea Shall Embrace Them: The Tragic Story of the Steamship* Arctic. New York: Free Press, 2002.

Simpson, A.W.B. *Cannibalism and the Common Law: The Story of the Tragic Last Voyage of the Mignonette and the Strange Legal Proceedings to Which It Gave Rise.* Chicago: University of Chicago Press, 1984.

——. *Leading Cases in the Common Law.* Oxford: Clarendon Press, 1995.

"ss *Great Britain.*" Accessed 23 September 2001. www.ss-great-britain.com.

Tappan, D.L. *Ancestors and Descendants of Abraham Tappan of Newbury, Massachusetts, 1606–1672.* Arlington, MA: Privately printed, 1915. Boston Public Library catalogue #c371/T175/1915).

Tappan, L. *The Life of Arthur Tappan.* Westport, CT: Negro Universities Press, 1970. 37–39.

Tappan, S.H. *Memoir of Mrs. Sarah Tappan: Taken in Part from the Home Missionary Magazine of November 1828, and Printed for Distribution Among her Descendants.* New York: West & Trow, Printers, 1834.

Trial of Alexander William Holmes, One of the Crew of the Ship "William Brown," for Manslaughter on the High Seas. Philadelphia: N.p., 1842.

United Kingdom. Public Record Office. Foreign Office 27/634.

United States Coast Guard. *International Ice Patrol/North Atlantic Iceberg Detection and Forecasting.* Accessed 12 October 1999. www.uscg.mil/lantarea/iip/home.html.

United States v. Holmes, 26 Fed. Cas. No. 15,383 (c.c.e.d. Pa. 22 April 1842).

Wallace, J. *Cases in the Circuit Court of the United States for the Third Circuit.* Philadelphia: Walker, 1849.

Wallis, H.M., and A.H. Robinson. *Cartographical Innovations: An International Handbook of Mapping Terms to 1900.* Tring, Herts, UK: Map Collectors Publications, 1987. 152–53.

Wangemann, G.W. "The *Titanic's* Unsung Heroes." Accessed 23 September 1999. www.execpc.com/~reva/html3c5.htm.

Yeo, E., and E.P. Thompson. *The Unknown Mayhew.* New York: Pantheon, 1971.

Zuckerman, L. *The Potato: How the Humble Spud Rescued the Western World.* New York: Farrar, Straus, and Giroux, 1998.

NEWSPAPERS AND PERIODICALS (in chronological order)

"Dreadful Shipwreck," *Journal de Havre,* 11 May 1841; reprinted *Times* (London), 15 May 1841, 6.

"Dreadful Shipwreck," *Galignani's Messenger,* 12 May 1841; reprinted *Times* (London), 15 May 1841, 6.

"The William Brown.—Havre," *London Morning Post,* 13 May 1841.

Hosken, James. "Extraordinary Fields of Ice in the Atlantic," *Times* (London), 17 May 1841, 5.

"The William Brown—Havre," *Times* (London), 17 May 1841, 6.

"Letter from English and U.S. Consuls," *Times* (London), 18 May 1841, 6.

Homo. "The Loss of the William Brown" (letter to the editor), *Times* (London), 18 May 1841, 7

"The Loss of the William Brown—Havre," *Times* (London), 20 May 1841.

"Melancholy Shipwreck—One hundred and forty-eight Lives Lost," *Quebec Mercury*, 22 May 1841; reprinted *Times* (London), 16 June 1841.

No title. *Times* (London), 16 June 1841, 6.

"Another Statement," *Philadelphia Public Ledger and Transcript*, 1 July 1841.

"The Ship William Brown," *Times* (London), 24 July 1841, 6.

"Maritime Herald," *New York Herald*, 11 October 1841, 5.

"Dreadful Shipwreck and Loss of Life," *New York Herald*, 11 October 1841, 5.

"Dreadful Shipwreck and Loss of Life," *Philadelphia Public Ledger and Transcript*, 11 October 1841.

"Postscript: Philadelphia," *New York Herald*, 11 October 1841.

"London Post Office," *Philadelphia North American*, 16 October 1841 (vol. 3, no. 796).

"Maritime Herald," *New York Herald*, 15 April 1842, 6.

"Shipping in Port—Stagnation in Business," *New York Herald*, 15 April 1842, 4.

"Local Affairs: Conviction of Holmes," *Philadelphia Public Ledger and Daily Transcript*, 23 April 1842.

"Philadelphia," *New York Herald*, 23 April 1842.

"United States Court: Before Judge Baldwin and Randall," *Philadelphia Public Ledger and Daily Transcript*, 23 April 1842, 1–2.

"Movements for Mr. Clay," *New York Herald*, 24 April 1842.

"Interesting Trial of a Shipwrecked Sailor for Throwing Passengers Overboard," *New York Herald*, 25 April 1842.

"The Holmes Case," *Philadelphia North American and Daily Advertiser*, 25 April 1842.

"To Certain Subscribers—Those Who Paid Curns the New Orleans Defaulter," *New York Herald*, 25 April 1842.

"The Wild Irish in the West, *Punch*, 19 May 1860, 200.

"The Right of Self-Preservation," *New York Times*, 28 September 1884, 8.

Hyne, C. "The Liner and the Iceberg," *McClure's Magazine*, August 1898, 333.

"The Titanic Crime," *New York Evening Journal*, 16 April 1912.

Hardin, G. "The Tragedy of the Commons." *Science* 162 (1968): 143–48.

Lasagna, L. "Mortal Decisions: The Search for an Ethical Policy on Allocating Health Care." *The Sciences* 43 (1991): 43–44.

Thomasma, D., S. Hellig and T. Kushner. "From the Editors," Cambridge Quarterly of Healthcare Ethics 8:2 (1999): 263.

Harris, P., and D. Lyon. "In New Bedford, a Return to the Days of 'Moby-Dick'," *Boston Sunday Globe*, 6 July 2001: L13–14.

Plagenz, G.R. "Lifeboat Ethics." *Joplin Globe* 22 February 2002. Accessed 20 May 2002. www.joplinglobe.com/archives/2002/020222/oped/story5.html.
Gladwell, M. "Political Heat: The Great Chicago Heat Wave, and Other Unnatural Disasters." *New Yorker* 12 August 2002: 76–80.

ACKNOWLEDGMENTS

WRITING MAY BE A SOLITARY CRAFT, but publishing is a communal task. In first researching and then preparing the manuscript that became this book, I received the assistance of a wide range of people. It is a pleasure to acknowledge those whose skills and knowledge have furthered this work.

A number of librarians and researchers generously assisted my pursuit of the documents on which this book is based. They include, in a partial list, librarians at the British Newspaper Library, the British Foreign Office, the British Maritime Museum, Harvard University and the University of British Columbia. My friend, Boston historian and geographer Arthur Krim, was supportive and helpful. Michael Phillips, formerly of the Plymouth Naval Base Museum (U.K.), was especially generous in my first attempts to gather data on this case.

Other historians and writers interested in nineteenth-century history gladly shared with me the benefits of their work. A.W. Brian Simpson, whose *Cannibalism and the Common Law* remains the principal legal text on this and related cases, generously provided me with his own notes on *United States v. Holmes*. Neal Hanson, author of *The Custom of the Sea*, was of material assistance in my thinking about this period. I was also fortunate to have the acquaintance of Maureen Ryan, whose work on the *Medusa*, and more generally on the place of the Irish in the greater British society of the day, was helpful indeed.

I am especially grateful to Brian Hill, the leading authority on the subject of shipwrecks and icebergs in the North Atlantic. He generously offered his research and his observations in a score of e-mail communications. Without his work, my understanding of these events would be the poorer. For the second time, Catherine Griffith assisted me in making my maps and illustrations presentable.

Without the resources of a committed publisher and publishing staff, none of the work that resulted would have seen the light of day. I am, therefore, especially indebted to James T. Sabin at Greenwood Publishing Group, who supported my first work in this area, *Scarce Goods*. My long-time friend Denis Wood ably served both as an editor of that and early drafts of the present manuscript. More importantly, he served as a sounding board against which to consider both how to understand and how to present this history.

For this work, it was Scott McIntyre of Douglas and McIntyre who, from the start, believed in a project that focussed on both Alexander William Holmes and the *William Brown* as a potentially engaging story. At Douglas and McIntyre, Becky Trewella and the book's editor, Saeko Usukawa, and the designer, George Vaitkunas, provided expert advice and support.

To all who assisted me in this work, and of course to the readers who support it, I am obliged.

INDEX